100 GREATEST™ U.S. MODERN COINS

5TH EDITION

SCOTT SCHECHTER and JEFF GARRETT

FOREWORD BY DAVID J. RYDER

Whitman™
SINCE 1934

100 GREATEST™ U.S. MODERN COINS

5TH EDITION

Whitman™ SINCE 1934

4001 Helton Drive • Florence, AL 35630

Correspondence concerning this book may be directed to the publisher, Attn: 100 Greatest U.S. Coins, at the address above.

ISBN: 0794851428
Ebook ISBN: 9780794839130
Printed in China.
ZT P1602-0824

Disclaimer: No warranty or representation of any kind is made concerning the accuracy or completeness of the information presented, or its usefulness in numismatic purchases or sales. The opinions of others may vary. The authors may buy, sell, and sometimes hold certain of the items discussed in this book.

Caveat: The price estimates given are subject to variation and differences of opinion. Especially rare coins trade infrequently, and an estimate or past auction price may have little relevance to future transactions. Before making decisions to buy or sell, consult the latest information. Grading of coins is subject to wide interpretation, and opinions can differ. Past performance of any item in the market is not necessarily an indication of future performance, as the future is unknown.

If you enjoy the fascinating history and color images of the *100 Greatest U.S. Modern Coins*, you will also enjoy the other books in this series, including *100 Greatest U.S. Coins*, *100 Greatest Ancient Coins*, *100 Greatest American Currency Notes*, *100 Greatest American Medals and Tokens*, *100 Greatest U.S. Error Coins*, *100 Greatest Women on Coins*, and *100 Greatest American Stamps*.

If you enjoy *100 Greatest U.S. Modern Coins*, visit www.greysheet.com for up-to-date news, pricing, and research.

For a complete catalog of numismatic reference books, supplies, and storage products, visit Whitman online at www.whitman.com

CONTENTS

FOREWORD

I am honored to write the foreword for the fifth edition of *100 Greatest U.S. Modern Coins.* Scott Schechter and Jeff Garrett, the authors, are very well known in the numismatic field and are extremely knowledgeable coin experts. Their lifetime dedication to the many facets of the industry is admirable. They have worked tirelessly over the years to educate and enhance the coin-collecting experience for both the savviest collector and young collectors alike.

Looking back at my tenure as the 34th and 39th director of the United States Mint, several coin programs stand out to me that fall in the category of great modern-day U.S. coins. I am proud to have been associated with the following programs: the 2021 new American Gold and Silver Eagle coins; the American Liberty 2021 High Relief gold coin; the re-introduction of the Morgan and Peace silver dollars; and the 2020-W American Liberty $50 Gold and $1 Silver Eagles with the V75 privy mark, symbolizing the 75th anniversary of victory in World War II. (An additional, limited mintage of the 2020 America the Beautiful quarters honoring the National Park of American Samoa were struck at the West Point Mint with both the W mintmark and the V75 privy mark.)

The End of World War II 75th Anniversary coin recognizes the end of the United States' involvement in the war. Inspiration for the privy mark's design was derived from the World War II Memorial, which is located on the National Mall in Washington, DC. At the time of the coin's development, I was riding my bike to work, and I always passed the memorial on my way. That particular morning, I actually stopped and got off the bike to look at the Rainbow Pool, and I knew we had the design. It took several weeks to get the U.S. Park Service to allow us to use it on our coin, as they were the owners of the memorial.

Within the World War II Memorial lies the Freedom Wall, with a message that reads, "Here We Mark the Price of Freedom." To me these words signify the importance of the V75 privy mark, which was chosen to honor the millions of Americans who served our nation during World War II; many of them gave the ultimate sacrifice in the fight for our freedom. It was a real privilege to have worked on this project with the many veterans who are employed at the United States Mint.

While 2020 and 2021 were exciting and busy times in the Mint's development of new coins, I also need to mention the Morgan and Peace dollars. The program required legislation to be passed by the U.S. Congress and then approved by the president, which was no small accomplishment. On January 5, 2021, President Trump signed H.R. 6192, the 1921 Silver Dollar Coin Anniversary Act, into law. It specifically states, "The conversion from the Morgan Silver Dollar to the Peace Silver Dollar design in 1921 reflected a pivotal moment in American history. The Morgan Silver Dollar represents the country's westward expansion and industrial development in the late 19th century. The Peace Silver Dollar symbolizes the country's coming of age as an international power while recognizing the sacrifices made by her citizens in World War I and celebrating the victory and peace that ensued." I believe these beautiful coins will live on for many years for all numismatists to enjoy and collect.

The 2021-W American Liberty High Relief gold coin, ranked at number 75 in this edition, is one of my favorites, and it adorns the cover of this book. The coin is part of an important U.S. Mint biennial program. Since its debut in 2015 the American Liberty gold coin has featured Lady Liberty in various depictions. For the 2021 issue, I encouraged the U.S. Mint and the Citizens Coin Advisory Committee (CCAC) to think creatively and put forward symbolic ideas as to what "liberty" meant to them, suggesting that we replace the standard depiction of Liberty with a fresh concept. Once a new direction for the program had been agreed upon, we engaged the talented artists from the Mint's Artistic Infusion Program to develop modern designs that would best embody what "liberty" meant to them. Many wonderful designs were submitted for consideration; however, one stood out, and that was the Bucking Bronco design by artist and illustrator Beth Zaiken. The design captures the essence of a western bucking horse symbolizing the breaking of the yoke of British rule during the American Revolution. The CCAC, the U.S. Commission of Fine Arts, and the Secretary of the Treasury unanimously approved the design. While the decision I made for this program was a bit controversial with some coin collectors, the 2021 American Liberty coin was awarded Best Gold Coin in the Coin of the Year (COTY) Award for 2021.

During my time as the director of the U.S. Mint, as well as before and after, I have had the opportunity to visit mints from all around the world. Unequivocally, I can assure you that each of the coins highlighted in this book was developed, designed, crafted, and minted by some of the world's leading artists in their chosen fields. As you flip through this book you will undoubtedly be enamored by the beauty of each coin and the creativity, talent, and skill that went into its design, earning it a place in *100 Greatest U.S. Modern Coins*, fifth edition.

David J. Ryder
Director of the United States Mint, 1992–1993 and 2018–2021

By John Feigenbaum

I hope you enjoy this fifth edition of *100 Greatest U.S. Modern Coins*, a modern classic painstakingly updated by authors Scott Schechter and Jeff Garrett. You will learn about the greatest and rarest of the United States Mint's modern issues, some of which were struck just a couple of years ago. Does that surprise you? Consider that American Eagles are the best-selling bullion coins in the world, attracting many new collectors.

As you can see, the concept of "modern" coinage is interesting. The term itself suggests an ephemeral state: What's modern today will be "classic" tomorrow, or next year. A good example is the 1955, Doubled Die Obverse, Lincoln cent. Nearly 60 years ago, in 1965, it was considered a modern rarity!

This book defines the modern era of numismatics as beginning in 1964. That was the landmark year in which silver last appeared in regular-issue U.S. coinage of dimes, quarters, and half dollars. From 1965 on, our coins were no longer supported by the silver standard. Thus, the modern era begins.

However, to a coin collector, "modern" may be seen through a different, more personal lens. I was born in 1969 and started collecting in 1975—yes, at the ripe old age of six. My first endeavor was a set of Indian cents, followed by a type set. Both were assembled in the classic blue Whitman folders of the era.

At the time, little of interest in circulation was coming out of the U.S. Mint. One exception was the 1976 Bicentennial issue. While this radical, one-year-only re-imagination of the reverse design was quite interesting to the general public, collectors yawned. The true collector knew these coins would never be valuable because they were struck in unprecedented quantity. Everyone seemed to hoard them as future valuables, and they quickly disappeared from circulation.

Back then, we collectors also snubbed Proof and Mint Sets, which the Mint was pushing in huge quantities. To this day, a typical Proof set issued in the 1970s has a lower value than its issue price. We collectors simply did not care about the contemporary coinage of the day.

As a young dealer in the 1990s, I held a loose definition of moderns, which broke down as follows: Lincoln cents with Wheat reverse (ending in 1958), Buffalo nickels (ending 1938), Mercury dimes (1945), Walking Liberty half dollars (1945), and so on, collectively marked the end of the "classic" era, and anything struck after these series was uninteresting. We made exceptions for the few key dates of that last series, and a gem 1949-S Franklin half dollar was considered a king of the era (though not today). The 1970-D Kennedy half dollars and 1950-D nickels were popular issues, but we were preoccupied with the coins of our fathers, like the 1909-S, V.D.B., cent, the 1877 cent, and the 1885 Liberty nickel. The term "key date" was a huge selling point, and it seldom applied to coins struck after World War II.

The market was slow to change in this regard. Even the advent of third-party grading in 1986 focused heavily on classic collectibles. In the early days of the "slab rush," everyone was trying to find high-grade coins from the 19th and early 20th centuries. Nobody spent time seeking high-grade Washington quarters, Roosevelt dimes, or Ike dollars.

This finally changed with the advent and popularity of competitive registry sets. First PCGS, then NGC designed elaborate software tools to help people track their collections and compete for top-graded sets of every issue from Lincolns to modern (starting in 1982) commemorative issues. That changed the mindset completely. As collectors sought top-quality examples of certain issues, it quickly became apparent that some do not exist in the highest grades. The Washington quarters of the 1980s are aesthetically boring, poorly produced in massive quantity in an industrial manner for use in vending machines and the like. Almost nobody was seeking to build a collection of these workhorse coins for a collection of high-grade specimens. You might have been laughed out of your coin club if you dared a slide-show presentation on "high-grade clad coinage."

Today, the sentiment has changed considerably. The coins we snubbed in the 1970s and 1980s are both highly sought-after and quite rare in top grades! Thanks to a series of engaged leaders, the U.S. Mint has evolved considerably in the past two decades, and it has experimented in many ways to create new coin designs and programs—none more popular than the 50 States Quarters Program, launched in 1999—that finally pushed the old Flanagan quarters off the cliff. The modern era is upon us, and the inspiration of these new issues has created unprecedented interest in the coins of our childhood. Of course, in 50 years, we will have to move this needle again and redefine what a "modern issue" is.

The Mint's foray into new and exciting programs, combined with the advent of registry sets, elevated clad coinage—like this Proof State quarter, graded PF-70DC—into the spotlight.

WHAT ARE MODERN COINS?

There is a very simple definition of modern U.S. coinage, which is a good starting point: modern U.S. coins are those struck from 1964 to date. All the coins described in 100 Greatest U.S. Modern Coins fall within this time period. The reader need go no further to have a very serviceable and accurate definition.

As with many things that seem simple on the surface, a deeper look reveals complexity. For example, it would be easy to mischaracterize the above definition simply as "coins of relatively recent vintage." This, of course, implies that the definition is a moving target, subject to change over time. In truth, it is not. Just as *modern art* defines a period of artistic production and connects works based on their content and character, *modern coinage* is more than a date range.

Coins minted in 1964 hint at this complexity. The date 1964 is hugely significant in American numismatics. It is the last year that U.S. coins struck for circulation contained 90% silver. It marks the end of a metallic composition that had been in use since the Mint Act of 1792 first established the standards for U.S. coinage. From 1965 forward, the formerly silver dimes and quarters struck for circulation would be sandwiches of copper and nickel. (For a short period, the post-1964 half dollar continued to be made with silver in its outer layer, but by 1971 no circulation issues would contain any silver.)

Not all Mint products from 1964 should be considered modern. In the *100 Greatest U.S. Modern Coins*, there are three entries from this year. One is the 1964 Special Mint Set—a set of coins with an unusual finish that replaced the Proof finish on coinage sets made for collectors from 1965 through 1967. The Proof set was put on hiatus while the Mint focused all its attention on the production of new-composition coinage. Another is the 1964-D, Reverse of 1965, Washington quarter, a coin that shows early use of a modified design created to suit the upcoming clad coinage. The third is the 1964, Accented Hair, Kennedy half dollar, a first-year variety of a new, distinctly modern coinage series. All of these coins relate directly to the changes that were coming to the new coinage, and are modern for that reason. They are coins not entirely stuck in the context of pre-1964 issues.

Proof 1964, Accented Hair, half dollar (no. 36).

So the era of modern coinage began with the Mint figuring out how to smoothly transition away from the silver issues of previous years. For years after the change, coin design remained stagnant, playing on the collective memory of past silver circulating coinage. Even when the Eisenhower dollar was introduced in 1971, a non-circulating version containing silver was also released, helping to create the still vitally important association between a coin's face value and its intrinsic worth. Not until 1979, nearly 10 years later, was this connection severed when a small-sized copper-nickel-clad dollar coin was issued replacing the original silver dollar of memory.

Subsequent new coinage programs similarly recalled the past before heading in a new modern path. In 1982, the U.S. commemorative-coinage program re-launched. (The last U.S. commemoratives had been struck in the 1950s.) The first coin was a silver half dollar, as nearly all the classic commemoratives issues had been. When Olympic commemorative three-coin dollar sets were sold in 1983, they were each composed of a Philadelphia, Denver, and San Francisco Mint issue, as the original commemorative P-D-S sets had been. At that time a new $10 commemorative coin followed, something novel enough to begin breaking ties with the commemorative coins of the past. In 1986, the first U.S. bullion coins were issued, in a program that had no historical antecedents in the United States. Even still, at this late date, designs were recycled from classic coinage issues for the obverses of both the American Gold Eagle and the American Silver Eagle.

1986 American Silver Eagle and Gold Eagle bullion coins.

The Mint continues to produce modern programs and designs, most recently with the America the Beautiful, Crossing the Delaware, and American Women quarters; the Native American and American Innovation dollars; and modern renderings of classic coins like the Morgan silver dollar.

Eventually, these gradual changes gave way to dramatic experimentation. By 1999, the era of modern coinage at last had hit its stride. New designs were introduced five times every year on the state quarters issued from 1999 through 2008. A brand-new-composition dollar coin was introduced in 2000. Only faint connections can be drawn to earlier coinage. There is no doubt that these latter series are singularly modern.

Throughout the modern era of coinage, a significant consideration has loomed in the background: every coin's design and composition needs to meet the demands of mass production. Modern coinage production is not an artisanal process. Instead, all modern coins are produced using very powerful, high-speed coinage presses in a refined mechanical process designed to create as many coins as needed. Technology and its limitations, therefore, also play a role in the story of modern coinage. No country produces nearly as many coins as the United States. The huge demand for coinage has been keenly felt throughout the era of modern coinage as the U.S. Mint has tested the upper limits of what is possible.

TYPES OF U.S. MODERN COINS

Describing the way that modern coins are made is not as straightforward as it might seem. It requires that we delve into the jargon of numismatics. When we do, we encounter terms that are polysemes, single words that have multiple meanings. Initially, this creates a confusing mess. It is helpful to be aware of this at the outset.

The Mint formally divides the coins it produces into three categories: circulation coins, numismatic coins, and bullion coins.

Circulation coins are coins produced to be used as money. Other common names for this category of coins are *business strikes* and *currency issues.* These coins receive a single strike from dies that the Mint hopes will, under the best of circumstances, make more than a million coins each. Coins are ejected from the coinage press into large bins and packed into enormous ballistic bags before being wrapped into rolls. Circulation-issue coins may have numerous contact marks from exposure to other coins and Mint equipment. They may be weakly struck, or struck from late-state or fatigued dies, which imparts a mushy impression of the design. Additionally, these coins are struck on planchets that have received no special care to preserve high quality. Roughness or abrasion on the planchets may still be evident on the final coins.

As a result, the process of producing coins for circulation does not necessarily yield an attractive specimen for collectors, and circulation-issue coins can be challenging to find in the highest states of preservation. This is true even of very recent issues.

For years, standard-issue coins were packaged into Mint sets (annual sets of coins sold by the Mint). From 2005 to 2010, the Mint replaced standard-issue coins in Mint sets with satin-finish examples that have a light, matte-textured finish and are usually found in much better condition than standard circulation examples.

Numismatic coins are coins that are struck at the Mint specifically for sale to collectors. These include special presentation versions of the circulating coins,

Mint sets have been issued since the 1940s, specially packaged by the government for sale as collectibles.

Proofs and commemoratives are designated by the Mint as *numismatic coins*, as opposed to bullion coins and coins struck for circulation.

The U.S. Mint launched its bullion coinage program in 1986, and has introduced several expansions and innovations in recent years.

issued annually in Proof sets. Since 1992, the Mint has also sold silver Proof sets that contain (in addition to other coins) a dime, quarter, and half dollar struck in 90% silver. The category of numismatic coins also includes commemorative, thematic coins that serve the dual purposes of honoring an event, person, place, or organization as well as raising money for a specific purpose in the form of surcharges assessed by the Mint at the time of sale. The coins themselves, as with all U.S. coins, must be authorized by act of Congress, which selects their themes, sets mintage limits, designates the benefactor, and can even inform their designs.

All numismatic coins receive extraordinary levels of special handling during the minting process. These coins are sold to collectors at a premium. Collectors—being a finicky bunch—demand quality. Numismatic coins are struck twice from fresh dies on planchets treated to yield the highest quality. The coins often are hand-packed into custom presentation cases. The Mint offers two finishes of numismatic coins: Proof and Uncirculated. The distinct characteristics of each are discussed in length in the next section.

The last category of coins produced by the Mint is *bullion coins.* Bullion is simply precious metal in coin form. Although bullion coins have a denominated face value, they actually trade based on their metal content. Scarce issues have become collectibles and do have a numismatic premium in addition to their bullion value, especially when they have been preserved in pristine condition. Normally, bullion coins have a matte-like or Uncirculated finish (in the Mint's parlance), but less care is taken in their production than for numismatic coins. Although they are always well struck from relatively new or fresh dies, they can have contact marks and hairlines. Bullion coins are quickly packed into tubes, and the tubes are placed in "monster boxes" of 500 ounces. This packaging is designed for the convenience of precious-metal transactions and not for coin preservation. Additionally, planchet preparation for bullion coins is not as meticulous as for numismatic coins. Often, planchets used to strike these coins are poorly rinsed, which later causes coins to spot or stain, especially on American Silver Eagles.

Bullion coins are produced for investors and do not have mintmarks. The Mint does make collector versions in Proof format with mintmarks (and special designs in the case of American Platinum Eagle coins). In most years since 2006, the Mint has made Uncirculated versions of American Gold Eagles and American Silver Eagles for direct sale to collectors. They are very similar in appearance to regular bullion coins except they include the W mintmark for West Point, New York, where they were struck. These coins did receive some extra attention during production, as their coin blanks were burnished at the Mint. This treatment is not visible in the final product except with respect to spotting and staining, which seems to be less prevalent in Mint-burnished coins. Additionally, these coins were individually packaged in capsules, and therefore tend to be comparatively devoid of contact marks.

U.S. MODERN-COIN SURFACE FINISHES

One of the biggest recent development in U.S. modern coinage is the introduction of new surface finishes appearing on modern numismatic coins, those produced for collectors rather than for commerce. Proof coins have mirrored fields (open areas) that contrast with frosted portions of their design, a visual effect achieved by polishing the flat areas and sandblasting the lettering and design elements on the die. Uncirculated modern numismatic coins have an even, matte-like finish, an effect created by sandblasting or acid-etching the entire die to texture the coins they strike and make them non-reflective. Confusion, of course, results from the Mint's use of the term *Uncirculated* as a surface finish. Uncirculated is more commonly a grading term used to describe coins that show no metal loss from circulation. In *100 Greatest U.S. Modern Coins*, we have observed the Mint's convention of describing these coins with the terms *Uncirculated finish* or *Uncirculated issue*. The potential for confusion, however, is noted here.

Beginning in 2006, the Mint added a third finish to their roster of numismatic coins—the Reverse Proof. Reverse Proofs are aptly named. Exactly the opposite areas of the coin are frosted than on conventional Proofs. The coin's design is rendered with a mirror-like reflectivity and sits atop a dull, matte-like field.

To create this effect the recesses of the die are polished while the flat field area is sandblasted. The final stages of the die creation process are meticulous, laborious, and were long done by hand. Starting in 2009, the Mint began laser-cutting dies rather than sandblasting or etching them to achieve these various finishes.

Not only did this new automated process make it easier for the Mint to create more Reverse Proofs, which they have for successive years since 2011, they could also explore even more finish types. This paved the way for the Mint's most recently introduced and named finish—the Enhanced Uncirculated. The Enhanced Uncirculated finish includes areas of light frost, heavy frost, and mirrored areas. This finish was first used on the 2013-W $1 American Silver Eagle, Enhanced Uncirculated (see no. 91). This coin's design is composed of both unfrosted and heavily frosted areas on a lightly frosted field. Together they are meant to "add sharp definition to the designs," according to the U.S. Mint sales catalog. The effect is indeed something outside of the traditional framework of Proof and Uncirculated surface finishes.

With new technology and an industry-wide interest in novel products, collectors should expect more Enhanced Uncirculated coins and even wholly new categories of surface finishes in the years ahead.

VARIETIES VS. ERRORS

An area of perpetual confusion involves the differences between these two related but distinct terms: *variety* and *error*. There are a number of varieties included within the 100 Greatest U.S. Modern Coins, along with a handful of error coins. It's fair to say that this is an important distinction to understand.

Variety is short for die variety. A die physically imparts a coin with its design by striking a coin planchet with great force. The die contains the inverted design of the coin. If something unusual occurred to that die when it was created, resulting in an unusual attribute such as a doubled legend, it will pass that attribute onto all the coins that it strikes. A number of coins will be produced with this exact same feature. If the feature is prominent and interesting, it can become collectible. These are varieties.

For example: in 1995, a Lincoln cent obverse die mistakenly received two misaligned impressions of the coin's design. All the coins struck from this die had a doubled image, like a two-color document printed with bad registration.

The 1995, Doubled Die Obverse, Lincoln cent—a popular variety.

This is a very popular type of variety called a doubled die, and the specific coin described here is the 1995, Doubled Die Obverse, Lincoln cent.

Because varieties are the result of a flaw or feature on a single die, they are said to be die specific. Sometimes, the same type of error will occur multiple times in the same year. For example, in 1972, the Mint produced a number of doubled-die obverse Lincoln cents. Some are quite minor, while one is very prominent and very famous. Each individual die variety is cataloged and assigned a unique reference number. A popular guide for collectible varieties is the *Cherrypickers' Guide to Die Varieties*, which illustrates and catalogs these coins. When you buy variety coins, it's important to know if there are multiple varieties for a year and exactly which one it is that you're purchasing. Major varieties can trade for huge premiums, while minor varieties often carry little or no premium. The most popular and coveted of all die varieties are those listed in the *Guide Book of United States Coins* (the annually issued reference known by coin collectors as the *Red Book*).

A Mint *error*, in contrast to a die variety, results when a mistake occurs during the production of a single coin. One common type of Mint error is an off-center coin. Such errors are created when a planchet is fed partway into the coinage press. When the hammer die comes to strike the coin, only a portion of the planchet receives an impression. This error is coin-specific—only that single coin is affected. The preceding coin and the following coin might be perfectly normal, well within the Mint's tolerances for acceptable production. This coin is an error because it falls outside those tolerances.

Even though an error results from a manufacturing mistake during the production of a single coin, some mistakes are repeated frequently. For example, minor off-center errors like those described above are common for most modern series even though they are created one-by-one when a single planchet is misfed into the coinage press. Occasionally, an error is repeated frequently enough to become a collectable adjunct to the standard set. One of the best examples occurred in 2007. The new Presidential dollar coins had a lettered edge. This feature is applied by a separate edge-lettering machine after the obverse and reverse of the coin are struck. For the first issue in this series, the George Washington dollar, several hundred thousand examples missed this step entirely and have blank edges. Although technically an error coin and not part of the regular series, the George Washington, Missing Edge Lettering, dollars are widely collected by Presidential dollar enthusiasts.

Both die varieties and Mint errors are the result of mistakes, and this can be a source of confusion. To draw the distinction between them it is important to know *where* during production the mistake occurred. If the Mint makes an error during die production, a variety coin is created. If the Mint makes an error producing a single coin, an error coin is created. This is the simple litmus test to determine whether a coin is a die variety or an error.

GRADING MODERN COINS

While grading modern coins is certainly similar to and related to grading classic coins, there are many specialized factors that come into play.

Grading is the art of condition analysis. Since the late 1940s, numismatists have used a 70-point numerical scale to describe coins' conditions. This system is called the Sheldon scale, after its originator, large-cent specialist Dr. William Sheldon. By analyzing the surface, luster, strike, and eye appeal of a coin, a grader assigns it an alphanumerical grade. Grades above 60 are reserved for coins that have no wear or evidence of circulation. These are called Uncirculated or Mint State coins. The grade of 70 is the highest grade assigned.

A single-point differential on the Sheldon scale can translate to a considerable difference in value between two examples of the same coin. (For example, a 1972, Variety 2, Eisenhower dollar in MS-64 might trade for $300, while an MS-65 trades for more than $1,300.) For that reason, collectors, investors, and dealers employ independent grading services that apply consistent standards and offer grade guarantees to draw these distinctions between grades. The most popular of such services are Numismatic Guaranty Company (NGC), Professional Coin Grading Service (PCGS), and Certified Acceptance Corporation (CAC) Grading. Both services assign grades on the 70-point scale and then encapsulate coins in sealed, tamper-evident holders with a grading certificate enclosed.

An abbreviation often seen in the market is OGP, which is short for "original government packaging." This is not a grading term per se, and it makes no comment on the condition of the coin(s) inside except to indicate that they are as they were when first purchased from the Mint. In this book's pricing charts, "OGP" appears in a column of its own alongside the numeric grading columns.

One distinction of modern coinage is that many numismatic and bullion issues are collectible in the 70 grade, the highest grade assigned. In 2001,

Independent third-party services grade and encapsulate coins for a fee. Because they are neither buyer nor seller, and because they have experience examining millions of coins, these services are highly trusted for their grading opinions.

NGC formalized the description of this grade as describing "a coin having no post-production imperfections at 5x magnification," a definition which has since been adopted industry-wide. Only special-issue coins such as Proofs, commemoratives, and precious-metal issues are regularly available in the 70 grade. Circulation or business-strike coins on this list can be found in Choice Uncirculated (MS-63) and Gem Uncirculated (MS-65) conditions. These coins will have some surface marks but no evidence of circulation. Learning to discern the differences between these grades requires years of experience but is a worthwhile pursuit for all collectors. For basic instruction in coin-grading technique, refer to the Modern-Coin Grading Essentials section of this book.

In addition to a numerical grade, some modern coins receive an extra designation indicating how well they are struck. Coins that have crisp, full details are said to be well struck. On Roosevelt dimes, graders will examine the horizontal bands on the coin's reverse, calling them Full Torch (FT) or Full Bands (FB) if these bands are clearly split. On Jefferson nickels, graders will actually count the number of steps present on Monticello, designating well-struck coins as having either five or six Full Steps (5FS or 6FS) or declaring them "Full Steps" if a certain threshold number of steps are present. Circulation-issue coins struck from highly polished dies are often called prooflike (PL).

A particularly important strike characteristic is used when grading Proof coins. Modern Proof coins have mirrored fields surrounding frosted design elements. The first coins struck from a Proof die will show the highest degree of contrast between these elements. Contrast gradually fades over the life of a die. Coins with heavy contrast are the most desirable, and, in addition to receiving a number grade, they are said to be either Cameo or Ultra Cameo (also called Deep Cameo), based on the depth of their contrast. Coins lacking contrast do not receive any special designator. Some Proof coins from the late 1960s and early 1970s are very scarce (and therefore coveted) with the Ultra Cameo designation. By the mid-1970s, Proof coins were, at minimum, predominantly Cameo in appearance while, since the early 1980s, almost all U.S. Proof coins are Ultra Cameo.

HOW THE 100 GREATEST U.S. MODERN COINS WERE CHOSEN AND RANKED

Since relatively few books have been written about modern coinage, when assembling the first edition of the *100 Greatest U.S. Modern Coins*, it wasn't entirely clear what the list of coins would look like once complete. After the idea for the book was first proposed, fundamental questions loomed. How collectible would the coins on the list be? Would they represent a broad cross-section of coinage types, or would they be mostly obscure issues and elusive die varieties?

The authors embarked on assembling a draft list as a launching-off point. Coins were chosen based on the authors' experience as professional numismatists. Both authors were aware of the trading values of these coins, the number of collectors actively adding them to their collections, and the buzz that certain coins created in the community. For each coin selected, the authors also wrote a brief explanation of why it should be included on the list. That first list quickly grew to include over 150 coins. It was sorted chronologically, without ranking, and was still by no means complete.

This grouping of coins had never before been presented in this way, and, unlike in classic coinage, there were no undisputed "kings of coins" like the

1804 Draped Bust dollar and 1913 Liberty Head nickel. Any ranking reflects a degree of personal opinion and is subject to debate. To cultivate a more universal view of the greatest modern coins, the authors consulted experts in the field. A draft of the list was discussed with leading dealers including Bill Gale, David Hendrickson, Robert Lecce (sadly, now deceased), and Lee Minshull. With information from these numismatists, the list became more focused, and an initial sequence was devised.

The next phase of ranking involved a survey of published works: books, specialized journals, numismatic periodicals, and Internet publications. While these sources are often-used tools of the authors, previously no efforts had been made to quantify the frequency with which certain coins were mentioned and how much attention was devoted to them. Books evaluated include works by researchers and dealers Bill Fivaz, Eric Jordan, Ken Potter, J.T. Stanton, Rick Tomaska, and John Wexler. Internet search engines and web-based news archives proved invaluable for determining how much attention had been given to various coins, allowing the authors to more accurately and objectively rank recent issues. As the manuscript was being prepared, numismatists David W. Lange (also, sadly now passed) and Richard S. Montgomery were consulted to add further refinement and nuance to the ranking.

In the initial aftermath of the publication of the first edition, the authors received a heavy wave of suggestions regarding the rankings. Seemingly no collectors or dealers were shy about telling the authors where they felt the order could be improved. Comments have continued to come in a steady stream, but the authors were proactive about engaging leading voices in the modern-coin field. Dealers John Maben and Mitchell Spivack were particularly gracious in responding to questions and providing wisdom from their deep experience in this field. From all this feedback, a new list was ready to be presented. The process was repeated with further nuance twice more to create the lists for the third and fourth editions. In addition to feedback from dealers and collectors, heavier emphasis was given to market factors, such as changing values and frequency of appearance at auction. Improved auction result reporting, introduced in the last few years, made this type of analysis possible. This data contributed to the new ranking that appears in the fifth edition.

The rankings that appear in this book are a reworking of the list that originally appeared in the previous editions. Ranking used in the prior four editions and a discussion of rank changes appears in the appendix. The authors firmly believe that the coins selected represent the most significant numismatic properties of the modern era. Going forward, new information and dialogue will certainly continue to shape the perspectives of these coins. In the final analysis, modern coinage will always be the most dynamic area of numismatics.

By Mark Salzberg

In the limited space that I have here, obviously I can't say everything that needs to be said about grading modern coins. One thing that seems to me to be among the most important of considerations is that the act of grading modern coins is identical to grading classic coins; in the mind of the collector, there should be no difference.

It is shorthand for how we communicate the condition of the coin. Coins issued within the last 10 years or so are generally described using just a small number of terms; "gem Uncirculated" and "gem Proof" describe almost all of them. For those coins that are especially well made and handled with extra care, the "superb gems," we often use the numerical grades MS-67, MS-68, MS-69, and MS-70 for Uncirculated coins and, correspondingly, PF-67 through PF-70 for Proof coins. In a sense, for very modern coins, the sum of our grading lexicon is reduced to a mere dozen or so words.

Yet a whole industry of modern-coin collecting has emerged around these very few categories of condition, and coins that differ only slightly in grade have vastly different values. Fortunately, almost anyone can learn how to examine coins and assign the correct grades following basic instruction. The three most basic and essential considerations are lighting, posture, and magnification.

Lighting. Coins must be examined under controlled lighting conditions. Each time you look at coins, you should do so under the same conditions to ensure an unchanging baseline for comparison. Coins should be examined under a single, focused light source. Excessive ambient light and overly diffuse light make it difficult to discern small details.

I recommend that coins be looked at under a desk lamp in an otherwise dark room. Draw the curtains and shut off the overhead light. Close the door. Some collectors like to look at coins under a halogen light but this can be too intense. It obscures faint hazing and spotting. Instead, a single 75- or 100-watt incandescent light (or watt-equivalent compact fluorescent) is best. This approach to lighting is simple, accessible, and economical.

Posture. In many disciplines, the fundamentals must be mastered or progress will ultimately plateau indefinitely. For example, the way you grip a golf club will affect aspects of your swing. An incorrect grip means that you may never get rid of that slice no matter how the swing is adjusted. To improve, the proper grip must first be learned and then the swing re-learned.

Grading coins is no different. You have to learn the fundamentals of how to sit and how to hold coins. The best graders all do this the same way. If you fail to master this fundamental technique, you'll only get so far.

Sit upright with the light source directly in front of you, about head height. Hold the coin out in front of you, at least 12 to 18 inches from your eyes. Gripping it by the edges—the only way to ever hold a coin!—with your thumb and index finger of one or both hands, examine the obverse. Turn it up to the left and to the right, a full 90 degrees in each direction, as though the top and bottom are a pivot axis. Then turn it to the front and back, using the sides as an axis. Look at the coin at each of these hard angles. Condition flaws, especially hairlines, may be visible from only one direction and when a coin is sharply angled toward or away from you.

Complete your examination of the obverse, flip the coin over, and examine the reverse the same way, hitting sharp angles of examination. Last, look at the edge the entire way around to examine flaws on the "third side" of the coin. By now, you should have a solid idea of what condition flaws are present on the coin and have formed an opinion of its grade. At this stage, you can examine flaws or problem areas under 5x magnification.

Magnification. Over the years, I've met with countless collectors face-to-face at conventions where I conduct in-person evaluations. They often tell me that they have looked over a coin "under a microscope" and can't understand why a third-party service graded it as they did. I always say the same thing: "Forget about magnification and look at the whole coin."

A common mistake made by collectors of all levels is micro-grading. They get overly focused on small details that are insignificant to the final grade. Or, they miss the big picture by looking at only small areas of the coin.

The first look at a coin should always be without magnification, and a preliminary determination of grade should be made. Then the grader should look over the coin with a 5x magnifier to refine or confirm the original grade assessment. A 70, the highest grade, is assigned to a coin that shows no post-production imperfections at 5x magnification.

Higher magnification should be used only for purposes of confirming authenticity and, when absolutely necessary, to attribute die varieties. It's not for grading.

Now, with these three primary considerations in mind, look at as many coins as you can. Re-examine the coins that you already own. Look at coins in holders from third-party grading companies with the same considerations in mind. Find the flaws and see how they accord to the grade that was assigned.

You're on your way to becoming a better grader.

***Mark Salzberg** is widely considered the industry's foremost grading expert, having played a central role in the formation and application of the grading standards used today by third-party certification companies. He is the founder of the Certified Collectibles Group.*

100 GREATEST™ U.S. MODERN COINS

1 1975, NO S, ROOSEVELT DIME, PROOF

Designed by John R. Sinnock. On the obverse, the head of Franklin Roosevelt faces left. LIBERTY appears in large letters along the left rim; IN GOD WE TRUST appears in small letters at the lower left, and the date appears at the bottom right. The reverse features a lit torch flanked by sprigs of olive and oak. UNITED STATES OF AMERICA arcs above, ONE DIME arcs below, and the motto E PLURIBUS UNUM runs in a straight line through the bottoms of the sprigs and torch.

Weight: 2.27 grams. *Composition:* Outer layers of .750 copper and .250 nickel over a core of pure copper. *Diameter:* 17.9 mm. *Edge:* Reeded. *GSID:* 81056.

Since 1968, all Proof coinage has been struck at the San Francisco Mint and bears an S mintmark to denote the mint of origin. However, several times dies made in Philadelphia were shipped to San Francisco without the mark. These dies produced the now highly coveted No S Proof coins. This happened during the first year of production, in 1968, when Proof No S dimes were produced (see no. 8). The same mistake was repeated in 1970. In 1971, Proof No S nickels were coined. And then there was a lull in No S production.

But why have no more been found? The most popular theory is that inspectors at the San Francisco Mint noticed the error and destroyed what coins they could.

But in 1975, an anonymous California collector who had purchased five Proof sets from the Mint made a lucky discovery: two of his sets contained Proof Roosevelt dimes without a mintmark. In 1977, the collector sent his discovery sets to *Coin World* for independent confirmation and to announce the discovery. The dimes were also independently certified at that time.

The collector eventually sold both sets to Fred J. Vollmer, a dealer based in Bloomington, Illinois, who specialized in Proof sets. In 1978, he sold the first of the sets containing a 1975, No S, dime to a collector in Ohio for $18,200. In 1979, during the midst of a coin-market boom, Vollmer offered the second set

for $38,550. Remarkably, since the sale of those two pieces, no further 1975, No S, dimes have surfaced.

Collectors and dealers have always had a great incentive to examine their 1975 Proof sets for No S dimes. In 1975, a total of 2,845,450 Proof sets were sold, and looking for a No S dime is something like searching for a needle in a haystack. But why have no more been found? The most popular theory is that inspectors at the San Francisco Mint noticed the error and destroyed what coins they could, allowing only two or so to be released.

In the intervening decades, the status of the famed 1975, No S, dime was called into question. It may even have added to its mystique that this coin was excluded from the first edition of *100 Greatest U.S. Modern Coins*, being mentioned only in the description of the more common 1970, No S, dime, where we wrote: "If it does exist, the 1975, No S, dime is one of the great rarities of the 20th century and will assume a vaunted position on the list of 100 Greatest U.S. Modern Coins—likely the number one spot. But until it's confirmed, it remains off the list."

At last, after more than 30 years of absence, in 2011, Stack's Bowers announced that it would be offering at auction an example of the landmark rarity 1975, No S, Roosevelt dime. Wonderful reporting and research by *Coin World* told the story of Vollmer's sales in rich detail and identified this coin as the second example he sold. The first-ever auction appearance of a 1975, No S, dime occurred at the ANA World's Fair of Money in Chicago on August 18, 2011. Its final price realized was the highest ever paid for a modern U.S. coin: $349,600!

Mintage: fraction of 2,845,450 (2 specimens confirmed)

PF-68
$528,000

2 1969-S, DOUBLED DIE OBVERSE, LINCOLN CENT

Designed by Victor David Brenner (obverse) and Frank Gasparro (reverse). The obverse continues the design of 1909. The reverse shows a frontal view of the Lincoln Memorial with UNITED STATES OF AMERICA and E PLURIBUS UNUM appearing above and ONE CENT below.

Weight: 3.11 grams. *Composition:* .950 copper, .050 tin and zinc. *Diameter:* 19 mm. *Edge:* Plain. *GSID:* Brown, 2366; Red-Brown, 2368; Red, 2376.

On October 3, 2007, Michigan collector Michael Tremonti made what is probably the greatest find from a Lincoln cent roll ever: a near-gem, fully red 1969-S, Doubled Die Obverse, Lincoln cent. Soon after, it was recognized by variety expert Ken Potter as the finest example known. It was auctioned three months later for $126,500.

This example reignited interest in this coin, which is now considered the king of all Lincoln cent varieties. It is definitely the most valuable Lincoln cent variety and among the most rare. With one of the more dramatic and visually splendid doubled-dies on U.S. coinage, it shows clear separation between the letters throughout the obverse legends. Perhaps because only a few dozen are known, over the years this coin has been less widely publicized than some of the other doubled-die Lincoln cents. It has one of the most fascinating stories of any 20th-century coin.

When the variety was first discovered in mid-1970, the U.S. Secret Service declared it a counterfeit, and even seized the first of these coins that were reported. Based on where and how the coins were found, numismatists objected—but the Secret Service held their position. The confusion surrounding the variety arose because two counterfeiters, Roy Gray and Mort Goodman, had created fake 1969 doubled-die cents, without mintmarks, to defraud collectors.

Pick-up point: Date.

When everything was sorted out, the Secret Service reversed their position and declared the 1969-S cent to be genuine, and returned the seized coins.

Over the years since then, finds of this coin remained scant. Freshly found examples were almost always circulated and did not retain their original Mint red color. Before Tremonti's discovery, no full-red examples had been graded by a major certification service, and only a couple of examples were Uncirculated.

The coin is one that is also notoriously frustrating to hunt for. *Die doubling* occurs when the design of the coin is duplicated on the die that strikes a coin, and the position of the doubling is exactly identical on all the coins that it strikes. Not all doubled dies are valuable, but when there is good separation between the design details, the variety is very desirable. Unfortunately, the relatively common and worthless occurrence of *strike doubling* can sometimes resemble die doubling. Strike doubling occurs when the die bounces on the surface of the coin during striking, creating a shelf-like shadow of the design that resembles die doubling. Strike doubling is especially common on 1969-S Lincoln cents. As Ken Potter notes on his web site, "It is *hard* to find a roll of cents for any of these dates without finding pieces exhibiting this affliction."

When looking for authentic 1969-S Lincoln cents, the searcher will find countless pretenders. Their abundance calls all stories of discovery into doubt until they can be verified by an expert. Nonetheless, recent auction transactions have intensified the hunt. The sale of Tremonti's coin was bookended by three others of slightly lower-grade coins that all traded in the $60,000 to $80,000 range. Doubtless, more examples will become known to collectors, but the overall rarity and mystique of this coin give the king of the Lincoln cent varieties a comfortable seat among the greatest modern U.S. coins.

Mintage: fraction of 544,375,000

Color	AU-50	AU-58	MS-60	MS-61	MS-62	MS-63	MS-64	MS-65
Brown	$14,400	$19,800	$21,600	$22,800	$25,200	$27,600	$45,600	—
Red-Brown	—	—	28,800	33,600	36,000	43,200	72,000	$144,000
Red	—	—	23,400	25,200	27,600	31,200	52,800	—

3 1976, NO S, BICENTENNIAL EISENHOWER DOLLAR, PROOF

Designed by Frank Gasparro (obverse) and Dennis Williams (reverse). The obverse features the head of Dwight Eisenhower facing left. LIBERTY arcs around the top and the date reads 1776–1976. On the reverse, the Liberty Bell appears superimposed on the moon. The outer legends include UNITED STATES OF AMERICA above and ONE DOLLAR below. The motto E PLURIBUS UNUM appears in small letters to the lower right of the Liberty Bell.

Weight: 24.59 grams. *Composition:* Outer layers of .800 silver and .200 copper nickel over a core of .209 silver and .791 copper (net weight .3161 ounce pure silver). *Diameter:* 38.1 mm. *Edge:* Reeded. *GSID:* 275425.

This coin is as mysterious as it is rare—extremely so in both cases! A solitary example is known and a great deal of speculation surrounds its origins. Two things make this coin unique. First, it is the only Proof Variety 2 Eisenhower dollar struck without an S mintmark. Second, it is the only Proof Variety 2 Eisenhower struck on a 40 percent silver planchet; all others are copper-nickel-clad.

According to the Coin World Comprehensive Catalog & Encyclopedia, *the unique coin was discovered in a cash register at a Washington, D.C., department store.*

The 1976 Eisenhower dollar was actually struck in both 1975 and 1976. No dollar coins dated 1975 were struck, but instead this special Bicentennial coin, dual-dated 1776–1976, was issued in both years. The design for the reverse was selected in a contest held in 1974, and the entry of sculpture student Dennis R. Williams was selected for the dollar. The coins issued in 1975 include the blocky letter style used in Williams's original design. These are called Variety 1. In late 1975, the U.S. Mint announced that a slightly modified Eisenhower dollar would be introduced in 1976. The new design had a narrower letter style to match the obverse and is called Variety 2. The difference is readily apparent.

When the first designs were selected, a handful of presentation examples of all the Bicentennial coins were struck at Philadelphia. One set was sent to be exhibited at a numismatic convention, while others were presented to government officials, including President Gerald Ford. These Variety 1 coins did not include the S mintmark, and a few examples survive. The Variety 1 dollar has been catalogued as a pattern in the standard reference, *United States Pattern Coins* by J. Hewitt Judd, and assigned the number J-2163. While the occasion for these Variety 1 dollars to be struck is clearly documented, no similar event is recorded for the Variety 2 dollar.

Proof Bicentennial Eisenhower dollars were struck in both silver-clad and copper-nickel-clad composition, but all silver coins were Variety 1. However, this particular Proof coin, already unique for not having a mintmark, is also struck on a silver flan, the only silver Proof Variety 2 dollar.

There are two popular theories as to why this coin was made. Many people assume that it was a test striking of the new Variety 2 design, and was created in mid-1975 to confirm that the new design was an aesthetic (or technical) improvement upon its predecessor. This coin is assigned a catalog number of J-2164 in the pattern reference, based upon the presumption that it is a trial coin. Others, however, speculate that, like the extant No S Variety 1 coins, this piece was coined for presentation to statesmen or dignitaries.

The discovery of the coin might support the latter theory, because it's unlikely that a test piece would leave the Mint. According to the *Coin World Comprehensive Catalog & Encyclopedia*, the unique coin was discovered in a cash register at a Washington, D.C., department store. The coin was last sold at auction in September 2002 and resides in private collection. Research efforts are ongoing to uncover the true story of its origin.

Mintage: unknown (1 specimen confirmed)

Value cannot be speculated, due to the extreme rarity of this variety.

4 2000 SACAGAWEA DOLLAR / WASHINGTON QUARTER MULE

Designed by John Flanagan, as modified by William C. Cousins (obverse) and Thomas D. Rogers (reverse). The obverse depicts a bust of President George Washington facing left, modified to include some of the wording previously used on the reverse that was displaced for the State-quarter designs. The reverse features an eagle in flight surrounded by 17 stars. UNITED STATES OF AMERICA arcs around the upper reverse; ONE DOLLAR arcs around the bottom. E PLURIBUS UNUM appears in small letters in the left field.

Weight: 8.1 grams. *Composition:* Outer layers of .770 copper, .120 zinc, .070 manganese, and .040 nickel over a core of pure copper. *Diameter:* 26.5 mm. *Edge:* Plain. *GSID:* 340426.

In late May of 2000, collector Frank Wallis, of Mountain Home, Arkansas, made an astonishing discovery. While searching a roll of new Sacagawea dollar coins he had acquired from the First National Bank & Trust, he found a single example that was different. The size, weight, composition, and reverse design were all correct for a Sacagawea dollar; the exciting discovery was that the obverse (which should have featured Sacagawea) was that of a statehood Washington quarter.

Their value has continued to escalate, with a handful of reported transactions in the low six figures.

During striking of this particular coin, a die for the Sacagawea dollar had been used for the reverse, and a statehood-quarter die was accidentally used for the obverse. Error coins that combine parts of different coins are called *mules*—and mules of two different denominations are exceptionally rare and valuable. They are so rare, in fact, that at the time of its discovery, this coin was the only known mule of a U.S. circulating coin—the first in 208 years of U.S. coinage production.

The discovery coin wasn't unique for long. A second example, dispensed in change by a Philadelphia post office stamp-vending machine, was found soon after in June, and yet another Philadelphia-area discovery followed. The finds

garnered widespread media attention, including feature showings on television news. The U.S. Mint acknowledged that the error was legitimate, and that, even though they'd known the mules had been created, a small, unknown number had been released. Media attention gained additional steam when the second of the newly found coins was placed on eBay for sale by prominent coin dealer Delaware Valley Rare Coin Company. The eBay auction ended on July 7, 2000, with a final bid of $41,395. Details of the auction circulated so widely that the transaction helped to legitimize eBay as a viable venue for coin sales. Today more than one billion dollars' worth of transactions occur each year in eBay's coin category.

In spite of the excitement, many saw the auction price as staggering. As with any circulating rarity, there was concern during the first blush of discovery that more would come to light and compromise the value of the coin. Ultimately, the concern about unknown caches of coins proved unnecessary. Since August 2001, no new specimens have been found, and today only 10 Sacagawea dollar / statehood quarter mules are known. Their value has continued to escalate, with a handful of reported transactions in the low six figures. On August 9, 2012, a high-grade example sold for $155,250.

For its rarity and influence, this is among the most important of the 100 Greatest U.S. Modern Coins. The coin is distinctly modern, as it combines the new-composition Sacagawea dollar and the obverse of the statehood quarter, two highly important, seminal coin series of the new millennium. Its first sale established eBay as a legitimate marketplace for coins in the eyes of many dealers. And, of course, it is among the most valuable of all modern U.S. coins and U.S. error coins of any era.

Mintage: unknown

MS-63	MS-64	MS-65	MS-66	MS-67
$96,000	$120,000	$150,000	$174,000	$204,000

5 1995-W $1 AMERICAN SILVER EAGLE, PROOF

Designed by Adolph A. Weinman (obverse) and John Mercanti (reverse). The obverse features Weinman's Liberty Walking design used on half dollars from 1916 through 1947. Weinman's initials are on the hem of the gown. The reverse design is a rendition of a heraldic eagle by John Mercanti.

Weight: 31.101 grams. *Composition:* .999 silver, .001 copper (net weight 1 ounce pure silver). *Diameter:* 40.6 mm. *Edge:* Reeded. *GSID:* 10684.

The king of the American Silver Eagles, the 1995-W American Silver Eagle is one of the most coveted and important of all modern U.S. coins. It is also among the most controversial. As a result of a surcharge placed on these coins by the U.S. Mint, Proof American Silver Eagles have been money-makers for the Mint since they were first issued in 1986. Roughly 500,000 of them were sold to collectors each year, making them a cash cow. Although Proof American Gold Eagles were also offered during the same period, their higher cost meant that their total sales volume would amount to only 10 percent of the number of Proof silver coins that sold each year.

These 1995 coins were the first Proof American Silver Eagles ever struck at West Point and the first to have the W mintmark. During the 10th year of the American Eagle Bullion program, the U.S. Mint created a 10th-anniversary set of five Proof coins. All four denominations of the 1995 American Gold Eagle were included: the $5 coin (tenth-ounce), the $10 coin (quarter-ounce), the $25 coin (half-ounce), and the $50 coin (one-ounce). As with all Proof American Gold Eagles from that year, each coin was struck at West Point and bore the W mintmark. Also included in the set, as the fifth coin, was a Proof 1995 American Silver Eagle. To match the others, it too was struck at West Point.

Previous Proof issues had been struck in either San Francisco or Philadelphia, with an S or P mintmark, respectively. In 1995, however, Proof American Silver Eagles were struck in both West Point and Philadelphia. If collectors ordered the coin for the issue price of $23 without the set, they received a 1995-P. The only way to get the 1995-W coin was to shell out the $999 for the complete anniversary set.

When the sales period for the 10th-Anniversary Proof Bullion Coinage Set ended, a total of 30,125 had been sold. This figure constitutes the entire mintage of the Proof 1995-W American Silver Eagle, making it tremendously rare. By contrast, more than 400,000 of the Proof 1995-P American Silver Eagle were sold.

Collectors were outraged. They accused the Mint of profiteering by forcing their loyal American Silver Eagle customers to shell out a thousand dollars to get a rare issue. There were, after all, 10 times more collectors of Proof silver than Proof gold, so this offering was viewed as a ploy to convert collectors of silver to gold. Sales of the 1995-W in the secondary market did little to quell collectors' frustration. Immediately, the Proof 1995-W American Silver Eagle was valued at a few hundred dollars, over 10 times more than previous issues. And as time passed, the price continued to climb. Collectors wrote to the Mint and even wrote open letters to numismatic publications announcing that they were no longer buying Proof American Silver Eagles.

Their threats proved idle, and collectors never abandoned the series en masse. Even as early as January 1997, U.S. Mint Director Philip N. Diehl noted the growth of the program in a U.S. Mint press release: "Despite the controversy and criticism surrounding the issue of the 'W' Mint mark Silver Proof Eagle and predictions in the numismatic community that customers would desert the coin wholesale, sales rebounded and rose 15 percent."

The mystique and desirability of this coin have only grown over time. To say that the 1995-W is the "key" to the series is an understatement. Its small mintage of 30,125 is dwarfed by that of every other Proof American Silver Eagle in the series. Its value is nearly equal to that of all the other coins in the series combined. By any measure, the Proof American Silver Eagle program is more popular today than at any point in its past, which only continues to bolster demand for its king rarity, the 1995-W.

Distribution: 30,125

PF-63	PF-65	PF-66	PF-67	PF-68	PF-69	PF-70	OGP
$2,220	$2,380	$2,440	$2,500	$2,560	$3,250	$16,200	$3,500

6 1964 SPECIAL MINT SET

GSID: cent (Red-Brown), 82063, (Red), 2202; nickel, 82044; dime, 4959; quarter, 5910; half dollar, 6988.

In 1993, an unusual set of coins appeared for auction in a sale conducted by the venerable coin auction house Stack's Rare Coins New York. They offered a set of specimen coinage dated 1964. Each of the five coins in the set—the cent, nickel, dime, quarter, and half dollar—had razor-sharp strikes. Rather than the deep, mirror-like surface seen on Proof coins, these coins had a satin sheen, possessing none of the reflectivity seen on Proof coinage. Swirling die polish was evident throughout the coins' fields, indicating that the dies that struck them had received special treatment. In fact, these coins looked nothing like other known coins dated 1964—they looked most similar to the Special Mint Set coins of 1965!

The obvious speculation was that these coins were produced as a trial version of the Special Mint Set coins that were to come in the following year. In 1965, circulating silver coinage was to be replaced with copper-nickel; to manage the metal transition, the Mint was forced to produce an unprecedented number of coins. To aid them in their task, two noteworthy accommodations were made. First, all coins were to be struck without mintmark, as it was widely believed that this measure would limit hoarding of coins by collectors and speculators. Second, no Proof coins were to be struck until enough coins could be produced to meet the requirements of circulation.

In lieu of selling Proof and Mint sets, from 1965 to 1967 the Mint sold Special Mint Sets. The sets consisted of just five coins, all circulating denominations without mintmark. Each coin had a special finish, often described as falling somewhere between Proof and Mint State coins. The dies that struck the coins received additional polishing, but coins received only a single blow from the coinage die—true Proofs receive multiple strikes to more sharply impress the design. The issues of 1965 usually have a satin-like surface, but later issues from 1967 have a shallow, mirrored surface, more closely resembling Proofs. They are all readily distinguishable from circulation issues of the period and are available in high grades.

But there was no way to explain the existence of a 1964 Special Mint Set, as Proof coins were produced that year and no documentation concerning the creation of a 1964 Special Mint Set exists. Two theories predominate. The first is that there would have been a need to test the process of creating these Special Mint Set coins as a way of assessing their feasibility for production. To do this, a

number of trial 1964 sets were made. Additionally, the examples that are known today are always found in high grade, a sign that they were preserved and maintained by their owners. That latter fact has led to a second possibility, that these coins were produced as special presentation sets, the last 90 percent silver coins. Whatever the case may be, either scenario contributes to their appeal.

When pressed about their origin, Stack's disclosed that the coins were from the estate of a coin dealer. Because of the timing of the sale, some speculate that these coins in fact came from the estate of former Mint Director Eva Adams. She served as director from 1961 to 1969 and passed away at the age of 80 in 1991. The coins first appeared at auction two years after her death, and she would have had access to them during her tenure at the Mint.

Initially, it was reported that 15 sets were produced in total, but as more 1964 Special Mint Set coinage appears, that figure has since been revised upwards to 50. They are still seldom offered, though. Their unique appearance, the clear attention to their production quality, and their mysterious origin make them among the most coveted of all U.S. coinage sets.

Mintage: unknown

Denomination	MS-63	MS-64	MS-65	MS-66	MS-67	MS-68
Cent (Red-Brown)	—	$6,900	$11,900	$14,400	—	—
Cent (Red)	—	13,200	16,800	19,200	$24,000	$42,000
Nickel	$7,500	8,100	8,750	10,000	12,000	14,400
Dime	5,600	6,250	6,900	7,500	8,100	11,250
Quarter	—	3,120	8,000	11,250	24,000	38,400
Half dollar	—	—	—	—	45,600	72,000

7 2009 (MMIX) ULTRA HIGH RELIEF DOUBLE EAGLE

Designed by Augustus Saint-Gaudens. This is a modern version of the famous U.S. 1907 Ultra High Relief double eagle gold pattern, and was made as a tour de force to demonstrate how technical advances in the minting process can now accommodate manufacturing such a coin. The 2009 version was made in a slightly smaller diameter and composed of 24-karat gold, thus making it easier to strike and maintain the fidelity of the design. The date was changed to 2009, and four additional stars were added to represent the current 50 states. Also included was the inscription IN GOD WE TRUST, which was not used on the 1907 version.

Weight: 31.1035 grams. *Composition:* .999 gold (one ounce pure gold). *Diameter:* 27 mm. *Edge:* Lettered. *GSID:* 69740; Prooflike, 70923; Deep Mirror Prooflike, 212321.

When President Theodore Roosevelt sought to redesign U.S. coinage during his presidency, he enlisted the services of Augustus Saint-Gaudens, one of the preeminent sculptors of the era. Beginning with the $20 gold piece in 1907, Saint-Gaudens produced a phenomenal design to be rendered in high relief. It was agreed that the coins were magnificent, but they were impractical for production because they required many, repeated strikes from coinage dies to show full detail.

During one experimental attempt to produce high-relief coinage, the diameter of the $20 coin was reduced from 34 to 27 millimeters, the size of a $10 gold piece, and its thickness was doubled. Mint officials recognized, though, that for this reduced-diameter version to enter production, Congress would need to legislate a change to the $20 coin's specifications. Testing along these lines was abandoned, and ultimately the coin was issued in lowered relief. Two of these reduced-diameter 1907 Ultra High Relief $20 gold coins were retained and are now in the National Numismatic Collection at the Smithsonian Institution.

In 2008, new Mint Director Edmund Moy wished to bring this coin back as a bullion issue to display the capabilities of today's modern Mints, as this early 20th-century work was widely considered the high-water mark of U.S. coinage design. The plan was announced in early 2008: a pure gold, .9999 fine version of the double-thick Ultra High Relief would be issued as part of the American Eagle Bullion Program. There was to be no cap on the coin's mintage.

Step by step throughout the year, the Mint reported on its progress. In a series of feasibility tests, they discovered that the coin could be struck with just two blows of the coinage dies. Test pieces were displayed amidst much fanfare at the

2008 American Numismatic Association's World's Fair of Money, and the exhibit became an interactive feature on the U.S. Mint's web site.

At noon on January 22, 2009, the coins went on sale. In a soaring bullion market, the one-ounce gold coin was priced at $1,189, with a limit of just one coin per household. The Mint would later announce that first-day sales alone totaled $33.7 million. In early February, the coins began to trickle out from the Mint and dribbled into the marketplace throughout the year. Significant back orders and fulfillment issues meant that customers didn't know when the coin they ordered would be received. Dealers wanting to make an active secondary market in the issue were hampered by the one-coin-per-customer order limit. It was a challenge to get any kind of quantity of the coin. Even though speculator buzz quelled, the coin remained the most-talked-about issue of 2009, more so than even the redesigned Lincoln cent.

By the end of the year, 115,178 had been sold. As a stand-alone $20 coinage issue and as a bit of an outcast from the rest of the American Gold Eagle series, the future prospects for this coin seem unclear. If eagle and modern commemorative collectors both embrace it, though, there is no doubt it will become a classic.

Mintage: 114,427

	MS-67	MS-68	MS-69	MS-70	OGP
	$3,180	$3,210	$3,280	$3,470	$3,280
Prooflike	—	—	3,530	4,000	—
Deep Mirror Prooflike	—	—	3,780	6,900	—

8 1968, NO S, ROOSEVELT DIME, PROOF

Designed by John R. Sinnock. On the obverse, the head of Franklin Roosevelt faces left. LIBERTY appears in large letters along the left rim; IN GOD WE TRUST appears in small letters at the lower left, and the date appears at the bottom right. The reverse features a lit torch flanked by sprigs of olive and oak. UNITED STATES OF AMERICA arcs above, ONE DIME arcs below, and the motto E PLURIBUS UNUM runs in a straight line through the bottoms of the sprigs and torch.

Weight: 2.27 grams. *Composition:* Outer layers of .750 copper and .250 nickel over a core of pure copper. *Diameter:* 17.9 mm. *Edge:* Reeded. *GSID:* 4972.

While the United States transitioned from circulating silver to copper-nickel-clad coins between 1965 and 1967, no mintmarks appeared on U.S. coinage. Mint officials and politicians blamed the hoarding activities of collectors and speculators for coinage shortages around the nation. It was thought that removal of these distinguishing marks, which indicated where a coin was made, would give the public fewer reasons to hoard, and coins would circulate more freely. Also at this time, and with a related rationale, no Proof sets or Mint sets were issued. Instead, only a simplified single release of Special Mint Sets having some prooflike characteristics was available to collectors.

Finally, in 1968, these dictums were lifted and the tradition of including mintmarks on coins and the production of Proof coinage both returned. From the time the first coins were issued in the United States until 1964, all presentation issues for sale to collectors had been made at the Mint in Philadelphia. The only noteworthy deviation from this had taken place from 1965 to 1967, when the production of Special Mint Set coinage occurred at San Francisco, but there was little fanfare or notice because these coins did not bear mintmarks. When Proof coinage returned, production remained in San Francisco and, for the first time, in 1968, Proof coins bore the S mintmark.

At some point during the production of 1968 Proof coinage, an unusual error occurred. Dimes were struck from an obverse die that lacked the S mintmark. It's easy to see how this error could have occurred. All dies are made at a single die shop in Philadelphia and then shipped to the branch mints where the dies are used in production. Coinage of this year was the first time that this missing-mintmark error could have occurred on a U.S. Proof coin because this

was the first year that these coins had mintmarks. The great irony of the 1968, No S, Proof dime is that it is missing the very feature that distinguishes 1968 Proof coinage from the Proof coinage of all previous years!

Proof coins missing their mintmark, several of which appear in this book, are an especially desirable category of coinage, and they are aggressively sought after.

Any error in the manufacture of a Proof coin is noteworthy because of the considerable amount of special care that is taken in their production. Indeed, Proof-coinage errors are rare across the board. Proof coins missing their mintmark, several of which appear in this book, are an especially desirable category of coinage, and they are aggressively sought after. They vary in their rarity, and the 1968, No S, dime is among the rarest. Even as late as 1988, noted historian Walter Breen knew of only six examples. Because of this, it is widely believed that the mistake was discovered by the Mint. Subsequently, almost all the mintmark-less coins were pulled from release, and only a handful escaped. New estimates suggest that as many as two dozen examples are in collectors' hands, and the finest examples can trade for as much as $50,000.

Mintage: fraction of 3,041,506

PF-65	PF-66	PF-67	PF-68	PF-69
$14,400	$16,200	$20,150	$26,400	$48,000

9 2007-W AMERICAN PLATINUM EAGLE, PROOF, "FROSTED FREEDOM" VARIETY

Designed by John Mercanti (obverse) and Thomas Cleveland (reverse). The obverse features a portrait of Lady Liberty. The reverse depicts a bald eagle with its wings spread wide to represent freedom, with a shield at the ready to enforce the laws that guarantee those freedoms.

$100: Weight: 1.0005 ounces. *Composition:* .9995 platinum. *Diameter:* 32.7 mm. *Edge:* Reeded. *$50: Weight:* 0.5003 ounces. *Composition:* .9995 platinum. *Diameter:* 27 mm. *Edge:* Reeded. *$25: Weight:* 0.2501 ounces. *Composition:* .9995 platinum. *Diameter:* 22 mm. *Edge:* Reeded. *GSID:* $25, 198091; $50, 198092; $100, 198093

The reverse design of Proof American Platinum Eagles changes each year. The design used in 2007 represents the executive branch of government. It shows an eagle's wings spread wide to represent freedom. A shield is placed before him, demonstrating a readiness to enforce the laws that guarantee those freedoms. And draped across the top of the shield is a banner inscribed with the word FREEDOM.

The Proof coin was produced in deep cameo contrast, with black mirrorlike fields and white frosted design elements. In the main illustration of this coin in the *Red Book*, the standard reference to U.S. coinage, and indeed in the illustration on the Mint's own web site, the word FREEDOM is frosted along with the rest of the design elements.

On the issued coin, however, the word FREEDOM is mirrored, showing in contrast to the rest of the design and making it more readable. No one attributed any significance to this anomaly, believing that the illustration was simply a U.S. Mint–generated rendering that predated actual production. No one, that is, until Florida-based dealer Jason Fishman made a surprising discovery in January 2011. He had purchased a one-ounce $100 Proof American Platinum Eagle. Unlike others he had seen, this coin indeed showed the word FREEDOM frosted, similar to the Mint's concept image.

In February, another discovery followed. This time it was a quarter-ounce $25 issue that showed the same variation, popularly referred to as "Frosted FREEDOM." Months later a third discovery emerged. Now a Frosted FREEDOM $50 American Platinum Eagle was identified.

Various theories circulated surrounding the mysterious origin of these coins, but the Mint did not wait too long to release the true story. Michael White of the Mint's Office of Public Affairs stated that a small number of coins were struck,

as originally designed, with the word FREEDOM frosted. Upon examining the actual coins, Mint officials decided that the coins would look better if this word were shown with a mirrored finish. New dies were prepared to strike coins for regular production, but the pre-production coins were never destroyed. In error, they were mixed among the production coins and released.

The Mint also released firm production figures for Frosted FREEDOM American Platinum Eagles:

- 12 one-ounce, $100 coins
- 21 half-ounce, $50 coins
- 21 quarter-ounce, $25 coins

No Frosted FREEDOM tenth-ounce, $10 coins were produced.

Only a very small number of these coins have been thus far identified. With only a few handfuls produced and released, the Frosted FREEDOM Platinum Eagles are among the rarest of all collectible modern U.S. coins. Inadvertent releases of pre-production coinage have only seldom occurred in the Mint's history. The 2000-P "Cheerios" Variety Sacagawea dollar with prototype reverse (no. 13) is the closest parallel to this coin. It is indeed another instance where a pre-production version was released before final changes were made to the design. Although only a small variation occurs on these coins, they will remain a standout in the American Platinum Eagle series and likely never be duplicated in terms of absolute rarity. In November 2022, the second known one-ounce $100 sold at GreatCollections auction for $232,624.12, an astronomical sum that has contributed to the legendary status of these coins.

Mintage: $25 coin, 21; $50 coin, 21; $100 coin, 12

Denomination	PF-70DC
$25	$48,000
$50	93,600
$100	240,000

10 1990, NO S, LINCOLN CENT, PROOF

Designed by Victor David Brenner (obverse) and Frank Gasparro (reverse). The obverse continues the design of 1909, featuring a bust of Lincoln facing right, the word LIBERTY to his left, and the date in the field in front of his coat. The legend IN GOD WE TRUST appears above his head. The reverse shows a frontal view of the Lincoln Memorial with UNITED STATES OF AMERICA and E PLURIBUS UNUM appearing above and ONE CENT below.

Weight: 2.5 grams. *Composition:* Outer layers of pure copper bonded to a core of .992 zinc and .008 copper. *Diameter:* 19 mm. *Edge:* Plain. *GSID:* Red, 315515; Red Cameo, 315516; Red Deep Cameo, 2619.

The 1990, No S, Lincoln cent is a Proof coin struck at the San Francisco Mint missing the obligatory and otherwise standard S mintmark. This omission had occurred several times in the past, including at least three times on the Roosevelt dime and once on the Jefferson nickel. This issue is the sole Lincoln cent missing its mintmark and represents the last time to date that such an omission occurred on a Proof coin. The first detail makes this coin especially coveted, while the second tells a particularly fascinating story.

The question remains as to how such a coin could have been produced in 1990. . . . A number of Mint employees handled and inspected the die without, apparently, noticing the missing mintmark.

Lincoln cents are collected by a large and enthusiastic group, a fact that makes this coin, the only Lincoln cent of its kind, very desirable. All collectors of Proof Lincoln Memorial cents want one. It also turns out that the coin is very rare, much rarer than many expected (more on that to follow), which makes it rather expensive, trading for as much as $7,000 in the highest grades.

All of these cents were issued in Proof sets and Prestige Proof sets—versions of the Proof set that included a Proof 1990-P Eisenhower commemorative dollar. In 1990, a Proof die struck approximately 3,700 cents, which is the estimated mintage figure of the 1990, No S, Lincoln cent. When this coin was discovered

not long after the Proof sets were issued, the U.S. Mint confirmed the error and announced that they had recovered and destroyed 145 examples. For this reason, the net mintage figure of this variety is often reported as 3,555. The total number of Proof sets issued in 1990 was nearly 2.8 million. To date, only about 250 examples are known, less than one-tenth the number thought to be struck. The discovery rate is so low that some numismatists suggest that many fewer than 3,555 ever actually left the Mint.

The question remains as to how such a coin could have been produced in 1990. Preparing a Proof die requires that the die be chrome-plated, polished, and, in 1990, sandblasted by hand to create the frosted design elements. A number of Mint employees handled and inspected the die without, apparently, noticing the missing mintmark. Another detail adds more intrigue to the story of this coin, as, starting in 1985, the master dies used to make dies for Proof coins included the S mintmark. When such errors had occurred previously, most recently in 1983, mintmarks were still being added by hand to individual dies, making this type of error more likely. Furthermore, Lincoln cent dies without mintmarks in 1990 would all have been clearly intended for the production of circulating coinage. In the case of the 1990, No S, cent, it appears that a die intended to strike circulating coinage was treated and used to strike Proof coins at San Francisco.

There are certainly still discoveries of these coins to be made. Most commonly, they are found in the Prestige Proof set, and the prize of finding one is significant. Additionally, a doubled-die nickel and a doubled-die quarter can be found in 1990 Proof sets (nos. 71 and 66 on this list, respectively). The prospect of finding one of three valuable varieties makes sets of this year irresistible to modern coin specialists.

Mintage: fraction of 3,299,559

Surface	PF-63RD	PF-64RD	PF-65RD	PF-66RD	PF-67RD	PF-68RD	PF-69RD
Normal	$1,880	$2,000	$2,120	$2,310	$2,500	—	—
Cameo	1,970	2,120	2,280	2,440	2,750	—	—
Deep Cameo	2,120	2,250	2,440	2,620	3,060	$3,440	$6,000

11 2006-W $50 AMERICAN GOLD EAGLE, REVERSE PROOF

Designed by Augustus Saint-Gaudens (obverse) and Miley Busiek (reverse). The obverse features a modified rendition of the Augustus Saint-Gaudens design used on U.S. $20 gold pieces from 1907 until 1933. The reverse displays a "family of eagles" motif.

Weight: 33.931 grams. *Composition:* .917 gold, .030 silver, .053 copper (net weight 1 ounce pure gold). *Diameter:* 32.7 mm. *Edge:* Reeded. *GSID:* 65313.

The $50 American Gold Eagle is the workhorse of the U.S. gold bullion program. This one-ounce coin is the largest gold coin in the series and accounts for the vast majority of gold units sold. Its obverse design is based on Augustus Saint-Gaudens's original design for the $20 gold coin that circulated from 1907 to 1933. The reverse is a more-contemporary arrangement by sculptor Miley Busiek and shows a male eagle returning to a nest containing a female eagle and hatchlings. Since it was first issued in 1986, this sequence has perennially been among the most popular bullion-coinage issues in the world.

To celebrate the 20th anniversary of the American Gold Eagle Bullion program, the Mint offered three different sets. The most expensive option was the three-coin gold set, which featured a 2006-W Proof American Gold Eagle, a 2006-W Uncirculated American Gold Eagle, and, for the first time ever, a 2006-W Reverse Proof American Gold Eagle; the set sold for $2,610. The offering was limited to 10,000 sets.

Normal Proof American Gold Eagles have frosted designs surrounded by mirrored fields. When this arrangement is inverted, and the fields of the coins are frosted while the design portion, including the lettering, is mirror-like and reflective, the coin is said to be a *Reverse Proof*. It's an unusual surface finish that can be both striking and exotic, especially when employed on a familiar coin-type for the first time, as it was with the 20th-anniversary eagles.

The announcement of the Reverse Proof American Gold Eagle was made nine days before the coin went on sale, and it was immediately clear that it would be something special. It was the only coin of its kind in the American Gold Eagle series, the most popular gold bullion-coinage sequence in history. Further, its mintage was limited to just 10,000 coins—far below what was then the lowest Proof one-ounce American Gold Eagle mintage, the 24,555 pieces of the 2001 issue. As expected, the coin was a quick and complete sellout (accounting for returns, the net mintage is now reported as 9,996). Prices doubled in the

secondary market, and the coins have retained their post-release premium while the value of gold has doubled.

The obvious question is why did the Mint produce only 10,000 coins? If the coin was so successful, why not make more? First, the Mint wanted to be sure that it would sell out. They produce collector versions of bullion coins only when production will not interfere with demand for bullion issues and when they can do so without creating expenses for taxpayers. A small program is more likely to sell out and easier to manage. Reverse Proof coins require special handling and die production; a much larger mintage would have made it difficult for the Mint to produce the coins.

Also, with gold valued at $617 per ounce on the initial sale date, the set of three American Gold Eagles had an intrinsic metal value of $1,851. Thus, its issue-price of $2,610 represented a large premium to gold weight and placed it among the most expensive sets ever sold by the U.S. Mint. With such a high original issue price, perhaps the Mint felt that if they produced more coins they would not sell or that the price premium to gold would be unsustainable.

The net effect of what appears to be an example of extreme caution is a modern rarity that will seldom be available on the market in large supply. Its unique appearance makes it always desirable and a standout precious-metal coin among modern U.S. issues.

Mintage: 9,996

PF-68	PF-69	PF-70	OGP
$2,630	$2,880	$3,750	$3,500

12 1972, DOUBLED DIE OBVERSE, LINCOLN CENT

Designed by Victor David Brenner (obverse) and Frank Gasparro (reverse). The obverse continues the design of 1909, featuring a bust of Lincoln facing right, the word LIBERTY to his left, and the date in the field in front of his coat. The legend IN GOD WE TRUST appears above his head. The reverse shows a frontal view of the Lincoln Memorial with UNITED STATES OF AMERICA and E PLURIBUS UNUM appearing above and ONE CENT below.

Weight: 3.11 grams. *Composition:* .950 copper, .050 tin and zinc. *Diameter:* 19 mm. *Edge:* Plain. *GSID:* Brown, 2231; Red-Brown, 2232; Red, 2233.

This strongly doubled die is one of the most visually dramatic varieties in the Lincoln Memorial cent series. It caused a sensation when it was first discovered in 1972 and collector interest has never faded. The entire obverse is fully doubled, with the doubling clear both on the legend, IN GOD WE TRUST and LIBERTY, and on the date. Each element shows a slightly offset replication of itself. The variety was created when the die that struck the coins was produced, and it received two misaligned impressions of the design from the hub. The doubling was then struck on each coin in the same way.

The coin was first spotted in the Mid-Atlantic states in 1972. Examples were offered for sale by prominent Philadelphia dealer Harry Forman. Almost immediately after the discovery of the variety, the price per coin jumped up to $30, allowing anyone who found one to turn a tidy profit. Unsearched 1972 cent bags, still Mint-sewn with 5,000 coins inside, traded at premiums as well.

Because the coin couldn't be found outside Philadelphia, Atlanta-based dealer John Hamrick contacted Forman for coins. To induce Forman to sell him a 50-coin roll, then priced at $1,500, Hamrick also agreed to buy ten Mint-sewn bags. The bags sat for a couple of months until Hamrick and his colleagues had time to sort them. When the job was completed, Hamrick had found 40 rolls of 1972, Doubled Die Obverse, Lincoln cents.

Pick-up points: Date, lettering.

The price and interest in the coin had blossomed during the months that led to Hamrick's discovery. Coin dealer Fred Balmer was paying $3,500 per roll at the time and bought Hamrick's entire find. In today's market, this would be a million-dollar cache of Lincoln cents—at the time, it made Hamrick the primary market maker in 1972, Doubled Die Obverse, Lincoln cents through the early 1970s.

The 1972, Doubled Die Obverse, Lincoln cent is one of the most desirable coin varieties found in circulation, although they are tough to find today. The strong interest in this coin from the time of issue means that a number of examples were located for the numismatic community, so they can be purchased from dealers. Condition plays a major factor in determining the value of this coin. Staining and carbon spots are common and finding a visually appealing example is not a simple task.

This coin can be easily mistaken for other, similar varieties—and subtle variety differences can mean a huge difference in value. A footnote to the Lincoln cent, Memorial Reverse section of *A Guide Book of United States Coins* (the *Red Book*), includes an important caveat: "Other slightly doubled varieties (worth far less) exist." Because so much time was devoted to searching for 1972, Doubled Die Obverse, Lincoln cents, other varieties that have been found are collectible. Very specialized collectors will pursue as many as nine different doubled-die obverse coins, but the coin properly referred to as the 1972, Doubled Die Obverse, Lincoln cent is very prominently doubled, easy to recognize, and worth the big premium.

Mintage: fraction of 2,933,255,000

Color	AU-50	AU-58	MS-60	MS-63	MS-64	MS-65	MS-66	MS-67
Brown	$260	$280	$290	$360	$390	$455	$680	—
Red-Brown	—	—	325	390	470	570	845	$2,440
Red	—	—	365	455	585	860	1,190	3,000

13 2000-P SACAGAWEA DOLLAR, "CHEERIOS" VARIETY

Designed by Glenna Goodacre (obverse) and Thomas D. Rogers (reverse). The obverse features the Indian guide Sacagawea and her infant son. LIBERTY appears above her head; IN GOD WE TRUST appears to the left, and the date is found on the right side. The reverse features an eagle in flight surrounded by 17 stars. UNITED STATES OF AMERICA arcs around the upper reverse; ONE DOLLAR arcs around the bottom. E PLURIBUS UNUM appears in small letters in the left field.

Weight: 8.1 grams. *Composition:* Outer layers of .770 copper, .120 zinc, .070 manganese, and .040 nickel over a core of pure copper. *Diameter:* 26.5 mm. *Edge:* Plain. *GSID:* 81740.

Acknowledging the failed prior attempts at getting a dollar coin into circulation, the Mint in 2000 wanted to remove all the possible barriers to their latest effort at introducing such a coin. They initiated a widespread media blitz that included television commercials and enlisting Wal-Mart to provide the new dollar coins to customers as change. One of the more novel efforts was a coinage give-away conducted with General Mills, which pictured the coin on every box of Cheerios.

Billed as a millennium promotion, a single example of the first 10,000,000 Lincoln cents struck bearing the date 2000 was included inside each marked box of Cheerios that year. One in every 2,000 boxes included both a cent coin and a Sacagawea dollar. According to a General Mills promotional release, "during the month of January, the only place to get either coin [was] in a box of Cheerios." We know this is a true statement regarding the Sacagawea dollar, as it was not released to Federal Reserve banks until January 26, 2000, and Wal-Mart had agreed not to release them until January 30, 2000.

In order to have the dollar coins delivered to General Mills in time for its promotion, the Mint struck 5,500 coins in late summer or early fall of 1999. Full-scale production of the finalized Sacagawea dollar did not begin until more than a month later, on November 18, 1999. During the intervening time, tests of the design were still ongoing at the Mint. A design variation other than the final circulation version had been used to strike the coins delivered to General Mills.

The so-called "Cheerios" or Reverse of 1999 Sacagawea dollar is easy to distinguish from a circulation issue by examining its reverse. The eagle's wings and tail show intricate feather detail, including raised central feather shafts and numerous veins. These details are absent on the final adopted design, on which the central tail feather shows an incuse shaft. This same level of reverse detail

is present on the 22-karat gold coins with the West Point mintmark that were struck in June 1999 and sent into space aboard the shuttle *Columbia.* Numismatic researcher Tom DeLorey speculates that the same die that was used to strike the gold Sacagawea dollars may have also struck the coins delivered to General Mills.

The timeline and story of this coin were pieced together by noted numismatic researchers, including DeLorey, David Lange, and David Camire. Collectors and hobbyists such as Pat Braddick and Mike Wallace also played a critical role in gathering information about this coin. But the discovery of this coin did not come until June 2005, five years after the coin was released. Two factors account for the late discovery of such an important coin. For one, the coin was mounted obverse-up in the holder, and the reverse with the extra tail-feather detail is not visible. Secondly, these coins were distributed in non-numismatic circles—to buyers of Cheerios—and few went to coin dealers. For years, no one wanted to remove them from their holders, thinking that it was the holder that imparted a small premium.

With only 5,500 examples extant and a wide distribution into mainstream commerce, this coin is a major rarity; there are fewer than a hundred examples in the numismatic marketplace. Discoveries are happening all the time, though, and these coins can turn up just about anywhere.

Mintage: 5,500

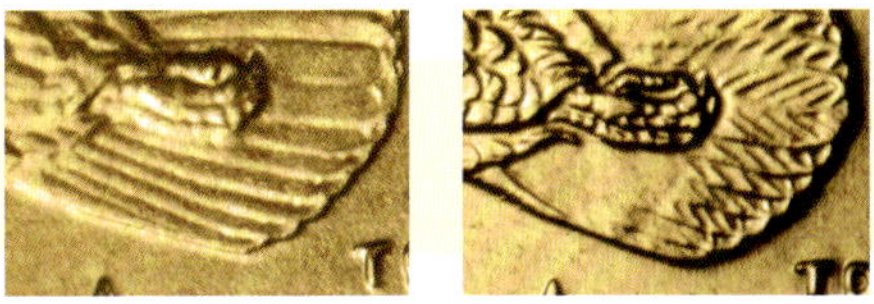

Pick-up point: Tail feathers (left, normal; right, boldly detailed).

MS-63	MS-64	MS-65	MS-66	MS-67	MS-68
$1,020	$1,440	$2,060	$2,620	$6,500	$10,000

14 2008-W $1 AMERICAN SILVER EAGLE, REVERSE OF 2007

Designed by Adolph A. Weinman (obverse) and John Mercanti (reverse). The obverse features Weinman's Liberty Walking design used on half dollars from 1916 through 1947. Weinman's initials are on the hem of the gown. The reverse design is a rendition of a heraldic eagle.

Weight: 31.101 grams. *Composition:* .999 silver (net weight 1 ounce pure silver). *Diameter:* 40.6 mm. *Edge:* Reeded. *GSID:* 197930.

Not long after the first 2008 American Silver Eagles came out, it was reported that the coins had been "re-hubbed." A hub is used to make dies, which in turn strike coins. *Re-hubbing*, therefore, meant that a new design template was being used to create all the dies that struck these coins. While the major design elements of the coin had not changed, subtle alterations had been made to the lettering and elsewhere. These changes were consistent across the entire American Silver Eagle production of 2008, including bullion, Proof, and Uncirculated versions of the coin.

In the course of producing modern coinage, these types of subtle changes occur over time. Technical aspects of minting, including attempts to prolong die-life and improve the clarity with which the design renders on the coin, find their way into the design process. According to the U.S. Mint, the changes seen on the 2008 American Silver Eagles were made because of the adoption of digital engraving in the production of American Silver Eagle dies. This was a more efficient and cost-effective method of production.

To accommodate this new process, a handful of modest changes were made to the coin. The most noticeable change occurred on the style of a single letter. In

Reverse lettering styles: (left) 1986–2007, with smooth curve at bottom right of U; (right) 2008 to date, with spur at bottom right of U.

2008, the U that appears in the word UNITED on the coin's reverse had a spur or foot on its right side, while on all previous issues the spur was absent—the old U was a simple bowl shape. Even though it affected just a single, small letter, this change was the tell-tale diagnostic that allowed the reverse hub of 2008 to be distinguished instantaneously from that used in previous years.

In mid-April 2008, only a couple of weeks after the first 2008-W American Silver Eagles were sold, collector John Nanney of Georgia noticed that a small number of coins had the old reverse style of 2007. This immediately ignited a search among collectors, and interest in this curious variety began to grow. When the variety was confirmed by the grading services, the search became a frenzy, and a number of collectors placed additional orders for coins from the Mint.

Numerous inquiries were directed to the U.S. Mint. The Mint responded quickly, acknowledging that during three production shifts for the 2008 coins, dies originally crafted for 2007-W American Silver Eagle production were used inadvertently. Approximately 47,000 American Silver Eagles had been struck with the reverse style of 2007. This type of variety is called *transitional* because it is a hybrid that combines the styles of coins used in two consecutive years. The 2008-W, Reverse of 2007, American Silver Eagle is the only significant die-variety in the entire American Silver Eagle series, and it is collected by enthusiasts as a required coin in the complete set.

The coins were crafted from designs by A.A. Weinman and John Mercanti. Weinman, who is responsible for the obverse design, originally created this composition for the Liberty Walking half dollar first released in 1916. It shows Liberty striding against the rising sun, and the design was long considered to be the most attractive ever used on a U.S. silver coin. The reverse heraldic eagle composition was designed and engraved by Mercanti.

Mintage: 47,000 (estimated)

MS-66	MS-67	MS-68	MS-69	MS-70	OGP
$290	$325	$360	$455	$1,080	$420

15 1999-S SILVER DELAWARE QUARTER, PROOF

Designed by John Flanagan, as modified by William C. Cousins (obverse), and William C. Cousins (reverse). The obverse depicting President George Washington was modified to include some of the wording previously used on the reverse. The reverse shows patriot Caesar Rodney on his historic 80-mile ride through terrible heat and thunderstorms to cast his vote in favor of Delaware signing the Declaration of Independence. Rodney's vote turned out to be the tie-breaker.

Weight: 6.25 grams. *Composition:* .900 silver, .100 copper.
Diameter: 24.3 mm. *Edge:* Reeded. *GSID:* 6046.

Many hyperbolic claims surround the 50 State Quarters® Program. For example, it's often asserted that these new circulating coins turned 100 million Americans into collectors, as they sought to complete sets of quarters from change. If that statement seems overreaching, it's important to consider the facts of the state-quarter series. For starters, it was certainly the most ambitious commemorative-coinage program and the most aggressive coinage-design program in U.S. history. Additionally, it produced some of the most important collectible quarters of the era, the most prized of which can trade for a few thousand dollars—yes, that's right, a few thousand!

At the outset, 50 different coins were to be struck honoring each state in the nation over the course of a 10-year period. Coins for each state were issued in the order that they achieved statehood. The first state in the union is Delaware, and its coin came first. Coinage legislation required that each state's governor select the coinage theme design. For Delaware, it was decided that the coin would honor early statesman Caesar Rodney. In 1776, hearing that his fellow Delaware representatives were deadlocked in the vote over independence, Rodney rode 80 miles on horseback (or at least partially on horseback) through a stormy night to arrive in Philadelphia in time to cast a deciding vote. Shortly thereafter, Rodney signed the Declaration of Independence.

As the first coin in the series, the Delaware quarter has some special cachet. But the silver Proof version is turning into a modern "classic." To begin with, the only way to get the Proof version at the time of issue was to purchase the complete silver nine-piece Proof set from the Mint, which included the cent and nickel, as well as 90 percent silver examples of the dime, half dollar, and all five 1999 quarters: the Delaware, Pennsylvania, New Jersey, Georgia, and Connecticut coins. The initial sales price for the set was $31.95, meaning that

these coins were premium items from the start. Slightly more than 800,000 silver Proof sets sold and they were widely dispersed. Today, it is challenging to find more than a handful of the sets on the market, and their price can be as high as $400 per set.

The packaging of 1999 statehood quarters Proof sets are different from those of subsequent years. The materials do little to protect the coins from toning, and most 1999 silver quarters are seen with a whitish haze. The Delaware quarter shows Caesar Rodney on horseback on an open field, with most of the margin of the coin flat and open. It may be this aspect of the coin that makes the Delaware quarter particularly prone to discoloration or spotting. As a result, it is far and away the hardest of the silver state quarters to find in the highest condition, Proof-70. There are fewer than half as many Delaware quarters graded at this level by the top grading services than for the next-scarcest quarter. In fact, the finest examples routinely trade for as high as $3,000 per coin!

The 50 State Quarters® Program started a trend in circulating-commemorative programs and caused many to take a closer look at their pocket change. There is no doubt that it contributed to a renaissance of coin-collecting in the United States. It also produced one of the most coveted of all modern coins in the Proof silver 1999-S Delaware state quarter.

Mintage: 804,565

PF-65DC	PF-66DC	PF-67DC	PF-68DC	PF-69DC	PF-70DC
$8.80	$11.50	$16	$20	$40	$405

16 1997-P JEFFERSON NICKEL, MATTE "SPECIAL UNCIRCULATED"

Designed by Felix Schlag. The obverse features a bust of Thomas Jefferson facing left. IN GOD WE TRUST appears inside the left edge, and LIBERTY and the date appear inside the right edge. On the reverse, Jefferson's home, Monticello, appears as the central device. E PLURIBUS UNUM arcs above. The word MONTICELLO captions the building, and the words FIVE CENTS and the legend UNITED STATES OF AMERICA appear below.

Weight: 5.00 grams. *Composition:* .750 copper, .250 nickel.
Diameter: 21.2 mm. *Edge:* Plain. *GSID:* 3606.

The 1997 U.S. Botanic Garden commemorative dollar was a coin that held a special interest for lawmakers. The museum and conservatory were created by an act of Congress in 1820, and together they are the oldest continuously operated garden in the nation. Although the U.S. Botanic Garden is little known outside of Washington, D.C., it sits at the foot of Capitol Hill and its trustees are Washington's elite. Given that the U.S. commemorative-coinage program was foundering under a swelling number of issues in the late 1990s, Congress intentionally acted to bring attention to this commemorative dollar in order to raise money for the National Fund for the U.S. Botanic Garden.

The Jackie Robinson commemorative coins (see no. 18 on this list) were scheduled to go on sale later that same year. One senator was so concerned about the competition caused by that coin that he took action. Senator J. Bennett Johnston, a Louisiana Democrat whose wife, Mary, was a vice chairwoman of the National Fund for the U.S. Botanic Garden, intended to block the Jackie Robinson coin unless a portion of the proceeds were diverted from the Robinson coins' surcharges to support the Botanic Garden. Instead of raising money for the Jackie Robinson Foundation, which gives college scholarships to poor inner-city youths, sales supported the garden. Needless to say, this was controversial and did not improve the image of the suffering U.S. commemorative-coinage program.

In a rare bit of irony, the Botanic Garden coin sold better than the Robinson coin. One reason was the 1997-P Jefferson nickel Matte "Special Uncirculated" coin. In an effort to spur sales, as they had done for the 1993 Thomas Jefferson dollar, the U.S. Mint offered a coinage and currency set that included a specially struck Jefferson nickel with a matte finish, minted in Philadelphia and

bearing a P mintmark. Thomas Jefferson, along with other founding fathers, had championed the concept of a botanic garden on the National Mall, so there was some historical relevance. Just 25,000 examples of the set were to be sold and the pre-issue price was $36. The only way to get the special-finish Jefferson nickel was in the set and the small premium over the $30 pre-issue price for the commemorative alone made the coin an unbelievable deal. Everyone predicted a sellout, and everyone was right.

It's easy to make an argument that the 1997-P Jefferson nickel Matte Finish coin was born of a special interest to boost the sales of another coin favored by Washington insiders, but that doesn't diminish its appeal. Within the context of the Jefferson nickel set, it is a standout key coin. Its mintage is a mere 25,000 pieces, the lowest of any U.S. coin belonging to a regular series since 1942. It is visually dramatic, with a sharp, Proof-quality strike but monotone dull surface shared in the series only by the 1994-P nickel Matte "Special Uncirculated"—yet this coin is nearly seven times scarcer.

Because it was issued in a commemorative set, almost all of these coins are well-preserved and high grade. It is not unusual to find examples that have toned to a golden hue. Untoned examples of the highest grade, 70 out of 70 on the Sheldon grading scale, command a premium and are highly sought-after.

Mintage: 25,000

MS-63FS	MS-64FS	MS-65FS	MS-66FS	MS-67FS	MS-68FS	MS-69FS	MS-70FS
$32	$35	$40	$47	$88	$120	$170	$360

17 2020-W $1 AMERICAN SILVER AND $50 GOLD AMERICAN EAGLES, V75 PRIVY MARK, PROOF

$1 American Silver Eagle: Designed by Adolph A. Weinman (obverse) and John Mercanti (reverse). The obverse features Weinman's Liberty Walking design used on half dollars from 1916 through 1947. Weinman's initials are on the hem of the gown. The reverse design is a rendition of a heraldic eagle by John Mercanti. $50 American Gold Eagle: Designed by Augustus Saint-Gaudens (obverse) and Miley Busiek (reverse). The obverse features a modified rendition of the Augustus Saint-Gaudens design used on U.S. $20 gold pieces from 1907 until 1933. The reverse displays a "family of eagles" motif.

Weights: 31.10 grams and 33.93 grams, respectively. *Compositions:* .999 silver and .001 copper (net weight 1 ounce pure silver); and .917 gold and .003 silver (net weight 1 ounce pure gold). *Diameters:* 40.6 mm and 32.7 mm. *Edges:* Reeded. *GSID:* Silver $1, 82111; Gold $50, 84815.

In 2020, the U.S. Mint released privy-marked versions of the American Gold and Silver Eagles to mark the 75th anniversary of the end of World War II. Privy marks have a long history in coinage. The term typically refers to a small emblem that denotes something significant about the origin, production, or issuing authority of the coin. The U.S. Mint has used privy marks on only a very limited basis in the past; the year 2020 marks the first time a privy mark appeared on the American Gold or Silver Eagle.

The privy mark itself is a small cartouche enclosing the insignia V75, to indicate "Victory" and "75 years." The shape is derived from that of the Rainbow Pool, a reflecting pool incorporated into the design of the World War II Memorial on the National Mall. Finding an evocative symbol that could be rendered on the coin in a small size had been challenging for the U.S. Mint's coin designers. Mint director David Ryder, passing the Memorial on his daily commute, exclaimed, "That's the shape."

In mid-2020, the full program parameters were announced. The coins were to go on sale on November 5. The V75 Silver Eagle had an authorized mintage of 75,000 pieces and a planned issue price of $69.50. The V75 Gold Eagle was to be exceptionally limited, at only 1,945 pieces. A nod to the year 1945, when the war ended, it was the lowest preset mintage limit of any numismatic product in the Mint's history. Its prospective issue price, based on the value of gold, was $2,400. In August 2020, the value of precious metals surged, pushing the actual issue prices of the silver and gold coins to $83 and $2,600, respectively.

Due to the Covid pandemic, no phone orders were taken; all coins were to be purchased on the U.S. Mint's website, with an order limit of one per household. When the coins went on sale at noon on November 5, the gold coin sold out in just seven minutes, and the silver coin lasted for an hour longer. The Mint, facing numerous complaints, described the event as the "highest website traffic we have ever experienced, which greatly exceeded our expected capacity."

The coins immediately because widely coveted and valuable. Aftermarket sales of V75 American Silver Eagles were reported at $300-plus, and certified coins traded for $500 or more. V75 Gold Eagles traded at more than $10,000, and soon reached $25,000 for PF-70 Ultra Cameo certified coins. These price levels have held, and the coins continue to be scarce and highly sought after. The popularity of the coins led to a slew of reported fakes, including outright counterfeits and genuine coins with added, fake privy marks. Buying from a known source and careful inspection is recommended.

Mintage: silver, 74,709; gold, 1,939

Denomination	PF-68DC	PF-69DC	PF-70DC	OGP
Silver, $1	$375	$410	$680	$420
Gold, $50	12,000	13,200	22,800	13,200

18 1997-W JACKIE ROBINSON $5 COMMEMORATIVE

Designed by William C. Cousins (obverse) and James Peed (reverse). The obverse depicts a portrait of Jackie Robinson in his later years as a civil rights and political activist. The reverse shows the detail of the seams on a baseball, Robinson's 1919–1972 life dates, and the inscription "Legacy of Courage."

Weight: 8.359 grams. *Composition:* .900 gold, .100 copper. (net weight .2418 ounces pure gold). *Diameter:* 21.6 mm. *Edge:* Reeded. *GSID:* 10588.

This coin is the best example of one of the many paths taken by coins in this book to earn their positions on the list of the 100 Greatest U.S. Modern Coins: "What is not desirable initially can become coveted in time." When the Jackie Robinson $5 gold commemorative went on sale on August 16, 1997, there was little interest. Congress had authorized that a maximum of 100,000 examples could be struck and that the sales period could extend for one year. By August 16, 1998, less than 30,000 had sold, divided between Proof and Mint State versions of the coin. Only 5,174 of them were of the Mint State, or Uncirculated, type, making it by far the lowest-mintage modern commemorative coin ever issued to that point.

The coin's poor sales record has survived, and today it is the second lowest-mintage modern commemorative. Although few were attracted to the coin at the time of issue, the Robinson commemorative's low mintage makes it the key to the series and it is now among the most-desirable coins in the series; it commands the highest price of any gold commemorative, trading for more than $5,000.

Thematically, this coin is interesting. Jackie Robinson's head is shown on the obverse in three-quarters profile, and the reverse shows a baseball inscribed with the dates of his life, 1919–1972, and the phrase "Legacy of Courage." It is a stark and modern design, if plain, but also singularly American. Robinson himself is an inspiring figure, the first black player in Major League Baseball when he joined the Brooklyn Dodgers in 1947, and should have generated widespread appeal.

So what accounted for the commemorative's infamous unpopularity? Primarily, two things are to blame: the overabundance of commemorative issues and the falling price of gold. In 1995, the U.S. Mint had sold three $5 gold commemoratives: one commemorating the end of the Civil War and two Atlanta Olympic commemoratives. Two more Olympic commemorative $5 coins followed in 1996, along with the Smithsonian coin discussed later, at no. 78 on this list. In 1997, there was a Franklin Delano Roosevelt $5 coin issued just a couple of

months before the Robinson coin. This meant the avid collector had already purchased seven different gold commemorative issues in the last three years when the Robinson coin came to market. This high a number of gold coins had never been offered to the modern coin collector in such a short time period before.

During that same time period, gold decreased in value by 25 percent. Throughout much of 1995, gold had teetered above the $400-per-ounce level, but then fell steadily, month after month, to $300 per ounce by mid-1998. Collectors were seeing commemorative coins trading at discounts to the original offering price in the secondary market, often by as much as $100 less than what they had paid. Frustrated by both the number of issues and the falling prices, collectors simply waited on the sidelines.

Despite the atrocious sales record, no one ever doubted the merit of this coin or the quality of the Mint's execution. Instead, it was acknowledged that too many coins had been issued in too short a time. Beginning in 1998, Congress limited the number of commemorative programs to two per year and also limited the number of coins that could be made under those programs. These steps contributed to the improved sales performances of future commemorative issues, and also helped cement this coin's place as the series key. What no one wanted in 1997 is now the most sought-after issue in the current market.

Mintage: 5,174

MS-68	MS-69	MS-70	OGP
$780	$860	$1,560	$880

19 2004-D, EXTRA LEAF, WISCONSIN QUARTERS

Designed by John Flanagan, as modified by William C. Cousins (obverse), and Alfred Maletsky (reverse). The obverse depicting President George Washington was modified to include some of the wording previously used on the reverse. The reverse features an agricultural theme: the head of a cow, a round of cheese, and an ear of corn, along with the motto FORWARD on a banner.

Weight: 5.67 grams. *Composition:* Outer layers of .750 copper and .250 nickel over a core of pure copper. *Diameter:* 24.3 mm. *Edge:* Reeded. *GSID:* Extra Leaf Low, 15340; Extra Leaf High, 15341.

At the time of its inception, the 50 State Quarters® Program was universally hailed as exciting and innovative, but by 2004, it was becoming old news. The program was already more than five years old and had passed its halfway-point. The coin market had certainly benefited from a rush of new collectors who entered the field by assembling quarter sets from pocket change; for the first time in a long time, Americans were looking at circulating coins. But outside of the design selection process, which made headlines in their respective states, these coins weren't a front page story anymore.

The 30th coin in the set would change everything. First released on October 25, 2004, the agriculturally themed Wisconsin quarter was well received. Shortly after the Wisconsin quarter's release, though, a Tucson, Arizona, collector named Bob Ford found a handful of Wisconsin quarters that were clearly something different.

Pick-up point: Corn on reverse.

For more than a decade, Ford had searched through circulating coins, looking for errors and varieties. On December 11, 2004, he noticed, unexpectedly, that some Wisconsin quarters appeared to have an extra leaf placed beneath the left leaf on the ear of corn, one of the central elements of the coin's design. This "extra leaf" could be found in two distinct varieties. One showed a thin extra leaf that ran from the base of the ear and connected with the larger, curved leaf above; this coin is now known as the "Extra Leaf High" variety. The other variety showed a thicker leaf that came out of the ear at a lower angle, never touching the leaf above, now called the "Extra Leaf Low."

Ford shared his find with coin dealer Rob Weiss of Old Pueblo Coin in Tucson. They realized that this was indeed something highly unusual and alerted the numismatic press. The extra leaves caused a flurry of speculation about their origin, and almost immediately Extra Leaf Wisconsin quarters were trading for hundreds of dollars. Quick on the uptake, collectors in Western states demanded rolls of Denver Mint Wisconsin quarters from their local banks, hoping to strike it rich. The story soon spread to the mainstream media. By mid-January 2005, it was front-page news on the Arizona *Daily Star*, and less than a month later it was reported in *USA Today*.

Questions regarding the irregularity remain unresolved. It is clearly the result of a *die-gouge*, an impression in the die that creates a raised element on the struck coin. Some people speculate that the gouge was created purposefully, to create an embellishment and stimulate waning collector interest. Other compelling evidence suggests that a misaligned die clash may have transposed elements of Washington's hair curls, which in radius and size resemble the shapes of the leaves. The exact cause of these varieties is unknown and certainly ranks among the most intriguing mysteries of modern coinage.

According to information from a Freedom of Information Act request made by *USA Today* and released in January 2006, approximately 50,000 coins displaying blemishes were struck on a Friday night in November 2004. Even though these coins had been detected by Denver Mint employees, they had already been bagged and prepared for shipment. Quite simply, it would have been too costly to separate them from regular coins, and thus they were released into circulation.

Although collectors around the country searched for these coins, most of their efforts were in vain. Their distribution appears to have been localized, and nearly all significant finds were in the Tucson area.

Mintage: fraction of 226,800,000

Variety	AU-50	AU-58	MS-60	MS-63	MS-64	MS-65	MS-66	MS-67
Extra Leaf Low (FS-5902)	$34	$68	$81	$100	$120	$160	$235	$585
Extra Leaf High (FS-5901)	54	88	110	145	160	275	390	780

20 2011-P $1 AMERICAN SILVER EAGLE, REVERSE PROOF

Designed by Adolph A. Weinman (obverse) and John Mercanti (reverse). The obverse features Weinman's Liberty Walking design, used on half dollars from 1916 through 1947. Weinman's initials are on the hem of the gown. The reverse design is a rendition of a heraldic eagle by John Mercanti.

Weight: 31.101 grams. *Composition:* .999 silver (net weight 1 ounce pure silver). *Diameter:* 40.6 mm. *Edge:* Reeded. *GSID:* 71375.

When the Mint celebrated the 20th anniversary of the American Eagle Bullion Program in 2006, they went big. They offered collectors three different anniversary sets: a silver dollar set, a silver and gold set, and a gold set. Above all, major excitement was generated by the first-ever Reverse Proof American Silver Eagle included in the silver dollar set. By almost every measure, the silver dollar set was a grand success, with final audited sales of 248,875 sets.

So everyone rightly expected a major celebration of the eagle's 25th anniversary in 2011. And they waited. And waited. Finally, in August 2011, Mint Deputy Director Richard Peterson announced that a 25th-anniversary set would be sold and that it would go on sale in October. True, the actual first release of American Silver Eagles had occurred on November 24, 1986, later in the year, but collectors and dealers had already been wondering for many months if there would be any anniversary coins at all.

The August announcement also included details of the sets' contents. Only a single five-coin American Silver Eagle set would be sold, which included the following coins:

- 2011 $1 American Silver Eagle, bullion coin without mintmark
- 2011-W $1 American Silver Eagle, Proof
- 2011-W $1 American Silver Eagle, Uncirculated
- 2011-S $1 American Silver Eagle, Uncirculated
- 2011-P $1 American Silver Eagle, Reverse Proof

Collectors were excited about the set, but it seemed like a bit of a mishmash. The first three coins described above were available individually outside of the set. The bullion coin had been available since the start of the year. The Proof went on sale in June and the Uncirculated coin in September. But the last two coins were special and unique to the set—the first-ever Uncirculated American Silver Eagle with an S mintmark, and the eagerly anticipated return of the

Reverse Proof. Reverse Proof coins have frosted fields and mirrored devices, the opposite of the cameolike Proof coinage traditionally issued in the United States. Only one other Reverse Proof American Silver Eagle had been issued to date, the enormously popular 20th-anniversary coin.

This solitary set was certainly scaled back compared to the coins offered in celebration of the 20th anniversary. Production details reinforced this feeling. Mintage was to be limited to 100,000 sets, less than half the number of silver dollar sets sold in 2006. There has never been a formal explanation for why the offering was so diminished, but a few reasons are plausible. First, because the Mint director was preparing to leave that office, perhaps the planning process for this program had been cut short. Second, following the broad financial collapse in 2008, austerity in celebration was the norm. In these circumstances, maybe Mint officials feared that a big release would fail and they would be criticized for their excess. Last, metal prices had boomed over the last five years. If a gold set had been offered, it would have been very expensive. Expensive Mint products are a target of criticism even in good times.

Compared to the 2006 silver dollar set, however, the price of the 2011 set was hardly restrained. It includes five American Silver Eagles, compared to three in 2006, but it was three times the price! While the 20th-anniversary silver dollar set cost $100, the 25th-anniversary set was priced at $299.95. But even with its comparatively high price and strict ordering limit of five sets per household, the coin sets sold out rapidly. Collectors could not resist the allure of the coins that were unique to this set, including the Reverse Proof. With only 100,000 minted, the 2011-P Reverse Proof is by far the scarcest of all Reverse Proof American Silver Eagles yet issued and is among the most highly sought after of all recent U.S. Mint releases.

Mintage: 100,000

PF-68	PF-69	PF-70	OGP
$215	$235	$365	$235

21 1999-W $5 AND $10 AMERICAN GOLD EAGLES, FROM UNPOLISHED PROOF DIES

Designed by Augustus Saint-Gaudens (obverse) and Miley Busiek (reverse). The obverse features a modified rendition of the Augustus Saint-Gaudens design used on U.S. $20 gold coins from 1907 until 1933. The reverse displays a "Family of Eagles" motif.

Weights: 3.393 grams; 8.48 grams. *Composition:* .917 gold, .030 silver, .053 copper ($5: net weight 1/10 ounce pure gold; $10: net weight 1/4 ounce pure gold). *Diameters:* 16.5 mm; 22 mm. *Edges:* Reeded. *GSID:* $5, 68755; $10, 71683.

These tenth-ounce $5 and quarter-ounce $10 American Gold Eagles are the first circulation-strike U.S. bullion coins that bear the W mintmark. Made by mistake, these coins were struck from Proof-coin dies that did not receive the final finishing steps before being mixed in with the bullion dies and sent to West Point. In 1999, all U.S. gold bullion coins were struck at the U.S. Mint in West Point, New York, but only the Proof versions included a mintmark. This variety is alternately called the 1999-W, "with W," and the 1999-W, "Struck from Unpolished Proof Dies."

It is said that Proof dies are individually accounted for and a number of manual quality-control steps occur in the production of these coins. Given the close management of the dies, errors are unlikely, but they do happen. In this case the blame rests on the enormous number of gold bullion coins struck in 1999.

Concerns about how computer systems would respond in the year 2000 was a constant and seemingly rational fear in 1999. Since a significant amount of software required only a two-digit date, the ramifications of a date recorded simply as "00" were unknown. Would computers, programmed to operate as though it were 1900, fail to execute scheduled tasks in the year 2000 (a.k.a. "Y2K"), causing systems to go offline and financial markets to tumble? Y2K fears caused a flight to tangible assets, and the popularity of the American Gold Eagle took off.

In most years, only 70,000 to 80,000 quarter-ounce $10 American Gold Eagle bullion coins are struck. In 1999, six times that figure, or a total of 564,232, were struck—a number that mintage figures have not approached since. Peak production of tenth-ounce American Gold Eagles was even more extreme in 1999, when a staggering 2.75 million examples were produced. To give some perspective, this figure is 10 times the typical number of sales; for example, in 2009 the net mintage for the tenth-ounce version was 270,000 coins.

The die-production facilities and the quality-control processes were so overworked that it's easy to understand how dies could have been mishandled. Based

on the coins' marketplace availability, it's widely thought that three dies were used in the production of the 1999-W tenth-ounce coins and two dies for the 1999-W quarter-ounce coins, although a comprehensive die study has never been undertaken. This leads to the estimated mintage figures of 14,500 and 10,000 for the $5 and $10, respectively.

Interest in these coins grew in 2006, when the U.S. Mint offered Uncirculated versions of the American Eagle Bullion Program coins directly to collectors. These coins had the same finish as the bullion issues and included the W mintmark. To construct a complete set, collectors needed to acquire two different American Gold Eagles: a coin with and a coin without the mintmark. The focus on mintmarks encouraged many collectors to take a second look at the 1999-W coins, but with only a few thousand in the hands of collectors, they've remained a hot commodity.

Distribution: $5, 14,500 (estimated); $10, 10,000 (estimated)

Denomination	MS-65	MS-66	MS-67	MS-68	MS-69	MS-70	OGP
$5	$780	$820	$845	$895	$1,020	$2,880	$1,220
$10	1,090	1,130	1,220	1,410	1,620	7,500	1,620

22 1972 EISENHOWER DOLLAR, VARIETY 2

Designed by Frank Gasparro. The head of Dwight Eisenhower faces left on the obverse. LIBERTY arcs around the top of the obverse, and the date appears below the head. IN GOD WE TRUST appears at the lower left. On the reverse, an eagle with an olive branch in its talons alights upon the surface of the moon. A tiny earth can be seen in the background, and 13 small stars surround the eagle. UNITED STATES OF AMERICA and E PLURIBUS UNUM appear above the eagle; ONE DOLLAR appears below.

Weight: 22.68 grams. *Composition:* Outer layers of .750 copper and .250 nickel over a core of pure copper. *Diameter:* 38.1 mm. *Edge:* Reeded. *GSID:* 7916.

This elusive and desirable coin demonstrates that testing and experimentation were components of the Mint's process to meet the demands of modern coinage production. Little more than a hundred years before this coin was struck, dies were individually handcrafted. The need for greater output and a focus on consistency and uniformity meant that the die-creation process also became mechanized. Errors that occurred during the mechanized process, such as doubled dies, account for some of the most compelling entries among this top-100 list. But there are also instances where the involvement of artists and craftsmen contributed to make an important modern coin. The 1972 Variety 2 Eisenhower dollar is the best example of this.

When the Mint was testing Eisenhower dollar dies, it was clear that the design as proposed was too high in relief to meet the challenges of production. To enable the large-scale minting of a dollar-sized copper-nickel coin, the U.S. Mint re-rendered the design in low relief. The higher-relief design was retained for production of Proof coinage, and a lower-relief version was used for circulating coins. This change allowed the Philadelphia and Denver Mints to strike more than 115 million circulation Eisenhower dollars in 1971, but the compromise was evident. The coins were very flat and otherwise poorly detailed.

The Proof coins, by contrast, were struck with the original, higher-relief design, and its effect and appearance were far superior. Herein lay the problem, however: a Proof die was used for only 4,000 strikes (or for making 2,000 coins, each of which got two blows from a die), while a circulation die struck 100,000 to 200,000 coins. How could the design be improved while still meeting enormous production demands?

In 1972, at the Denver Mint, the original, low-relief dies were used to strike all 92 million coins made there that year. At Philadelphia, however, the tinkering

began. Of the 75 million coins produced there that year, an estimated 50 million are of the original, low-relief design, called Variety 1. Enthusiasts also discovered that a higher-relief design normally used to make Proofs was prepared to make circulation strikes, testing the design and performance. This is the so-called Variety 2, and it is very rare relative to the other types. Just two die pairs have been identified, called the "March" and "August" dies because each is found singly among coins released during these months in 1972. Based on die life, approximately 300,000 coins were struck in this variety. Later in the year, a modified design was introduced, called Variety 3, which was used for all Proofs and circulation strikes of this design at all Mints in subsequent years. According to estimates, 25 million or so of the Variety 3 were struck.

The best way to tell the three varieties apart is to look at the earth as depicted on the reverse of the coin. On Variety 1 coins, the earth shown on the reverse of the coin is not round, but rather is flattened in its upper left from 9:00 to 11:00. Additionally, the islands beneath Florida are all directly underneath it or to the right. None are to the left of it. On the Variety 2 examples, the earth is round and there are no islands beneath Florida. Instead, delicate inset lines strengthen the outlines of the continents. On the Variety 3 coins, the earth is again round, but three islands are visible beneath Florida and extend well to the west of the state into the Gulf of Mexico.

In the realm of modern coinage, these details distinguishing the various types constitute dramatic and deliberate design changes. The Variety 2 Eisenhower dollar is legitimately scarce, and adding to its allure is its absolute rarity in high grade—it is so elusive that gem examples trade for thousands of dollars when they can be found.

Mintage: fraction of 75,890,000

AU-58	MS-60	MS-62	MS-63	MS-64	MS-65	MS-66	OGP
$74	$81	$100	$120	$195	$1,620	$9,400	$88

23 1998-S KENNEDY HALF DOLLAR, SILVER, MATTE FINISH

Designed by Gilroy Roberts (obverse) and Frank Gasparro (reverse). On the obverse, the head of John F. Kennedy faces left. LIBERTY arcs across the top of the obverse; the date arcs along the bottom of the obverse and IN GOD WE TRUST runs in a straight line beneath Kennedy's head. The reverse features a heraldic eagle, similar to that seen on the 1801 through 1807 and 1892 through 1915 half dollars, within a circle of 50 stars. UNITED STATES arcs around the top and HALF DOLLAR arcs along the bottom of the reverse.

Weight: 12.50 grams. *Composition:* .900 silver, .100 copper.
Diameter: 30.6 mm. *Edge:* Reeded. *GSID:* 6975.

By the late 1990s, the U.S. Mint was under pressure to boost commemorative coin sales. Coins for the 1994 World Cup and the 1996 Olympics had performed miserably. Although today's collectors salivate when they see the low mintage figures of commemoratives from this era—making them among the most desirable of all the issues—at the time it was disastrous for the Mint. Millions of dollars were lost. For example, the U.S. Mint paid nearly $9 million to the World Cup Organizing Committee from collected surcharges on the sale of the 1994 commemorative coins, even though the Mint itself netted a loss of $5 million on the coins.

To boost sales, the Mint tried new things. In one experiment, special versions of circulating coins were paired with other Mint products. This was done to great effect in 1998, when the Uncirculated Robert F. Kennedy silver dollar was paired with a silver John F. Kennedy half dollar from the San Francisco Mint. Sold in the "Brothers Set," this Kennedy half dollar is a significant coin for many reasons. To match the appearance of the commemorative dollar it was paired with, the Kennedy half dollar was given a dull matte surface, the first time that this finish had ever been used on a Kennedy. Further, unlike circulating coins, the Kennedy half dollar issued in this set is 90 percent silver. Although 90 percent silver Kennedy half dollars had been sold since 1992 in special Proof sets, this was the first Kennedy of this composition since 1964 that wasn't strictly a Proof.

Adding another unusual element, the Brothers Set was only offered for sale during a six-week window. Rather than limiting the number of sets that could be produced, the Mint limited the sales period and therefore did not need to strike coins until it knew exactly how many were sold. Referring specifically to

this facet of the program in the U.S. Mint's Annual Report, Director Philip N. Diehl wrote, "[The six-week sales window] created urgency among collectors and brought us cost and production benefits from knowing how many coins to produce. This innovation served us and the hobby, and it's a win-win option for the future. The program will close profitably on December 31, 1998."

A profitable commemorative program was indeed something to celebrate in 1998. But the program's success may have had more to do with the convenient thematic relationship of two siblings on coins combined with the rather high issue price of $59.95 for the set—a lofty $30 premium for the silver half dollar—than anything else. Despite the success, this type of initiative has not been repeated by the Mint.

The $30 spent on the coin back in 1998 has generated a nice return, as this coin is worth several hundred dollars today. Its mintage of approximately 62,000 is very low for the series and the unique attributes of the coin give it a broad base of appeal. Issued in special sets and created with extra care, the coin frequently survives in pristine condition, making this a key date that can be acquired in the very highest grades.

Mintage: 62,000 (estimated)

MS-60	MS-63	MS-65	MS-66	MS-67	MS-68	MS-69	MS-70
$68	$81	$88	$92	$97	$105	$155	$360

24 2001-P AMERICAN BUFFALO DOLLAR COMMEMORATIVE

Designed by James Earle Fraser. The obverse and reverse designs are based on the original 1913 Buffalo nickel, with modified inscriptions on the reverse. The obverse features a portrait of a Native American facing right with the inscription LIBERTY in front and the date on the shoulder. The reverse features a full figure of the American bison, standing, facing left. The inscription reads UNITED STATES OF AMERICA, IN GOD WE TRUST, E PLURIBUS UNUM and ONE DOLLAR.

Weight: 26.73 grams. *Composition:* .900 silver, .100 copper. (net weight .77344 ounces pure silver). *Diameter:* 38.1 mm. *Edge:* Reeded. *GSID:* 10538.

One major characteristic of modern U.S. coinage is that it frequently borrows from previous coinage designs. The obverse of the American Gold Eagles and American Silver Eagles recast, respectively, Saint-Gaudens's design from his eponymous $20 gold piece and Weinman's design for the Liberty Walking half dollar, both issued at the turn of the 20th century. The First Spouse series similarly depicts adaptations of Liberty from earlier coinages when a particular president was not married while in the White House. Following in this tradition, James Earle Fraser's Buffalo nickel design has been recast on a series of .9999 fine gold coins since 2006, but its first reuse came in 2001 on the American Buffalo commemorative coin.

The coin was sold to benefit the National Museum of the American Indian (NMAI), a new Smithsonian museum then under construction on the National Mall. The authorizing legislation stipulated that a $10-per-coin surcharge be used to supplement the new museum's endowment. It also stated that James Earle Fraser's design for the Buffalo nickel, "which portrays a profile representation of a Native American on the obverse side and a representation of an American buffalo on the reverse side, is a distinctive and appropriate model for a coin to commemorate the NMAI." The design of the new coin followed Fraser's original in near-replica, making adjustments for its different relief and size, and the addition of requisite legends left off the original.

Whether or not it was Congress's original intention, its design selection created a blockbuster. A new Fraser Buffalo coin proved incredibly popular, and the authorized mintage of 500,000 was a complete and rapid sellout. Prices quickly escalated in the secondary market, with coins almost immediately selling for double and triple their issue price. So many people were shut out of the ordering process that legislators examined whether it would be feasible to authorize an

increase to the mintage of an additional 500,000 pieces. After all, they reasoned, proceeds should benefit the NMAI and not market speculators who had purchased coins solely to quickly resell.

Others questioned whether such a move would be legal. Many had purchased the coin with an understanding that it was to be limited to 500,000 pieces. Would an increase in mintage constitute a misrepresentation of the edition size? The debate played out well in the numismatic press and added interest to the coin. Ultimately, no increase in the mintage was authorized and the number produced remained at half a million coins. The Proof version had proven slightly more popular, selling 272,869 examples versus 227,131 for the Uncirculated format. All controversy aside, this coin ranks among the most sought-after of all modern U.S. commemorative coins, being one of the highest-priced silver issues in the series.

Distribution: Uncirculated, 227,131; Proof, 272,869

MS-67	MS-68	MS-69	MS-70	OGP
$89	$105	$110	$235	$110

25 2008-W AMERICAN GOLD EAGLE SET, UNCIRCULATED

GSID: 77945

Ask most collectors or dealers what the lowest-mintage American Gold Eagle is, and often they will respond quickly, "It's the 2006-W $50 Reverse Proof." At the time it was issued, few could believe the Mint would offer a coin with a maximum mintage of just 10,000 pieces. The final net audited sales figure for this coin is even lower, 9,996 pieces. So this low-mintage coin is the one that people think of first, but it is not actually the correct answer to the question.

The lowest-mintage American Gold Eagle is, in fact, the Uncirculated quarter-ounce 2008-W $10. Just 8,883 were produced.

The year 2008 was a huge year for gold. Spot broke the $1,000-per-ounce mark in the first time in history, after two straight years of gains in excess of 20%. U.S. Mint sales of gold bullion would be the fifth highest to date, topped only by the first two years of the American Gold Eagle Program and 1998 and 1999, when concerns over Y2K encouraged heavy purchases of hard assets.

At the same time, the Mint was offering a very large number of different gold products: Proof and Uncirculated American Gold Eagles, the Bald Eagle $5 commemorative coins, the First Spouse coins, and the gold Buffalo coins. With the rising price of gold, all these coins were more expensive than they had ever been before. Something had to give. Sales of the 2008-W Uncirculated American Gold Eagle coins were devastating. For the first time ever, the gold Buffalo coins were offered in fractional-ounce denominations, and that head-to-head competition was probably the biggest factor accounting for the sales decline.

The Uncirculated American Gold Eagles are the collector version of American Gold Eagles sold directly by the Mint. They are similar in appearance to the bullion issues but include a W mintmark, for West Point, where they are struck. They are commonly referred to as the "burnished" eagles because the Mint advertises them as being "specially burnished," a pre-striking process that does not affect the coins' final appearance. Sales were never great, but in 2008, they reached new lows:

- 2008-W $50: 11,908 coins, the second lowest one-ounce mintage in the entire series, in any format.
- 2008-W $25: 15,682 coins, the third lowest for the half-ounce denomination. This coin was also included in the "8-8-08 Prosperity Set," which contributed to uncharacteristic high sales.

- 2008-W $10: 8,883 coins, the lowest mintage of any American Gold Eagle (excluding the 1999-W varieties struck from unfinished Proof dies).
- 2008-W: $5, 12,657 coins, the lowest mintage of the denomination (excluding the 1999-W variety struck from unfinished Proof dies).

Sales were so devastatingly low that the Mint cancelled the Uncirculated Bullion Program entirely for 2009 and 2010, before bringing it back in its current form, offering only one-ounce versions of these bullion coins to collectors.

The 2008-W American Gold Eagles are most commonly collected as a four-coin set. It is much easier to buy the quarter-ounce $10 coin with its three companion coins than singly. All four coins are downright scarce in their own right. Individually or as a set, they occupy this position on the list of 100 Greatest Modern U.S. Coins.

Mintage: $5 coin, 12,657; $10 coin, 8,883; $25 coin, 15,682; $50 coin, 11,908

OGP
$5,950

26 2000-W LIBRARY OF CONGRESS $10 COMMEMORATIVE, BIMETALLIC

Designed by John Mercanti (obverse) and Thomas D. Rogers (reverse). The obverse features the hand of Minerva raising the torch of learning. The Library of Congress Jefferson Building's dome is visible in the background. The inscriptions around the ring state LIBERTY, 2000, and LIBRARY OF CONGRESS. The motto IN GOD WE TRUST appears in the platinum portion of the coin to the left of the hand and torch. The reverse features the seal of the Library of Congress surrounded by a laurel wreath. The outer ring carries the inscriptions UNITED STATES OF AMERICA and TEN DOLLARS. The motto E PLURIBUS UNUM appears in the platinum center below the eagle.

Weight: 16.2590 grams. *Composition:* Outer ring of .900 gold and .100 copper around a core of .999 platinum (total 48% gold, 48% platinum, and 4% alloy). *Diameter:* 27 mm. *Edge:* Reeded. *GSID:* 10602.

One sentence inserted into the authorizing legislation for this commemorative yielded one of the most intriguing coins made by the U.S. Mint. According to the law, the secretary of the Treasury was given the option of producing a $5 gold commemorative that conformed to the specifications of previous commemorative issues or, instead, could produce a $10 bimetallic gold and platinum commemorative. Thankfully for collectors, the Treasury elected to make the bimetallic coin.

The reasons for this selection are not entirely known, but there are a few likely causes. For one, the $10 platinum coin would be sold at a higher surcharge of $50 per coin compared with $35 for the alternative gold issue, and it was likely that this would raise more money for the Library of Congress Trust Fund Board, which supports outreach programs for the Library. More likely, however, is awareness that this would be the first commemorative coin issued in the new millennium and a desire to celebrate with a coinage "first" as well.

While the composition of the coin is unique, the design itself is relatively staid. The central portion of the obverse, in platinum, shows a hand holding a torch before the dome of the Library's Jefferson building. The legend surrounds on a golden ring and, cleverly, the flame of the torch rests fully on the gold portion as well. The reverse shows a compact version of the Library's seal in platinum, with legends surrounding on the golden ring. The coin was issued in both Uncirculated and Proof versions.

This ambitious bimetallic concept was only attempted this one time. It's widely thought that production of this coin was a huge challenge because the gold and platinum parts did not meld together well during striking. Indeed, platinum and gold bimetallic-coinage issues are very few in number. Despite the obviously complementary nature of the metals, the disparate densities of gold and platinum make them difficult to strike in concert. Indeed, on many specimens of the Library of Congress $10 commemorative, the inner platinum core can be heard rattling inside its golden ring. In the end, the Mint was spared from producing them in large numbers because the coin did not sell very well.

While a total of 200,000 examples were authorized to be struck, only 7,261 of the Uncirculated version and 27,455 of the Proof version were sold. Today, its low mintage makes the Uncirculated, Mint State coin one of the most sought-after issues in the commemorative series and commands the second highest price of any modern commemorative, trailing after only the Uncirculated version of the Jackie Robinson $5 coin.

The reason for the commemorative's unpopularity at the time of production really isn't clear either. Perhaps this issue did not resonate very well thematically because it commemorates the anniversary of an institution rather than a person or an event. The novelty of its composition doesn't appear to have been much help, either. Most likely, the issue price was just too high at nearly $400 per coin, when previous U.S. Mint offerings of $5 gold commemoratives were offered for little more than $200 per coin. As one of the keys to the series, their original issue price now seems like an absolute steal!

Distribution: Uncirculated, 7,261; Proof, 27,445

MS-68	MS-69	MS-70	OGP
$1,180	$1,250	$1,560	$1,250

27 1965–1967 SPECIAL MINT SET COINAGE, ULTRA CAMEO

GSID: 1965—cent (Red), 2614; nickel, 3555; dime, 4965; quarter, 5916; half dollar, 7000; *1966*—cent (Red), 2616; nickel, 3558; dime, 4968; quarter, 5919; half dollar, 7003; *1967*—cent (Red), 2618; nickel, 3561; dime, 4971; quarter, 5922; half dollar, 7006.

This particularly scarce group of highly coveted coins was struck during a three-year period, from 1965 to 1967. The Coinage Act of 1965 mandated replacing circulating silver coinage in favor of copper-nickel-clad, an enormous undertaking for the U.S. Mint. They were tasked with producing quantities of copper-nickel-clad coins to replace the silver coins presently in circulation. Because it was impractical to completely replace all the currency at once, silver coins continued to be struck until 1966. Working furiously, the Mint created an unprecedented number of coins in Philadelphia, Denver, and San Francisco.

The statistics for this period of production are staggering: before 1964, only three mintage figures of quarters exceeded 100 million. In 1965, however, more than 1.8 billion quarters were struck! In the *entire prior history* of the silver quarter dollar, a total of 4.4 billion coins were struck for circulation. Between 1965 and 1967, more than 4.1 billion quarters were struck, so that in just three years, the U.S. Mint nearly matched the production of the previous 168.

To enable this enormous increase in production, the Mint cut back in other ways from 1965 to 1967. First, they removed mintmarks from coins. Then the Mint created no Proof sets or Mint sets in these years. To satisfy collectors, they issued Special Mint Sets, a hybrid of two with less emphasis on packaging and production quality but specially struck coins. Possibly as a measure to curb demand, their issue price was set at $4, nearly double the price of Proof sets or Mint sets in previous years.

The coins within these sets vary considerably in their appearance. Some of them present a rather gray satin surface with striated die polish unique to Special Mint Set (SMS) coinage, particularly those coins dated 1965. Others resemble regular circulation-strike coins with few distinguishing characteristics, while others yet resemble true Proof coinage with highly reflective, mirrorlike fields and contrasting frosted devices. These are said to be early strikes from fresh dies.

Coins that display contrast between their devices (the design area of the coins) and their fields (the blank portions) are referred to as cameo. Coins with the strongest or sharpest level of contrast are referred to as ultra cameo or deep

cameo. While most SMS coins are relatively available and affordable, the SMS coins with this strongest level of cameo contrast are particularly valuable. These coins are so desirable because they resemble the highest-quality Proof coins, and SMS coinage is today sought by Proof coinage collectors. Only a few dozen ultra cameo examples have been identified for each of the cent, nickel, dime, and quarter dollar. The Kennedy half dollar, especially the 1967 issue, is slightly more available with very deep cameo contrast; a few hundred exist.

Mintage: unknown

Denomination	MS-64DC	MS-65DC	MS-66DC	MS-67DC	MS-68DC	MS-69DC
1965						
Cent (Red)	—	$2,500	$4,000	$6,250	—	—
Nickel	—	340	420	3,250	—	—
Dime	$520	845	1,690	3,500	—	—
Quarter	—	1,500	2,500	4,380	—	—
Half dollar	390	585	2,000	4,060	—	—
1966						
Cent (Red)	845	2,000	3,120	5,600	—	—
Nickel	180	260	390	1,380	$5,600	—
Dime	—	—	960	1,880	3,120	$5,600
Quarter	—	520	960	2,250	5,000	—
Half dollar	285	340	470	1,250	6,250	—
1967						
Cent (Red)	960	2,250	3,750	5,600	—	—
Nickel	51	68	130	520	3,000	—
Dime	—	390	585	1,090	5,000	9,400
Quarter	160	260	455	715	2,750	—
Half dollar	68	100	210	415	3,880	19,200

28 2021 MORGAN DOLLARS

Designed by George T. Morgan. This coin served as the circulating dollar from 1878 to 1921 and features a capped head of Liberty on the obverse and an eagle with wings spread on the reverse. Mintmarks and privy marks, when present, appear below the eagle.

Weight: 26.73 grams. *Composition:* .999 silver (0.858 ounce pure silver). *Diameter:* 38.1 mm. *Edge:* Reeded. *GSID:* 2021-(P), 85110; 2021-(CC), Privy Mark, 85111; 2021-D, 85112; 2021-(O), Privy Mark, 85113; 2021-S, 85114.

Morgan dollars are often said to be the most widely collected U.S. coin. The original series, issued from 1878 to 1904 and again in 1921, is a staple of the numismatic marketplace. The key dates to the series—the 1895 (a Proof-only issue), the 1889-CC (the rarest Carson City issue), and the 1893-S (the undisputed key)—are dream coins for many collectors and occupy coveted spots in dealer showcases when they are lucky enough to have one. In anticipation of the 100th anniversary of the last Morgan dollar, the Mint authorized a centennial recreation of the coin.

The 2021 issue featured careful renditions of the original design. Chief engraver Joseph F. Menna said that the U.S. Mint used original models to render the design digitally so that it would be a faithful recreation. The relief was lowered to a correct proportion between rim and design elements for modern production. Its composition is pure silver, as opposed to the historical .900 fine version, but its weight and diameter are otherwise identical. The 2021 coins contain .858 troy ounces of silver rather than .773 troy ounces, due to the higher fineness.

Historically, the Morgan dollar was issued from five different Mint facilities, including two that are no longer in service, New Orleans and Carson City. To celebrate the issue, one version was struck in Denver with the D mintmark and another in San Francisco with the S mintmark. Three versions were struck at Philadelphia: one with no mintmark, like the original Morgan dollar, and two with privy marks in lieu of mintmarks—an O for New Orleans or a CC for Carson City.

The coins were minted in quantities of 175,000 each and offered in three different sales windows for $85 apiece. Initially the household order limit was set at 25 coins for each issue, but anticipating high demand, this was lowered to 10 coins. Regardless, on May 24, the CC and O privy-marked versions went on

sale and sold out on the first day. On August 3, the Denver and San Francisco coins sold out. And on August 10, the Philadelphia version went on sale at the same time as the Peace dollar, again setting a record when the coins sold out in one day.

Orders started shipping in October 2021. As indicated by the rapid sellouts, demand outstripped the limited supply. The higher household ordering limits meant that many collectors had duplicates to sell, and coins appeared for resale at 50- to 100-percent premiums over their issue price. While initially demand seemed strongest for the CC privy marks, this subsided, as the coins had identical mintage figures and availabilities. Ultimately, however, the Denver issue proved to have some modest condition deficiencies and was notably tougher to find in the top MS-70 grade. It now can trade for double the other Mint issues when certified at this grade level.

The authorizing legislation permitted the minting of the coins to begin any time after January 1, 2021, but did not provide a termination date. Mint director David J. Ryder was quick to recognize this and proclaimed that Morgan (and Peace) dollars might become regular offering of the Mint in future years. While no Morgan Dollars were issued in 2022, due to a shortage of silver planchets, they returned in 2023 and 2024, creating a new following for this beloved series.

Mintage: No Privy Mark, 174,498; CC Privy Mark, 173,781; O Privy Mark, 173,530

Issue	MS-68	MS-69	MS-70	OGP
2021-(P)	$160	$175	$245	$175
2021-(CC), Privy Mark	235	275	300	245
2021-D	160	175	1,090	175
2021-(O), Privy Mark	160	175	240	175
2021-S	160	175	235	175

29 2021 PEACE DOLLAR

Designed by Anthony de Francisci, this coin served as the circulating dollar coin from 1921 to 1935. It features a radiate head of Liberty on obverse and a eagle at rest on reverse with the word PEACE below.

Weight: 26.73 grams. *Composition:* .999 silver (0.858 ounce pure silver). *Diameter:* 38.1 mm. *Edge:* Reeded. *GSID:* 85116.

The Pittman Act, passed in 1918, called for the melting of up to 350 million silver dollars. The purpose was to generate a supply of silver bullion that could be sold to the United Kingdom to support the value of their currency during World War I. The legislation also required that melted dollars be replaced, leading in 1921 to the resurrection of the Morgan dollar, which had not been produced since 1904. Although it saw record production that year, by 1921, the Morgan dollar was an old coin. All other U.S. coins issued for circulation had been redesigned in a new American style between 1907 and 1916.

The Treasury was pressured to create a new dollar coin. The Peace-dollar design was finalized as the year was ending, and the first coins of this type were produced on December 28, 1921. According to the U.S. Mint, the "Peace silver dollar symbolizes the country's coming of age as an international power while recognizing the sacrifices made by her citizens in World War I and celebrating the victory and peace that ensued." Indeed, the word PEACE appears on the reverse below an eagle at rest, looking east toward a rising sun. The coin was designed by Anthony de Francisci, an American medalist who had studied under famed coin designers James Earle Fraser, Hermon MacNeil, and Adolph Alexander Weinman, whose iconic coinage has continued to be recast on numerous top-ranking modern coins.

For collectors of modern U.S. coins, a new Peace dollar represented an exciting opportunity. The original Peace dollar of 1921 was rendered in high relief, but the design elements are seldom fully present. Further, its original mintage figure of 1,006,473 makes it just scarce enough that uncirculated examples are expensive, with those in Gem Uncirculated condition commanding four-figure prices. Its pre-issue cost of $85 was a reasonable price point to get a pristine legal-tender example. Further, the gold 1916 Centennial issues and the 2009 High Relief double eagle had proved the Mint could recreate old designs faithfully.

The new Peace coin was limited to 200,000 pieces and was sold alongside 2021 Morgan dollars. Despite an order limit of three per household, when sales opened at noon on August 10, they sold out in a mere 30 minutes. The net mintage remains at 199,940, or one-fifth that of the original coin it is modeled after.

Coins finally came to market in October. Coins in original Mint packaging traded at a 50-percent premium to their issue price. Certified examples graded MS-70 traded at more than $300, indicating strong demand beyond the authorized production limits. In 2023 and 2024, the Mint released additional uncirculated, Proof, and Reverse Proof versions, all with higher mintage limits than for the 2021 issue. This continuation of a centennial coinage issue is a novelty among U.S. Mint products, but they have been well received, thereby sustaining collector interest and giving special appeal to this comparatively low-mintage 2021 issue.

Mintage: 199,543

MS-68	MS-69	MS-70	OGP
$235	$245	$340	$245

30 1996-W ROOSEVELT DIME

Designed by John R. Sinnock. On the obverse, the head of Franklin Roosevelt faces left. LIBERTY appears in large letters along the left rim; IN GOD WE TRUST appears in small letters at the lower left, and the date appears at the bottom right. The reverse features a lit torch flanked by sprigs of olive and oak. UNITED STATES OF AMERICA arcs above, ONE DIME arcs below, and the motto E PLURIBUS UNUM runs in a straight line through the bottoms of the sprigs and torch.

Weight: 2.27 grams. *Composition:* Outer layers of .750 copper and .250 nickel over a core of pure copper. *Diameter:* 17.9 mm. *Edge:* Reeded. *GSID:* 4876; Full Bands, 4875.

It may not always be recognized as an important milestone, but the United States has often observed the 50th anniversary of a coin's design. The best such example is, of course, the Lincoln cent. First issued in 1909, the Lincoln, Wheat Ears Reverse, cent got an update in 1959 on the occasion of its 50th anniversary. In that year, a reverse design featuring the Lincoln Memorial was first released. When the Lincoln cent had aged another 50 years, in 2009, it got another update, this time with four new reverse designs featuring snapshots of Lincoln's life.

The Roosevelt dime was similarly honored on the occasion of its 50th anniversary. First issued in 1946, the Roosevelt dime honored President Franklin Delano Roosevelt, who had died in 1945 while serving his fourth consecutive term as president. The dime was an especially fitting tribute to Roosevelt, as throughout his life he had been a leader of the March of Dimes' fundraising efforts to combat polio. Although originally issued in silver, the dime underwent no significant design changes throughout its entire 50 years of workman-like service. The only noteworthy design change was the movement of the mintmark to the coin's obverse in 1968.

In 1996, to celebrate the 50th anniversary of the Roosevelt dime, the West Point Mint was chosen to strike a special dime issue. The coin of course shows its usual austere design, except the W mintmark sits just above the numeral 6 in the date. It is the first "circulating" coin to bear the West Point mintmark. This coin was not released into circulation, but instead was included as part of the 1996 Mint set, the Uncirculated coinage set sold by the U.S. Mint. The only way to get this coin was as part of the Mint set. A total of 1,457,000 sets were sold, which is correspondingly also the mintage figure of the 1996-W Roosevelt dime.

This low mintage figure gives the 1996-W Roosevelt dime the lowest mintage of any Mint State Roosevelt, including the 1946 to 1964 silver issues. In fact, the so-called key date of the silver series, the 1949-S, has a mintage of more than 13 million pieces! But the 1996-W Roosevelt dime is an anomaly in many ways. It is the only coin struck in copper-nickel-clad composition to bear the W mintmark. All other coins with this mintmark are precious-metal coins struck in silver, gold, or platinum. It is one of only three commemorative issue dimes issued by the U.S. Mint, as it was joined in 2015 by two special Proof silver issues to celebrate the 75th anniversary of the March of Dimes.

Like most Mint set coins of the era, the 1996-W dimes received very modest special handling and therefore can show contact marks from knocking against other coins and machine-sorting and packaging. Although most are gem Uncirculated, a disparity of quality does exist among them.

Mintage: 1,457,000

Strike	MS-64	MS-65	MS-66	MS-67	MS-68	MS-69
Normal	$14.00	$15.00	$20	$27	$54	$340
Full Bands	19.00	21.50	30	49	81	370

31 1971, NO S, JEFFERSON NICKEL, PROOF

Designed by Felix Schlag. The obverse features a bust of Thomas Jefferson facing left. IN GOD WE TRUST appears inside the left edge, and LIBERTY and the date appear inside the right edge. On the reverse, Jefferson's home, Monticello, appears as the central device. E PLURIBUS UNUM arcs above. The word MONTICELLO captions the building, and the words FIVE CENTS and the legend UNITED STATES OF AMERICA appear below.

Weight: 5.00 grams. *Composition:* .750 copper, .250 nickel. *Diameter:* 21.2 mm. *Edge:* Plain. *GSID:* 3562; Cameo, 3563; Deep Cameo, 3564.

In 1971, all Proof coins were struck at the San Francisco Mint and included an S mintmark. All, that is, except for a small number of nickels that were mistakenly struck without mintmarks. According to the Mint Bureau, some 1,655 coins were struck and released without the S mintmark. This figure was released after the initial discovery in 1971 of examples of these nickels. To date, only about 400 are known. They were found among the 3.2 million Proof sets issued that year.

Proof coinage is made with special care and attention, which makes No S Proof issues fascinating to collectors. They find a wide following, stretching well beyond collectors who specialize in a series. There are only five No S Proof coins in existence: three dimes struck in 1968, 1970, and 1983; a cent struck in 1990; and the 1971 No S Jefferson nickel, the lone nickel on the list.

Designed by Felix Schlag, the winner of a design contest in 1938, the Jefferson nickel was issued continuously without a design change for 66 years. The design itself demonstrated public support for the portrayal of a president and a monument on coinage, a pattern that would be repeated on the Lincoln Memorial cent as well as a number of commemorative issues. Despite the success of the Jefferson nickel, it is Schlag's only coin design; he did, however, also design a number of medals. In 1966, the initials FS were added to this coin for the first time, and they remain on the reverse to this day (the current obverse design no longer belongs to Schlag).

The Jefferson nickel series includes more than one interesting issue for collectors of Proof coinage besides the 1971, No S, variety. In 1942, when Proof coins were still struck in Philadelphia, the Jefferson nickel was the first U.S. Proof coin to include a P mintmark. A large P was added to silver-alloy nickels struck from 1942 to 1945 to distinguish them from their regular copper-nickel-alloy

counterparts. Nickel was needed for the war effort and thus was removed from use in coinage. The key Proof coin of the series, however, is unquestionably the 1971, No S, nickel.

This coin usually grades at least gem Proof and more often superb gem Proof. Significant premiums are paid for the highest-condition coins. Most often, these coins are *cameo*, exhibiting medium contrast between the design and the field area. Very deeply contrasted coins, sometimes called *ultra cameo*, are less common, as are coins with minimal contrast. The degree of contrast is normally greater on the obverse than the reverse. Certification is strongly advised when paying a premium for condition.

Mintage: fraction of 3,220,996

Surface	PF-63	PF-64	PF-65	PF-66	PF-67	PF-68	PF-69
Normal	$715	$750	$780	$880	$990	$1,250	$2,250
Cameo	780	805	860	960	1,050	1,380	2,620
Deep Cameo	940	990	1,120	1,220	1,380	2,620	4,190

32 1982, NO MINTMARK, ROOSEVELT DIME

Designed by John R. Sinnock. On the obverse, the head of Franklin Roosevelt faces left. LIBERTY appears in large letters along the left rim; IN GOD WE TRUST appears in small letters at the lower left, and the date appears at the bottom right. The reverse features a lit torch flanked by sprigs of olive and oak. UNITED STATES OF AMERICA arcs above, ONE DIME arcs below, and the motto E PLURIBUS UNUM runs in a straight line through the bottoms of the sprigs and torch.

Weight: 2.27 grams. *Composition:* Outer layers of .750 copper and .250 nickel over a core of pure copper. *Diameter:* 17.9 mm. *Edge:* Reeded. *GSID:* Strong Rims, 4779, with Full Bands, 4780; Weak Rims, 4782, with Full Bands, 4781.

While, historically, coins made at the Philadelphia Mint did not have mintmarks, a change began in 1979. When the newly issued Susan B. Anthony dollars came out that year, they all had a mintmark, including those struck at Philadelphia, which were branded with a P. In 1980, this practice extended to all coins except for the cent. Just two years after this practice began, the first inadvertent omission occurred. In 1982, an obverse die without a mintmark was put into use, creating the 1982, No Mintmark, dime.

Because dimes were struck for circulation at both Philadelphia and Denver, the missing mintmark could be either a P or a D. The uncertainty leads to the more general name No Mintmark. In the early 1980s, coinage hubs did not include mintmarks. All dies were made in Philadelphia, and mintmarks were added before the dies were put into use or shipped to a branch mint for use elsewhere. This by-hand process accounts for the variations in mark sizes, positioning, and, as in this case, omissions.

1982, No Mintmark, dime (left, Strong Strike; right, Weak Strike).

Overwhelming evidence, however, suggests that the coins were, in fact, struck in Philadelphia, and thus this variety is also called the 1982, No P, dime. Examples were first discovered in late 1982 in northern Ohio. A cache thought to number several thousand coins funneled from local banks through a coin shop in Toledo, Ohio, according to researcher and author Walter Breen. A subsequent discovery in Pennsylvania added a few thousand more coins to the total number available to collectors.

Numismatists distinguish between strong and weak varieties of the 1982, No Mintmark, dime. The strong is properly struck and essentially fully detailed. The weak variety shows soft detail and, diagnostically, the 2 in the date is indistinct and melds with the rim of the coin. The same dies were used to strike both varieties, and the weak is variously attributed by researchers to either misaligned dies or weak striking pressure. Even though it is less common than the strong variety, the weak trades for much less, and price guides usually report only the price for the strong. Grading services do distinguish between the varieties.

The number of 1982, No Mintmark, dimes produced is not known precisely. It is estimated that a single obverse dime die produces as many as 150,000 coins. Roughly 10,000 examples are known to collectors, a sizable percentage of the original mintage for a circulation-issue variety. No other mintmark omission of any kind occurred on a circulating coin until 2007, and during the 25-year interlude, the 1982, No Mintmark, dime grew in status. This coin is much sought after and especially elusive in high grades, making it a key to the long-running Roosevelt dime series.

Mintage: fraction of 519,475,000

	MS-60	MS-61	MS-62	MS-63	MS-64	MS-65	MS-66	MS-67
Strong Rims	$130	$145	$150	$160	$190	$210	$490	$715
with Full Bands	—	—	—	—	305	365	545	1,500
Weak Rims	74	81	92	110	130	180	290	520
with Full Bands	—	—	—	190	215	240	520	960

33 2006-P $1 AMERICAN SILVER EAGLE, REVERSE PROOF

Designed by Adolph A. Weinman (obverse) and John Mercanti (reverse). The obverse features Weinman's Liberty Walking design used on half dollars from 1916 through 1947. Weinman's initials are on the hem of the gown. The reverse design is a rendition of a heraldic eagle.

Weight: 31.101 grams. *Composition:* .999 silver (net weight 1 ounce pure silver). *Diameter:* 40.6 mm. *Edge:* Reeded. *GSID:* 68427.

On August 21, 2006, the U.S. Mint announced the 20th-anniversary eagle sets—special collector editions being sold to celebrate the 20th anniversary of the American Eagle Bullion Program. One of the options was a three-piece silver coin set, including a Proof coin, an Uncirculated coin, and a Reverse Proof coin. The announcement described the Reverse Proof coins as featuring "a unique finish which results in a frosted field, or background, and a brilliant, mirror-like finish on the raised elements of the coin, including the design and inscriptions."

It's difficult to imagine exactly the environment into which this coin was released. Silver had roughly doubled in price, from $6 to $12 an ounce, in the two years leading up to this coin's release. There was a tremendous baseline of interest in the American Silver Eagle generally. Add to that articles in the numismatic press and blogosphere, which were intimating that the Reverse Proof would be a successful coin—not only would it be the only Reverse Proof in the American Silver Eagle series, but its mintage would be limited to 250,000. At the time of issue, with the exception of the Proof 1995-W (ranked at no. 5), this was the lowest-mintage American Silver Eagle; the next closest was the Proof 1994-P American Silver Eagle, with a mintage of 372,168.

Also in 2006, more advanced and intricate finishes were appearing on foreign issues of silver and gold bullion coins. Mints in Australia, Canada, China, and Great Britain were all producing precious-metal Reverse Proof coinage for collectors (as well as holographic coins and privy-marked, limited-edition coinages). The U.S. Mint had, in prior years, used the Reverse Proof finish: American Platinum Eagle bullion issues from 1997 through 2000 were struck with frosted fields and mirror-like devices. Nonetheless, in the context of 2006 and the American Silver Eagle series, this felt like a very unique American silver coin, and the only way to get it was as part of the three-coin set.

Few collectors were willing to miss the opportunity. To defend against speculators, the U.S. Mint set an order limit of 10 sets per household. The issue price of the set was $100. A flood of orders began at noon on Wednesday, August 30, and the flurry of activity slowed the Mint's web site to a halt. The Mint's toll-free order hotline reached a continuous busy signal. Devoted collectors, dealers, and speculators spent furious hours trying to complete their orders. After the maddening rush of orders, collectors waited two months before Reverse Proof American Silver Eagles began to ship in earnest from the Mint. Those who received their coins in early October were already able to double their money and resell the sets for $200.

The price of Reverse Proof American Silver Eagles continued to climb to the end of the year as they trickled out of the Mint and were absorbed into the marketplace. Prices and demand appear to have stabilized not far from those original post-release levels, keeping one of the key issues of the series within reach of collectors. Its look is so distinctive within the series that the Reverse Proof will always be a curious standout among American Silver Eagles—but of course, other special anniversaries are ahead.

Mintage: 248,875

PF-68	PF-69	PF-70	OGP
$110	$130	$340	$130

34 2006 $100 AMERICAN PLATINUM EAGLE

Designed by John Mercanti (obverse) and Thomas D. Rogers (reverse). The obverse features a portrait of Lady Liberty. The reverse (bullion issues) features an eagle soaring above America.

Weight: 1.0005 ounces. *Composition:* .999 platinum.
Diameter: 32.7 mm. *Edge:* Reeded. *GSID:* 65118.

In 1996, legislators passed a minor amendment to section 5112 of Title 31, U.S. Code, which prescribes the legal requirements and specifications for all U.S. coinage. Added to the U.S. Code was the following, in full: "Secretary may mint and issue bullion and proof platinum coins in accordance with such specifications, designs, varieties, quantities, denominations, and inscriptions as the Secretary, in the Secretary's discretion, may prescribe from time to time. : *Provided*, That the Secretary is authorized to use Government platinum reserves stockpiled at the United States Mint as working inventory and shall ensure that reserves utilized are replaced by the Mint."

With those two sentences, the American Platinum Eagle was created. First issued from 1997 until 2008, the bullion coin had a new design. The obverse, created by then–U.S. Mint sculptor and engraver John Mercanti, features a portrait of Liberty reworked from the Statue of Liberty in clean, modern lines. The reverse, conceived by U.S. Mint sculptor and engraver Thomas D. Rogers Sr., shows a composition named "Eagle Soaring Above America" and displays a gliding eagle with its wings fully outstretched above the sun's rays. This same design is used on all bullion issues, while collector versions of the coins (Proof and Uncirculated issues) have a different design that changes each year.

Like the American Gold Eagle, coins were available in one-ounce, half-ounce, quarter-ounce, and tenth-ounce weights, but with a face value double that of their gold counterparts. This gave the one-ounce platinum coin a $100 face value, the highest of any U.S. coin ever issued. Also, like the other bullion issues, the coins were sold only through authorized distributors who, in turn, sell them to other dealers, investors, and collectors.

The first few years of the American Platinum Eagle showed banner sales: more than 50,000 one-ounce coins sold in the first and third years, and a mind-boggling 133,002 coins sold in year two, among the highest mintage figures for any platinum coin. Bullion sales declined steadily thereafter, reaching a nadir of only

6,000 examples of the 2006 $100 American Platinum Eagle bullion one-ounce coin, the single lowest mintage figure for any U.S. bullion coin ever issued.

Why was there such a precipitous drop? One answer is that platinum increased in price, making these coins more expensive and therefore less obtainable by a broad spectrum of collectors. Throughout 2005, platinum flirted with the $1,000-per-ounce price level, but on January 9, 2006, it broke through and never looked back, spiking to more than $1,300 per ounce in May. More significantly, however, in 2006 the U.S. Mint issued the Uncirculated American Platinum Eagle coins for collectors, and offered versions of these coins directly for sale to collectors. The Uncirculated coins have a different reverse design, as do the Proof issues. Only 3,068 of the 2006-W $100 Uncirculated American Platinum Eagle coins were sold. Likely, this accounted for much of the collector demand for platinum and fewer units of the bullion counterpart were needed to meet the requirements of investors.

Mintage: 6,000

MS-68	MS-69	MS-70	OGP
$195	$205	$285	$190

35 1983, DOUBLED DIE REVERSE, LINCOLN CENT

Designed by Victor David Brenner (obverse) and Frank Gasparro (reverse). The obverse continues the design of 1909, featuring a bust of Lincoln facing right, the word LIBERTY to his left, and the date in the field in front of his coat. The legend IN GOD WE TRUST appears above his head. The reverse shows a frontal view of the Lincoln Memorial with UNITED STATES OF AMERICA and E PLURIBUS UNUM appearing above and ONE CENT below.

Weight: 2.5 grams. *Composition:* Outer layers of pure copper over a core of .992 zinc, .008 copper. *Diameter:* 19 mm. *Edge:* Plain. *GSID:* Brown, 2267; Red-Brown, 2268; Red, 2269.

Almost all of the important doubled-die Lincoln cents share a common feature: they were struck from doubled obverse dies, meaning that the best features of the coin are present on the front. The major exception in the series is the 1983, Doubled Die Reverse, which has prominent, well-separated doubling throughout all of the reverse legends. There is a second impression on all of the reverse wordings, shifted upwards, above the image below.

The 1983, Doubled Die Reverse, Lincoln cent is the most dramatic of any doubled-die reverse (DDR) in the entire Lincoln cent series. Even though it is of relatively recent vintage, it is comparatively scarce. Authors have reported that two caches of these coins were found, in Pennsylvania and Florida, but they likely amounted to only a few thousand coins in all, the estimated number available to collectors.

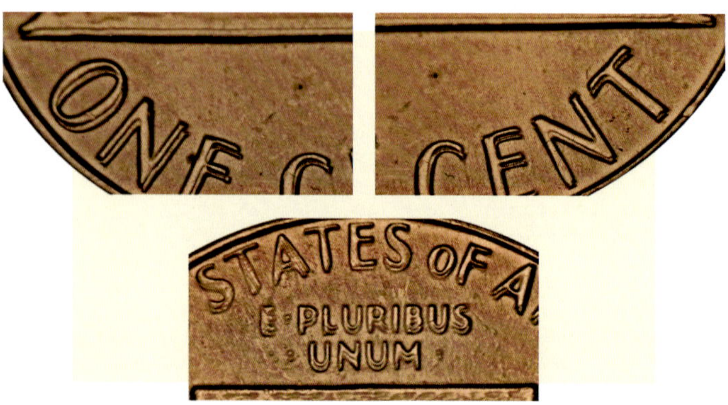

Pick-up point: ONE CENT.

The obverse of this coin features heavy die polishing, giving it a very characteristic appearance. This obverse has been found paired with two different reverse dies other than the doubled reverse, which suggests that the doubled die was removed from service before the end of its functioning life. Further evidence confirms this theory: correspondence quoted in an Associated Press story from June 3, 1984, quotes George Hunter, assistant director for technology at the Mint, as stating that the error was discovered and the die destroyed before 50,000 total coins were struck, and that only 5,000 or so entered circulation.

In addition to contending with this coin's scarcity, collectors seeking it have another issue to deal with: condition. The transition from a solid Lincoln cent to a coin with a copper-coated zinc core had begun in 1982, and the Mint was still plagued by serious production difficulties. Tiny gas bubbles often became trapped beneath the surface of the plating, causing small blisters to appear throughout the coin and damaging its aesthetics. Because these flaws are "as made," they are present even in high-grade examples and do not affect a coin's value unless they are severe. In areas where plating is too thin or, in rare cases, where the zinc core became exposed during striking, coins can discolor or corrode and, unfortunately, these effects are irreversible. Fortunately, most other condition issues affecting early copper-coated zinc-core Lincoln cents are manifest on these coins by now, and as long as collectors exercise proper care in storing their coins, further extreme changes are unlikely to occur.

The relative rarity of this coin and the condition factors affecting coins of the highest grade make this coin comparatively expensive at the very highest end of the grade range. Mid-range Uncirculated examples can be purchased at more modest prices, making them a fairly good value for the best DDR in the series.

Mintage: fraction of 7,752,355,000

Color	AU-50	MS-60	MS-63	MS-64	MS-65	MS-66	MS-67	MS-68
Brown	$130	$175	$235	$260	$305	$370	—	—
Red-Brown	—	195	260	285	340	420	—	—
Red	—	215	290	360	390	500	$1,250	$4,060

36 1964 KENNEDY HALF DOLLAR, ACCENTED HAIR, PROOF

Designed by Gilroy Roberts (obverse) and Frank Gasparro (reverse). On the obverse, the head of John F. Kennedy faces left. LIBERTY arcs across the top of the obverse; the date arcs along the bottom and IN GOD WE TRUST runs in a straight line beneath Kennedy's head. The reverse features a heraldic eagle, similar to that seen on the 1801 through 1807 and 1892 through 1915 half dollars, within a circle of 50 stars. UNITED STATES arcs around the top and HALF DOLLAR arcs along the bottom of the reverse.

Weight: 12.50 grams. *Composition:* .900 silver, .100 copper. *Diameter:* 30.6 mm.
Edge: Reeded. *GSID:* 6993; Cameo, 6994; Deep Cameo, 6995.

Some of the most intriguing stories in numismatics involve major personalities (often politicians) who had the ability to influence coinage design with just a few words or pen strokes. There is such a tale about this coin, the Proof 1964 Kennedy half dollar Accented Hair variety.

After the president's assassination on November 22, 1963, discussion immediately began about how to commemorate his life with a circulating coin. Within only a few days of Kennedy's death, Mint Director Eva Adams contacted the Mint chief engraver, Gilroy Roberts, and told him to begin work on a design. Roberts quickly adopted his profile portrait for the Kennedy presidential medal. While this design work was ongoing, a new coinage bill was passed by Congress on December 30, 1963, allowing Kennedy to replace Benjamin Franklin on the circulating half dollar.

The first trial strikes were shown by Adams to the president's widow, Jacqueline Kennedy, and to his brother, Attorney General Robert F. Kennedy. They provided comments on the design and a modified version was prepared. It's this exchange, which took place less than a month after the president's death, that has implanted itself in the annals of numismatic lore. It is thought that Mrs. Kennedy objected to the heavily inscribed lines that showed the direction of the president's delicately coiffed hair, and that this aspect of the design was changed because of

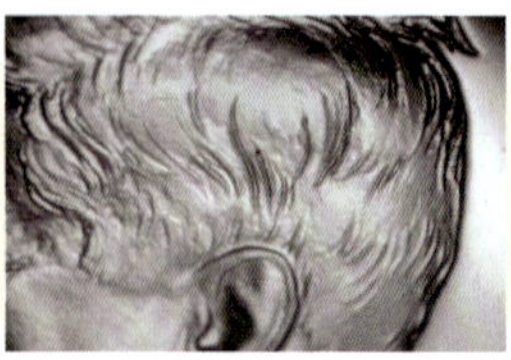

Pick-up points: Hair, I of LIBERTY.

her personal recommendation. In fact, this is a striking dissimilarity between the otherwise-parallel portraits used on this coin and Paul Manship's design of the Kennedy inaugural medal, in which the hair detail is only faintly hinted.

The very first examples struck were Proofs; the Mint rightly recognized that many would want the new coins as souvenirs, and nearly four million Proofs were struck. Two distinct varieties could be seen. One, known from only one Proof die, was the Accented Hair version, best distinguished by a series of accented hair lines in the area above Kennedy's ear. The other showed much-reduced detail and depth of lines in this area. Although not exactly rare, this Accented Hair variety accounts for fewer than 1 in 20 Kennedy half dollars struck in 1964 (less than five percent); many estimate that about 120,000 were struck. Clearly, some coins had been produced with this original feature still in place. Perhaps during the rush, dies for Proof coinage had already been prepared relying on Roberts's original design.

Although we do know that the Kennedys were consulted about the coin's design, any specific objection to this aspect of the coin, or how these Accented Hair examples came to be released, is left open to speculation. Numismatists, quite frankly, enjoy the good story. Another theory posits that the deeply incised grooves in the original version caused production problems, such as reduced die life, and the design was quickly changed so that the Mint would be better able to accommodate the aggressive demand for this coin in 1964.

Sometimes, spotting an Accented Hair Kennedy half dollar without another specimen for comparison can be tricky by looking at the hair detail alone. A tell-tale flaw at the bottom of the I in LIBERTY is the best diagnostic. On the Accented Hair variety, the lower-left serif will always be missing.

Mintage: fraction of 3,950,762

Surface	PF-64	PF-65	PF-66	PF-67	PF-68	PF-69
Normal	$51	$76	$115	$150	$245	$935
Cameo	88	120	155	275	715	2,000
Deep Cameo	415	780	1,080	3,250	7,000	51,000

37 1964-D WASHINGTON QUARTER, REVERSE OF 1965

Designed by John Flanagan. The obverse features the head of George Washington facing left, the word LIBERTY above his head and the date below it. The motto IN GOD WE TRUST appears in small letters in the left field. On the reverse, an eagle, with wings outspread, perches on a tight bundle of arrows. Two olive sprigs are joined beneath the eagle. The outer legends include UNITED STATES OF AMERICA above and QUARTER DOLLAR below. The motto E PLURIBUS UNUM appears in smaller letters above the eagle's head.

Weight: 6.25 grams. *Composition:* .900 silver, .100 copper.
Diameter: 24.3 mm. *Edge:* Reeded. *GSID:* 374378.

The Washington quarter's design was successful from the outset. It was first produced in 1932, and its clean geometry recalls the art deco fashion of the time. To today's tastes, the design may appear overly sculptural and idealized, but it is classically well-balanced. It was also a remarkably easy design to coin, a feature perhaps more important than its aesthetics. The relief is low, and late-state die damage (a break or crack) is seldom seen on Washington quarters. It was a design that held up well to the high demands of production.

However, the low-relief design required that the Washington quarter be re-hubbed more frequently than other coinages, creating subtle variations among coins in the series. Hubs are used to create dies, and dies are then used to strike coins. When a coin is re-hubbed, a design change is made that is replicated throughout the entire coinage production. The Washington quarter was famously re-hubbed in 1934, when the relief on the obverse motto, IN GOD WE TRUST, was so low that the inscription could barely be read. A subsequent change (in two iterations) strengthened the letters. While several very subtle alterations were made to the design in the years that followed, these changes were essentially imperceptible until the final year of silver coinage in 1964.

In 1965, the reverse of the Washington quarter was re-hubbed to strengthen the detail on the reverse, most notably on the eagle's tail feathers. This very shallow element of the coin's design was almost indiscernible on many of the Washington quarters of the early 1960s produced prior to this re-hubbing. In addition to sharpening the outline of the feathers, the Mint also added the rachis, or shaft of the feather. This feature was absent from the design in previous years and makes the Reverse of 1965 Washington quarter readily distinguishable.

This new reverse hub with strengthened feather detail was intended for use on 1965 coinage. However, new-style dies were impressed with D mintmarks and used to strike 1964-D quarters. The name given to this variety is "Reverse of 1965," or sometimes "Type C Reverse." While it is not known exactly how many of these coins were produced, they appear to account for only a small fraction of 1964-D Washington quarters. To date, only two different reverse dies that struck these coins have been identified. These dies minted approximately 400,000 "Reverse of 1965" quarters out of the total 1964-D quarter mintage of more than 704 million, or 1 in 1,760 coins.

This coin belongs to a class called transitional varieties, which occur when two design types, an old and a new, can be seen on a single coin. They are all very collectible, but this one is doubly special. The 1964-D quarter was the last silver quarter, while the 1965 version is the first copper-nickel-clad quarter. This transitional variety is actually the copper-nickel-clad reverse style used on a silver quarter. All 1965 quarters, even those struck in Denver, were made without mintmarks. When mintmarks resumed in 1968, they were placed on the obverse of the coin rather than the reverse, and this coin is thus also the only "Reverse of 1965"–style quarter to have a mintmark on that side.

Even though all these details make this coin interesting, there is not too much mystery about how it was produced. In 1965, the public began to pull silver coins from circulation as the Mint was striking copper-nickel-clad coins to replace them. In order to meet aggressive demand for coins, however, silver coinage was struck alongside copper-nickel-clad until 1966, but the silver coins were still dated 1964. These coins, then, could very well have been made at the same moment or even after the new reverse style came into general use. Rather than the new design being brought into use early, as some speculate, it is just as likely that these coins were produced alongside the 1965 issues or even as late as 1966.

Mintage: fraction of 704,135,528

MS-65	MS-66
$420	$650

38 2008-W $50 AMERICAN PLATINUM EAGLE

Designed by John Mercanti (obverse) and Joel Iskowitz (reverse). The obverse features a portrait of Lady Liberty. The reverse depicts Justice, blindfolded and holding her scales aloft, in front of an eagle.

Weight: .5003 ounces. *Composition:* .9995 platinum.
Diameter: 27 mm. *Edge:* Reeded. *GSID:* 70659.

Starting in 2006, the U.S. Mint began offering Uncirculated versions of the bullion American eagles for direct sale to collectors. Historically, bullion coins were sold only through dedicated distributors who purchased in bulk from the Mint. For collectors, Proof versions of the coins were offered at price premiums. The Uncirculated coins were meant to be sold at more modest prices than their Proof counterparts, a prospect that became more appealing as metal prices accelerated.

The Uncirculated versions differed from bullion coins in a few ways. First, Uncirculated coins had a W mintmark, for West Point, while bullion coins are issued without mintmark, even though they, too, are struck at West Point. Secondly, the Mint advertised that Uncirculated coins were struck on "specially burnished blanks," although the effects of this treatment, which occurs prior to striking, are not visible on the finished coins. Finally, for the American Platinum Eagles, the reverse design is not the bullion version but rather the Proof design.

Each year, the Proof American Platinum Eagle has a different reverse design, an element that makes this coin different from other coins in the American eagle series. In 2006, the Mint began a three-year thematic sequence, creating reverse designs emblematic of the three branches of government, beginning with the legislative branch in 2006, followed by the executive branch in 2007, and finishing with the judicial branch in 2008. The reverse for the 2008 coin shows a personified image of Justice holding a scale from her fingers to represent the balance of the law. She wields a sword to symbolize the power of reason, and a vigilant eagle, symbol of the nation, stands behind her as the protector of Justice.

Of all weights of the American Gold Eagles and American Platinum Eagles, the half-ounce and quarter-ounce coins have always been the worst sellers. The lion's share of their sales comes from purchases of four-coin sets that include the one-ounce, half-ounce, quarter-ounce, and tenth-ounce coins. In 2008, platinum metal was experiencing unprecedented price volatility, starting off the year at $1,500 per ounce and climbing to $2,100 per ounce at mid-year before settling

back at $900 per ounce. When the half-ounce 2008-W American Platinum Eagle $50 Uncirculated coin went on sale on July 1, 2008, it was priced at $1,199.95, and the four-coin set was $4,289.95, among the most expensive products ever offered by the Mint. Platinum's price fluctuation worked against collector demand for these coins, as did the somewhat duplicative offerings of bullion, Proof, and Uncirculated versions.

These coins are produced to meet demand, and there is no pre-set order limit. Only 1,283 four-coin sets and 970 individual Uncirculated 2008-W American Platinum Eagle $50 coins were sold, making a total mintage of 2,253. This figure is the lowest of *any* modern U.S. coin. In fact, to find a lower-mintage U.S. coin, one has to go back more than 70 years to 1939, to the Arkansas Centennial half dollar. Sales of the Uncirculated American Platinum Eagles were deemed so poor that the Mint put the program on hiatus after 2008 and it's unclear if they will be offered again. Being the lowest-mintage regular-issue coin of its era, however, earns this coin a unique place in the mind of collectors.

Mintage: 2,253

MS-65	MS-66	MS-67	MS-68	MS-69	MS-70	OGP
$630	$640	$645	$650	$2,090	$2,880	$1,750

39 2016 CENTENNIAL GOLD COINS

GSID: dime, 74059; quarter, 74060; half dollar, 74061.

Throughout the list of 100 Greatest U.S. Modern Coins are new coins that repurpose older designs. Numismatists favor both tradition and nostalgia. This means there will always be collector interest in coins that honor the past with familiar designs. The 2016 Centennial Gold Coins hit that mark very precisely.

Relying on its authority to produce gold coins at its discretion, the United States Mint announced that it would honor the coinage issues of 1916 with three coins in 2016. These coins recreated very precisely the designs of the Mercury or Winged Liberty Dime (used from 1916 to 1945), the Standing Liberty Quarter (1916–1930), and the Walking Liberty Half Dollar (1916–1947). The designs are iconic and formed the latter part of an extensive, expressive redesign of coinage initiated by President Theodore Roosevelt, which began with the 1907 Saint-Gaudens High Relief Double Eagle. That coin was honored in 2009 with the release of the Ultra High Relief Double Eagle, and in many ways these three coins are a continuation of that program.

All three 2016 Centennial coins were struck at West Point and offered in a single format that the United States Mint refers to as "Uncirculated." The Mint did later reveal that dies were wire brushed, and that each die pair was used to strike fewer than 2,000 coins. These coins thus have a very uniform look and their surfaces have a matte-like finish. Grading services designated them as Specimen using the "SP" prefix rather than Mint State or "MS."

The appearance of the coins earned very high praise, and the accuracy with which the coin designs were recreated was widely lauded. One substantive complaint was that the coins were 10% smaller than the designs as originally issued. Wanting to reuse previously developed planchets, the Mint used the standard .9999 fine gold planchets created for the American Gold Buffalo. The gold dime was therefore 15.0 mm rather than the standard dime diameter of 16.5 mm. The variance became more noticeable as the coins get larger. The 1/4 oz. Standing Liberty coin is 22.0 mm versus 24.3 mm as issued, and the 1/2 oz. Walking Liberty is 27.0 mm compared with 30.6 mm for the original coin.

The coins were not sold as a set, but offered singly throughout the year, beginning with the dime. The mintage limit was set at 125,000. The household order limit—the maximum number of coins any individual can purchase—was 10. When they went on sale on April 21, they sold out in 40 minutes! Naturally many collectors complained they had lost out to speculators.

The Mint sought to fine tune their ordering process, limiting households to just one Standing Liberty Quarter. The mintage of that issue was capped at 100,000. It went on sale on September 21, but new limits meant total sales were just a trickle; ultimately, 91,752 were sold.

With the final coin, the Walking Liberty Half Dollar, the Mint sought middle ground. Its mintage was 70,000 coins and three could be purchased by each household, with final sales reaching 65,509.

Minor missteps with the ordering process probably prevented these coins from being a massive runaway success at time of issue. Since all three coins were sold at significant premiums to their gold content in an environment very sensitive to price which also slightly tampered their appeal. But these are short term considerations. The design quality of all three coins and their long-term collectability earn them a place among the 100 Greatest U.S. Modern Coins.

Distribution: Dime, 124,885; Quarter Dollar, 91,752; Half Dollar, 65,509

Denomination	MS-68	MS-69	MS-70	OGP
Dime	$320	$350	$470	$320
Quarter	870	935	985	935
Half dollar	1,750	1,800	1,920	1,800

40 2000-D SACAGAWEA DOLLAR, "MILLENNIUM" VARIETY

Designed by Glenna Goodacre (obverse) and Thomas D. Rogers (reverse). The obverse features the Indian guide Sacagawea and her infant son. LIBERTY appears above her head; IN GOD WE TRUST appears at the left, and the date appears on the right side. The reverse features an eagle in flight surrounded by 17 stars. UNITED STATES OF AMERICA arcs around the upper reverse; ONE DOLLAR arcs around the bottom. E PLURIBUS UNUM appears in small letters in the left field.

Weight: 8.1 grams. *Composition:* Outer layers of .770 copper, .120 zinc, .070 manganese, and .040 nickel over a core of pure copper. *Diameter:* 26.5 mm. *Edge:* Plain. *GSID:* 375899.

Among the product offerings included in the U.S. Mint's 2000 Holiday Catalog was a novel grouping called the United States Millennium Coinage and Currency Set. The set included a 2000-D Sacagawea dollar, a 2000 silver eagle, and a $1 note with the first four digits of its serial number being "2000." The edition was limited to 75,000 sets. Combining these items into a single set may have been thematically important to the Mint because the silver dollar and the dollar bill are clearly the most recognizable dollars. Now joining the ranks in the new millennium was the golden-colored Sacagawea dollar. Regardless of the intent or the message, there wasn't too much collector interest in the set—until the sets started arriving in collectors' hands, that is.

When buyers received the sets, they saw that the 2000-D Sacagawea dollar in the set was deeply reflective. It had clearly received special handling from the Mint, having been struck on polished planchets and from polished dies. This fact had not been promoted in the Mint's literature when they were offered for sale, and the presence of "prooflike" Sacagawea coins ignited a frenzy among collectors. The sets then quickly sold out from the Mint.

These coins are referred to as "prooflike" because they have some of the attributes of Proof coinage but are not true Proofs. For example, unlike Proof coins, they are not struck multiple times from the coinage dies, and therefore their striking detail is no sharper than a regular circulation-strike coin's detail. They also don't have true mirror-like reflective fields, and unlike current Proofs they are mirrored throughout their surface and don't display cameo contrast between fields and the design area. Normally these attributes can be quite subtle; however, the differences between the Millennium Set Sacagawea dollar

and the regular issue 2000-D Sacagawea are stark enough that they are readily distinguishable.

Most collectors consider the Millennium Set Sacagawea dollar to be a required element of the Sacagawea dollar series, and therefore a complete set will have two 2000-D coins: a regular Mint State example and the Millennium Set issue. Its status as a required element of any Sacagawea dollar collection has assured its enduring popularity. While the coin is often found in gem Uncirculated to superb Uncirculated condition, the best examples have very deeply reflective fields and are untoned and virtually free of contact marks or blemishes. Specialist collectors will pay substantial premiums for coins that have especially deep mirrors and are at the highest grades of preservation.

In retrospect, the most interesting aspect of this coin may be that the special finish, and therefore the desirability, of this coin was completely unexpected, and that the U.S. Mint had a special surprise for collectors who ordered the set. With 75,000 struck, it remains widely available for today's collectors, but since it's now required for set completion, demand certainly isn't going away.

Mintage: 75,000

MS-66PL	MS-67PL
$20	$43

41 2021-W $10 AMERICAN GOLD EAGLE, FROM UNPOLISHED PROOF DIES

Designed by Augustus Saint-Gaudens (obverse) and Jennie Norris (reverse). The obverse features a modified rendition of the Augustus Saint-Gaudens design used on U.S. $20 gold pieces from 1907 until 1933. The reverse shows the head of an eagle.

Weight: 8.48 grams. *Composition:* .917 gold, .030 silver, and .053 copper (net weight 1/4 ounce pure gold). *Diameter:* 22 mm. *Edge:* Reeded. *GSID:* 226243.

"That which has been is what will be, that which is done is what will be done, and there is nothing new under the sun."—Ecclesiastes 1:9

In late September 2021, coin dealer Gerald Medel from San Diego was examining a complete roll of 2021 quarter-ounce $10 American Gold Eagles from a bullion box. He discovered that all 40 coins included the W mintmark for West Point. Bullion coinage in the United States is issued without mintmarks, which are included only on the versions of the coins made for collectors. The U.S. Mint had inadvertently used an unpolished Proof die, which included the mintmark, to strike bullion coins. The exact same error had also occurred in 1999.

Medel and fellow numismatist Todd Pollock began a frenzied search through as many rolls as they could and were able to locate 61 examples of the coin. They announced their discovery with Ian Russell of auction house Great Collections, where the first pieces would be sold. Coins from the initial roll were labeled as discovery coins and commanded strong prices in late-October and early-November auctions, with pieces certified at MS-69 trading for around $6,000, and at MS-70 for more than $15,000—prices similar to their 1999 counterparts.

The U.S. Mint soon confirmed the error. Todd Martin, deputy chief of the U.S. Mint's Office of Corporate Communications, related that 7,924 of these coins were produced in error on August 24. That was only the second month of production of the new design for the quarter-ounce coin.

What led to the errors? Updates to dies and a push to produce more coins faster. In 1999, production was booming at the U.S. Mint, and record numbers of fractional American Gold Eagles were being produced. The sheer volume of production at that time contributed to the Mint's error. While 2021 mintage figures weren't as high, 2021 saw a frenzy of activity related to the redesign of

the 2021 issues, which may have contributed to the wrong die being put into use. Today it's estimated that 10,000 examples of the 1999-W $10 American Gold Eagle bullion coins were produced, an upward revision from original estimates. The revised estimate is based on a combined certified population of 5,870 examples, which makes this new discovery slightly lower mintage than originally thought. A total of 4,841 examples have been certified to date.

These mintmarked versions of the American Gold Eagle bullion coin are highly desirable. When the error initially occurred in 1999, few anticipated that it would ever happen again. Incredibly, history repeated itself, now giving us two unique errors—and creating an extremely valuable entrant to the list of 100 Greatest U.S. Modern Coins.

Mintage: 7,924

MS-65	MS-66	MS-67	MS-68	MS-69	MS-70	OGP
$2,500	$2,620	$2,750	$3,000	$3,620	$4,380	$3,250

42 1983-P WASHINGTON QUARTER

Designed by John Flanagan. The obverse features the head of George Washington facing left, the word LIBERTY above the head, and the date below. The motto IN GOD WE TRUST appears in small letters in the left field. On the reverse, an eagle with wings outspread perches on a tight bundle of arrows. Two olive sprigs are joined beneath the eagle. The outer legends include UNITED STATES OF AMERICA above and QUARTER DOLLAR below. The motto E PLURIBUS UNUM appears in smaller letters above the eagle's head.

Weight: 5.67 grams. *Composition:* Outer layers of .750 copper and .250 nickel over a core of pure copper. *Diameter:* 24.3 mm. *Edge:* Reeded. *GSID:* 5719.

The Mint was looking for ways to cut costs in the early 1980s, and one product that found itself on the chopping block in 1982 was the once-popular Mint set. Issued since 1947, Mint sets include an example of each coin struck for circulation at each mint. These sets have served as one of the primary sources of Uncirculated coins for collectors and they were enormously popular. More than two million sets were sold each year from the late 1970s through 1981.

In the absence of Mint sets, a number of private companies took up the challenge of supplying demand, and thus, for 1982 and 1983, privately issued sets can be found. The other source of Uncirculated Mint-set coins is Souvenir sets. After receiving a tour of a mint, it's not unusual that visitors should want examples of the coins struck there. The Souvenir set was designed to meet this demand. Sold primarily in mint gift shops, it includes circulation examples of coins struck at a single mint. The problem with both Souvenir sets and privately issued sets is that the coins included seldom match the quality of Mint-set coins, and are often low-end Uncirculated examples. They are also comparatively scarce. Just 15,000 Souvenir sets were made in Philadelphia in 1983 and 20,000 were made in Denver, compared to 2.9 million Mint sets in 1981.

Bags and rolls of 1983 Washington quarters were rarely saved by collectors, meaning that the other obvious source for these coins is circulation. Many album sets assembled by collectors include blank spaces for this date. Collectors seeking high-quality examples face a further challenge. The 1983 Washington quarters from the Philadelphia Mint in particular tend to be heavily abraded. Production quality was low (possibly further indicative of cost-cutting at the time), and most

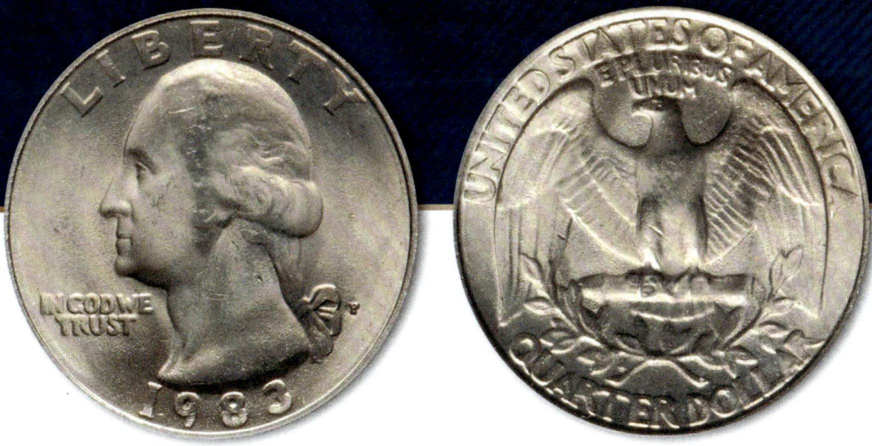

coins are struck from late-state, heavily fatigued dies that imparted weak, mushy detail. Contact marks and other forms of abrasion, including die burn, are common. They are typically not attractive coins.

Widely known to be scarce, 1983-P quarters are worth many times the value of equivalent coins from years with Mint-set examples. In fact, non-collectors are often surprised to discover that if a particularly nice Uncirculated example can be found in pocket change, it's easily worth a hundred times its face value. Fewer than a dozen superb gem Uncirculated (MS-67) examples have been professionally certified.

The move to drop Mint sets was timed in concert with the re-launch of the commemorative-coinage program in 1982, which likely mitigated complaints from collectors at the time. But the complaints grew louder over time, and in response the Mint reversed their policy; they began issuing Mint sets once again in 1984 and have done so each year since. As the half dollar and dollar coin are seldom used in circulation, a few sets from subsequent years included coins that were struck for sets only and not for circulation. These inclusions, along with the role of the Mint set as the most convenient source of high-quality examples of circulating coins, have sustained the sets' popularity and collectibility as well as their secondary-market value.

Mintage: 673,535,000

MS-63	MS-64	MS-65	MS-66	MS-67
$18.50	$27	$54	$88	$650

43 1983, NO S, ROOSEVELT DIME, PROOF

Designed by John R. Sinnock. On the obverse, the head of Franklin Roosevelt faces left. LIBERTY appears in large letters along the left rim; IN GOD WE TRUST appears in small letters at the lower left, and the date appears at the bottom right. The reverse features a lit torch flanked by sprigs of olive and oak. UNITED STATES OF AMERICA arcs above, ONE DIME arcs below, and the motto E PLURIBUS UNUM runs in a straight line through the bottoms of the sprigs and torch.

Weight: 2.27 grams. *Composition:* Outer layers of .750 copper and .250 nickel over a core of pure copper. *Diameter:* 17.9 mm. *Edge:* Reeded. *GSID:* 4980.

When this coin was first discovered in a Proof set in mid-1983, it was widely believed that it would be more common than it has ultimately proved to be. Since its initial discovery, only a few hundred examples have been found, certainly less than 400 in all. This figure makes it a bit scarcer than the 1970, No S, Roosevelt dime.

No S Proof coins are made when the S mintmark is omitted from the die. A number of steps are involved in the creation of Proof dies, during which they are inspected, or at least handled, by many different people in the process. It surprises many that this type of error can occur, and by 1983 it had happened at least three times already.

It is clear when this error occurred. In 1983, as in all previous years, dies were created from working hubs that did not contain a mintmark. The working dies themselves received an impression from a mintmark punch before being prepared to strike Proof coins—a very involved process.

To strike Proof coins, first the working dies are cleaned with solvents to remove grease, metal dust, and oil. Next, they are sandblasted. This task is performed by hand with the field areas marked off by tape, undoubtedly a tedious process. The field areas are then polished to a high shine. To increase die life and retain the effects of the polish and sandblasting, dies are then chromium plated. Every 500 to 1,000 strikes, dies are examined and refreshed by reprocessing if needed; if they are too worn, they are discarded. Over the years, the exact sequence of preparation has varied. This overview of the process, though, had been in use for the production of U.S. coins since 1970, according to Proof-coinage specialist Rick Tomaska. Sandblasting was ultimately replaced in 2009 by laser-frosting.

Like most Proof coins of its era, the 1983, No S, Roosevelt dime is almost always seen with a notable deep or ultra cameo contrast. It is clear that, as with regular Proof dimes, its obverse die was handled and inspected many times before and during the coinage process. To make the Proof 1983, No S, Roosevelt dime, then, a number of individuals failed to note the omitted S mintmark. In fact, the nature of the oversight is what makes these coins so interesting to collectors, and the rarity of the error makes them valuable.

This coin is the most recent issue of No S Proof dimes reported to date. To avoid mistakes like this in the future, starting in 1985, Proof dies were created from a production hub that included the mintmark. It is likely that this is the coin that led to the change in this process. While this change has prevented another No S dime from being made, a No S Lincoln cent was still produced in 1990 and is no. 10 on this list.

Mintage: fraction of 3,279,126

PF-65DC	PF-66DC	PF-67DC	PF-68DC	PF-69DC	PF-70DC
$455	$490	$550	$585	$650	$6,250

44 1992 AND 1992-D LINCOLN CENT, CLOSE AM

Designed by Victor David Brenner (obverse) and Frank Gasparro (reverse). The obverse continues the design of 1909, featuring a bust of Lincoln facing right, the word LIBERTY to his left, and the date in the field in front of his coat. The legend IN GOD WE TRUST appears above his head. The reverse shows a frontal view of the Lincoln Memorial with UNITED STATES OF AMERICA and E PLURIBUS UNUM appearing above and ONE CENT below.

Weight: 2.5 grams. *Composition:* Outer layers of pure copper over a core of .992 zinc, .008 copper. *Diameter:* 19 mm. *Edge:* Plain. *GSID: 1992*—Brown, 312941; Red-Brown, 312942; Red, 80831; *1992-D*—Brown, 312945; Red-Brown, 312946; Red, 70065.

On the reverse of this aptly named variety, the letters AM in the word AMERICA are close together, nearly touching. What makes this noteworthy is that all Lincoln cents produced from 1959 to 1991 had a comparatively broad spacing between these two letters. The design change was planned for release in 1993, and indeed all 1993 Lincoln cents, both Proof and Mint State issues, are of the Close AM variety.

The year 1992 marks a transitional year. All 1992 Proof coins are of the normal Wide AM variety, as are nearly all the currency-issue coins. But a very small number of 1992 cents from both Denver and Philadelphia are known to have the Close AM reverse. Fewer than two dozen Denver Mint examples are reported, and only two 1992, Close AM, cents from the Philadelphia Mint are known. The rare Philadelphia variety carries a catalog value in excess of $10,000.

While the payoff from finding a 1992, Close AM, would be akin to winning the lottery, the odds of finding one are slim. In 1992, more than 4.6 billion cents were struck in Philadelphia, and another 4.4 billion were struck in Denver. If a single full die-run were used to strike each coin, the chance of finding a Close AM may be on the order of 1 in 10,000. Based on average attrition rates, probably fewer than 60,000 survive from each Mint. To find one, you need to be deliberately looking for it.

That said, this variety isn't too hard to spot, and magnification makes the hunt a bit easier. To help with the attribution, there is a second clear difference that distinguishes the Close AM from the Wide AM variety. On a Close AM coin, the designer's initials, FG, are spaced farther away from the lower right side of the Lincoln Memorial. On the Wide AM variety, the G nearly touches the monument. It's worth confirming this diagnostic as well if attribution is ever in doubt. Of course, since most coins prior to 1992 are Wide AM and most coins

dated after are Close AM, it's very easy to have coins of both reverse types for comparison.

The reason for all these minor design changes was never explicitly revealed by the Mint. They were likely aimed at improving die life to make the coin easier and more economical to produce. As numismatic author David W. Lange has noted in his *Complete Guide to Lincoln Cents*, beginning in 1992 such changes as this became a nearly annual occurrence, but most were imperceptible. The most noticeable of the changes has been this repositioning of the AM. Since all the 1993 cents, both Proof and Mint State, are of the Close AM reverse variety, many have speculated that the 1992, Close AM, coins were struck as a test run before the change was implemented on full-scale production. Adding further credence to this theory, tests appear to have been conducted at both Mints producing these coins, Philadelphia and Denver.

For circulating Lincoln cents, the design appears to have been an improvement, as the Close AM reverse remained in use until the final year of the Memorial reverse design in 2008. For Proof issues, the Close AM reverse was used in 1993, but in 1994 the Wide AM returned for use on all Proof issues until the end of the series. But as a boon to collectors, these rules were not applied with perfect consistency, and other Close AM and Wide AM varieties appear on the top-100 list. As some experts speculate that yet-undiscovered varieties may also exist, the hunt continues.

Distribution: 1992, fraction of 4,648,905,000; 1992-D, fraction of 4,448,673,300

Color	AU-58	MS-60	MS-61	MS-62	MS-63	MS-64	MS-65	MS-66
				1992				
Brown	$8,100	$10,000	$11,500	$13,500	$15,000	—	—	—
Red-Brown	—	12,000	13,200	15,000	18,000	$21,600	—	—
Red	—	13,200	15,000	16,800	21,000	27,000	$30,000	$36,000
				1992-D				
Brown	1,380	1,560	1,620	1,810	2,000	—	—	—
Red-Brown	—	—	—	2,000	2,250	3,250	—	—
Red	—	2,500	2,810	3,120	4,190	5,000	8,750	11,250

45 2008 $50 AMERICAN PLATINUM EAGLE, PROOF

Designed by John Mercanti (obverse) and Joel Iskowitz (reverse). The obverse features a portrait of Lady Liberty. The reverse features the final design in the three-year series entitled "The Foundations of American Democracy," and celebrates our nation's Judicial Branch of government.

Weight: .5003 ounces. *Composition:* .9995 platinum.
Diameter: 27 mm. *Edge:* Reeded. *GSID:* 71029.

In 2007, platinum tested new heights, briefly breaking through the $1,000-per-ounce price barrier. The year 2008 was even more volatile. The metal's value surged well past $2,000 per ounce and then tumbled back to $800 per ounce by the end of the year. This extreme volatility in its value was a reflection of global economics—the downturn in the stock market that year caused an aggressive flight to tangible assets. Sales doubled for almost all of the bullion versions of the American Silver Eagles, American Gold Eagles, and American Platinum Eagles in 2008 from their 2007 numbers.

Curiously, the exact opposite is true of the collector versions of these coins. The Proof and Uncirculated versions offered directly by the Mint to collectors almost all sold at half the level in 2008 that they had sold in 2007. This is very well illustrated by the 2007 and 2008 $100 American Platinum Eagle one-ounce coins. Sales of the bullion coins were 7,202 in 2007 and 21,800 units in 2008, while the Proof version declined from 8,363 in 2007 to only 4,769 in 2008.

There is a likely explanation. Investors sought exposure to precious metals, causing the surge of interest in bullion. Collectors, meanwhile, buying coins with discretionary money, were much more sensitive to price. In 2003 the price for the half-ounce $50 American Platinum Eagle Proof was $587. In 2007, the Mint offered the $50 American Platinum Eagle Proof coin for $810, a leap of $223 in five years. When the next year's Proof coin went on sale on May 5, 2008, its price was $1,175, an increase of $365 in just one year. This aggressive pricing on collectibles in an uncertain economy discouraged collectors from buying.

There is also one more consideration. Of all the Proof American Platinum Eagles, the single-lowest mintage has always been the $50 American Platinum Eagle half-ounce coin. In every year since its first offering in 1997, the half-ounce Proof American Platinum Eagle has been the lowest-selling issue, except in 2003 when 87 more units were sold than its platinum quarter-ounce compatriot. In 2008, when collectors were skittish or unwilling to buy Proof platinum

coins at platinum's new-found dizzying heights, the $50 American Platinum Eagle was most affected. Being the lowest-mintage Proof American Eagle in nearly every year meant that it found a new low of just 4,020 coins in 2008, the lowest mintage figure of a Proof American Eagle in any weight or metal. With so few to go around, this coin is already seldom found in the marketplace and is widely thought to be a major key issue.

Mintage: 4,020

PF-68DC	PF-69DC	PF-70DC	OGP
$740	$825	$1,310	$825

46 1999 LINCOLN CENT, WIDE AM

Designed by Victor David Brenner (obverse) and Frank Gasparro (reverse). The obverse continues the design of 1909. The reverse shows a frontal view of the Lincoln Memorial with UNITED STATES OF AMERICA and E PLURIBUS UNUM appearing above and ONE CENT below.

Weight: 2.5 grams. *Composition:* Outer layers of pure copper over a core of .992 zinc, .008 copper. *Diameter:* 19 mm. *Edge:* Plain. *GSID:* 2322.

While the precise purpose of these changes is not 100 percent clear, whether it might have been for either aesthetic reasons or to improve die life, the Mint experimented with different letter positioning on the reverse of the Lincoln cent throughout the 1990s. The most notable of these changes were adjustments to the spacing of the letters AM in AMERICA. In 1993, all coins had a "Close AM" reverse, with the letters nearly touching. This reverse was used for almost all circulation-strike coins until the end of the series in 2008. A reverse style with more spacing between the letters, the "Wide AM" reverse, was used for nearly all Proof issues from 1994 to 2008.

The compelling feature of these hub changes is that they were not followed with perfect consistency, and variations exist. In 2001, die-variety expert John Wexler found a circulation 2000 Lincoln cent with a Wide AM reverse, the version intended for Proof coinage. Shortly thereafter, a 1998, Wide AM, Lincoln cent was also found. Both were discovered in roll quantity, and, although not common, they are available. Sometime later, the 1999, Wide AM, Lincoln cent was found to fill in the gap. Today, only about 500 examples are known and they are by far the rarest of the Wide AM circulation Lincoln cents of this era.

Subtle and delicate hub variations of this type are usually not collectible because they are too minor to be noteworthy or interesting. These varieties, however, *are* noteworthy and interesting for two clear reasons. First, the difference in letter spacing is very easy to see. Reference coins for both the Wide AM

Pick-up point: AMERICA.

and Close AM configurations can always be found from previous years' issues for comparison. Second, one hub style was used for Proof coinage, while the other was used for circulation coinage, suggesting to some that the wrong die or hub was used accidentally.

To add to the intrigue of these coins, Proof coins also exist with the Close AM reverse for the 1998-S and 1999-S issues. In other words, the circulation-strike-style reverse was used to make Proof coins. Enthusiasts will seek to complete the set of all reverse types for both Proof and Mint State issues. In the case of the Proof issues, the 1999-S is more common than the 1998-S, while the opposite is true for the Mint State issues.

It isn't known how many 1999, Wide AM, Lincoln cents were made. Reverse dies can strike many hundreds of thousands or even a million Lincoln cents for circulation. The challenge with circulating Lincoln cent varieties is that if they are discovered well after their time of mintage, they become widely distributed and very difficult to find in quantity. While the number of known 1999, Wide AM, Lincoln cents will certainly increase from today's levels, it's uncertain that a huge cache will ever be found.

Mintage: fraction of 5,237,600,000

MS-60RD	MS-63RD	MS-64RD	MS-65RD	MS-66RD	MS-67RD	MS-68RD
$155	$190	$195	$210	$275	$1,020	$4,810

47 1970-S, DOUBLED DIE OBVERSE, LINCOLN CENT, LARGE DATE

Designed by Victor David Brenner (obverse) and Frank Gasparro (reverse). The obverse continues the design of 1909. The reverse shows a frontal view of the Lincoln Memorial with UNITED STATES OF AMERICA and E PLURIBUS UNUM appearing above and ONE CENT below.

Weight: 3.11 grams. *Composition:* .950 copper, .050 tin and zinc. *Diameter:* 19 mm. *Edge:* Plain. *GSID:* Brown, 2376; Red-Brown, 2377; Red, 2378.

Doubled dies are a very collectible type of die variety. They are created during the production of coinage dies. Die blanks are imparted with their design, a reversed impression of the coin they will ultimately strike, by a hub. Although die production processes have changed, it used to be that during hubbing a die blank received multiple strikes from a hub to ensure a complete transfer. If there was any misalignment, elements of the design would be shifted and duplicated, and this doubling would then appear on every coin that that die struck.

The misalignment can occur in multiple ways. So-called Class I doubled dies occur when there is a rotation between strikes of a hub with the central area of the design as the primary axis for doubling. These coins characteristically show doubling in one direction (either clockwise or counterclockwise). Doubling will be most evident toward the periphery of the struck coin. On the Lincoln cent obverse this is where the date, the word LIBERTY, and the motto IN GOD WE TRUST can be found. Class I rotated-hub doubling accounts for several of the most dramatic doubled dies in the Lincoln cent series.

The value of doubled-die variety coins is usually determined by two factors: the amount of separation between designs and the overall scarcity of the coin. The first factor contributes to the visual drama. Collectors want major doubled dies where duplicated design elements are readily distinguishable and visible under low magnification or, better yet, to the naked eye. And collectors want coins that are hard to find. Dramatic and rare doubled dies are worth big money.

The 1970-S, Large Date, Doubled Die Obverse, Lincoln cent meets all these requirements. It is a Class I doubled die with dramatic duplication on the date,

Pick-up points: Lettering, mintmark.

LIBERTY, and IN GOD WE TRUST. By most measures it is among the top five doubled-die Lincoln cents with Memorial reverse in terms of visual drama along with the 1969-S, Doubled Die Obverse; 1972, Doubled Die Obverse; 1983, Doubled Die Reverse; and 1984, Doubled Die Obverse. Of any major doubled-die variety, it is the second scarcest with only about four dozen known, bested only by the 1969-S, Doubled Die Obverse.

It surprises many that more 1970-S, Large Date, Double Die Obverse, Lincoln cents have not been found. Among 1970-S Lincoln cents, there are both Small Date and Large Date logotypes. The 1970-S, Small Date, is comparatively scarce and trades for big premiums in high grade. That means rolls and rolls have been searched for Small Date and Large Date DDOs alike, but still not many have been found.

All known examples exhibit a large die defect—a raised line emerging from the top of the zero in the date and extending all the way down to the mintmark. Looking for an explanation for this coin's rarity, some have described this die line as a crack that ultimately caused this obverse die to be taken out of service early, thereby limiting the number of coins it produced. In fact, this is not a crack, but it is possible that the defect of the doubling was discovered and thus this die was taken out of service early. The scarcity of this coin is, indeed, a true mystery.

Because it is so rare, it is also valuable. Gem red examples in the finest states of preservation can carry a $20,000 price tag. A pleasant choice Uncirculated red coin will cost more than $5,000. Third-party certification is recommended here. Valueless die doubling abounds on San Francisco cents of this era, and a much less desirable minor DDO is also known for this date; mixing up the two coins is a mistake that can cost thousands.

Mintage: fraction of 690,560,004

Color	AU-50	MS-60	MS-61	MS-62	MS-63	MS-64	MS-65	MS-66
Brown	$845	$1,560	$1,690	$1,880	$2,120	$2,380	$4,000	—
Red-Brown	—	1,750	1,940	2,190	2,440	2,750	4,750	—
Red	—	2,120	2,250	2,380	2,560	2,900	5,000	$10,600

48 2001-W CAPITOL VISITORS CENTER $5 COMMEMORATIVE

Designed by Elizabeth Jones. The obverse depicts a section of a Corinthian column. The obverse inscriptions read LIBERTY, 1800, FIRST CONVENING OF CONGRESS IN WASHINGTON, IN GOD WE TRUST, and 2001. The reverse features a view of the 1800 Capitol with the inscriptions UNITED STATES OF AMERICA, E PLURIBUS UNUM, and FIVE DOLLARS.

Weight: 8.359 grams. *Composition:* .900 gold, .100 silver (net weight .24187 ounces pure gold). *Diameter:* 21.6 mm. *Edge:* Reeded. *GSID:* 10593.

For well over a decade this was the second lowest mintage commemorative coin in the entire series, a fact from which it derives its considerable allure and scarcity. The cause of its small mintage was poor sales. It was known before the coin was issued that it could encounter some challenges. The coin commemorated the first convening of Congress in the Capitol building in 1800; this made it the fifth commemorative program in 11 years to recognize Congress either directly or through an affiliated institution. Since surcharges from the sale of this coin went to construct and maintain a new 446,000 square-foot U.S. Capitol Visitor Center, some collectors viewed this issue as Congress passing a tax on collectors for its own benefit.

The program was also large—a three-coin commemorative program with large mintage limits, making it similar in scale to the unsuccessful 1995 and 1996 Olympic coinage. There was no reason to think that the commemoration of the 6th Congress's first meeting in the Capitol building would merit a coin program with such a large scale.

Lastly, the coin subject met with little enthusiasm. Legislation only stipulated that the design be "emblematic of the first meeting of the United States Congress in the United States Capitol Building." Buildings on coins are seldom well received, but the $5 coin showed only the portion of the building that was complete in 1800: an unrecognizable, and unbalanced, square building. The Capitol building is certainly best known for its dome, which was actually the third dome to grace the building and was only completed in 1868. All three coins in this set display the partially finished building. The $5 gold coin smartly puts it on the reverse.

The design was the last United States commemorative created by former chief engraver Elizabeth Jones, who came out of retirement for the project. As did her

previous designs for the 1983 Olympics silver dollars and the 1988 Olympics $5 gold—both enormously successful coins—she placed an element inspired by classical Greece as the dominant feature of the obverse. This time it's the cap of a Corinthian column, another widely recognized feature of the Capitol. It is both characteristic of her work and may well be the saving grace of this coin.

Just 6,761 of the 2001-W Capitol Visitors Center $5 coin were sold in the Uncirculated format. Only four coins in the series have lower mintage figures: the 2016-W National Parks $5, the 1997-W Jackie Robinson $5, 2013-P 5-Star Generals $5 Gold, and the 2015-W U.S. Marshals $5 Gold, all Uncirculated. Three are comparatively recent issues which are much easier to locate in the marketplace and therefore command smaller premiums. For whatever criticism it may have received, the Capitol Visitors Center $5 coin certainly does recognize a very worthwhile moment in U.S. history; the Capitol is, after all, among the world's greatest symbols of democracy.

Distribution: 6,761

MS-69	MS-70	OGP
$745	$780	$750

49 2011-S $1 AMERICAN SILVER EAGLE

Designed by Adolph A. Weinman (obverse) and John Mercanti (reverse). The obverse features Weinman's Liberty Walking design used on half dollars from 1916 through 1947. Weinman's initials are on the hem of the gown. The reverse design is a rendition of a heraldic eagle by John Mercanti.

Weight: 31.101 grams. *Composition:* .999 silver (net weight 1 ounce pure silver). *Diameter:* 40.6 mm. *Edge:* Reeded. *GSID:* 74464.

To celebrate the 25th anniversary of the American Eagle Program in 2011, the Mint offered a five-coin set of American Silver Eagles. Three of the coins were of the same type that had formed the three-coin set offered in 2006 to celebrate the American Eagle's 20th anniversary: a West Point Proof American Silver Eagle with W mintmark, a West Point Uncirculated American Silver Eagle with W mintmark, and a Philadelphia-made Reverse Proof American Silver Eagle with P mintmark. The 2011 set also included a bullion American Silver Eagle, which has no mintmark, and an Uncirculated American Silver Eagle struck at San Francisco and bearing an S mintmark.

Wow! This was the coin that really got everyone talking. Everything else in this set had been seen before, but this coin was truly a first: the first-ever Uncirculated American Silver Eagle with an S mintmark. Sure, Proofs had been struck at San Francisco from 1986 to 1992, and they all included an S mintmark. But that was almost 20 years ago, and this coin was still something different, something unique. Proofs from the late 1980s and early 1990s had mintage figures ranging from nearly half a million to well over a million coins. This coin was limited to 100,000 pieces, among the lowest mintage in the series!

Even with so much enthusiasm about this coin, to many it seemed odd or somewhat arbitrary that a San Francisco–made American Silver Eagle was included in the set at all. Why San Francisco? There are two reasons. First, to Mint personnel, the San Francisco Mint is closely associated with the early history of the American Silver Eagle. In 1986, the first American Silver Eagles were struck there. Proof American Silver Eagles, the only American Silver Eagles sold directly to collectors, were made at San Francisco exclusively from 1986 to 1992. Second, starting again in 2011, San Francisco joined West Point in the production of bullion American Silver Eagles. The press release came as a big surprise: "The United States Mint announced today that, effective May 31,

it will fulfill orders for American Eagle Silver Bullion Coins with coins minted at its San Francisco facility, in addition to its facility at West Point. Demand for American Eagle Silver Bullion Coins remains at unprecedented high levels. . . . Adding production at the United States Mint at San Francisco provides manufacturing flexibility across the bullion and numismatic product lines to meet customer needs."

In the eyes of Mint officials, San Francisco was an important part of the history and future of the American Silver Eagle, which is why they included an Uncirculated 2011-S $1 American Silver Eagle in the set. For collectors, it was a unique coin and maybe a once-in-a-lifetime opportunity. With 100,000 sets offered and a limit of five sets per household, a sellout was assured. The only thing that was uncertain was how long it would take. That question was answered in a matter of hours—five, to be exact. After going on sale at noon on October 27, 2011, the set was listed as "backordered" by 5:00 p.m. By the next morning, orders placed after 5:00 p.m. were cancelled, and the sellout was announced.

The 2011-S American Silver Eagle is still the only Uncirculated American Silver Eagle with an S mintmark ever released. And, as it was from its release date, it's still a hot seller.

Mintage: 100,000

MS-65	MS-66	MS-67	MS-68	MS-69	MS-70	OGP
$100	$110	$115	$130	$145	$235	$155

50 1991 $25 AMERICAN GOLD EAGLE

Designed by Augustus Saint-Gaudens (obverse) and Miley Busiek (reverse). The obverse features a modified rendition of the Augustus Saint-Gaudens design used on U.S. $20 gold pieces from 1907 until 1933. The reverse displays a "family of eagles" motif.

Weight: 16.966 grams. *Composition:* .917 gold, .030 silver, .053 copper (net weight 1/2 ounce pure gold). *Diameter:* 27 mm. *Edge:* Reeded. *GSID:* 10764.

The American Gold Eagle was created so that Americans would have an American product to buy if they wanted to own and invest in gold. Nationalism certainly played a role in passing the legislation that created this coin, and patriotism heavily informed its designs. For these reasons, and also because of its status as the only U.S. gold coin, the American Gold Eagle found a loyal following among collectors who purchased bullion-issue coins for their collections.

Since the inauguration of the series in 1986, the American Gold Eagle was issued in four sizes: one-ounce, half-ounce, quarter-ounce, and tenth-ounce weights. The most popular issues were always the one-ounce and tenth-ounce sizes, which carried $50 and $5 face values, respectively. The other weights were poor sellers; in many years, 10 times more one-ounce coins were struck than half-ounce or quarter-ounce coins.

Other than interested collectors, the other purchasers of those fractional sizes—so called because they consist of a fraction of an ounce of gold—are small investors. This group was most heavily hit by a recession at the start of the 1990s. Deficit and inflation concerns, spurred by rising oil prices during the first Persian Gulf War, should have pushed U.S. investors towards gold. True gold-bugs had bought into the American Gold Eagle program when it was first opened, only to watch the price of gold fall by 30 percent from $500 to $350 an ounce during the late 1980s. More casual investors would have been aware of gold's tumble during the past decade from its short-lived dizzying highs of 1980. In 1991, when signals suggested that gold investments would be popular, they weren't.

Interest from collectors wanting to complete a set likely accounted for a significant portion of the interest in the half-ounce 1991 $25 American Gold Eagle. Only 24,100 were produced; not only is this the lowest mintage figure for

half-ounce bullion-issue American Gold Eagles, it's the lowest mintage figure for any bullion-issue American Gold Eagle. As a result, today it is, by a good margin, the most valuable half-ounce American Gold Eagle, eclipsing even the Proof and Uncirculated (with mintmark) collector issues.

Bullion issues are sold by the U.S. Mint through official distributors, who buy coins in large quantities primarily to service investor demand. When purchasing coins in the secondary market, often it's not possible to request coinage of a specific year other than the current year. Coins of prior years become intermixed or are not tracked by date by bullion dealers. This is doubly true because American Gold Eagles issued from 1986 through 1991 included a date in Roman numerals. This number form was so difficult to work with that bullion dealers avoided date-specific sales for these coins, and the MCMXCI issue can't be purchased from investor sources. Instead, collectors are reliant on the small number available through numismatic channels, where its scarcity is always recognized.

In 1992, the date format was changed to conventional Arabic-style numerals for the American Gold Eagle, which has, in a small way, improved the accessibility of these coins. They, along with all subsequent issues, are also of a higher mintage. Some of the Uncirculated coins issued to collectors do have lower mintage figures, but they are more available in collectors' circles and do not yet garner the price premium of the 1991 issue.

Mintage: 24,100

MS-65	MS-66	MS-67	MS-68	MS-69	MS-70	OGP
$1,510	$1,520	$1,530	$1,800	$5,950	$6,750	$5,600

51 1998-S LINCOLN CENT, CLOSE AM, PROOF

Designed by Victor David Brenner (obverse) and Frank Gasparro (reverse). The obverse continues the design of 1909. The reverse shows a frontal view of the Lincoln Memorial with UNITED STATES OF AMERICA and E PLURIBUS UNUM appearing above and ONE CENT below.

Weight: 2.5 grams. *Composition:* Outer layers of pure copper over a core of .992 zinc, .008 copper. *Diameter:* 19 mm. *Edge:* Plain. *GSID:* 315589; Cameo, 315590; Deep Cameo, 70860.

Proof coinage is struck purposefully for presentation purposes and not for use as money in circulation. Both historically and presently, the goal of Proof coinage is to showcase a nation's coins both to demonstrate artistry and to show off the technical capabilities of the Mint. Proof coins are made using a controlled process, with considerable attention paid to each step of their production. Specially prepared blanks receive multiple blows from a coinage die that has been treated to render the design in the best possible way. Proof coins are then sold in sets that include Proof versions of all coins struck during a given year.

Because of the careful scrutiny they receive, there are relatively few collectible die varieties of Proof coins. The few that do exist seem to have slipped through the cracks without explanation, suggesting that an error occurred at the Mint. This last point plays a major role in collectors' fascination with Proof die varieties.

This is especially true of a curious die variety found on some Proof Lincoln cents from 1998, the Proof 1998-S, Close AM, Lincoln cent. For one year, 1993, the reverse of all Proof Lincoln cents showed the letters AM in AMERICA nearly touching. This was part of a subtle design modification meant to improve die life (a cost-saving measure) and was put into use on both Proof and circulating coins. In 1994, the design modification was retained for circulating coins, but the Wide AM reverse, which showed the letters more widely spaced, was resumed for all Proof Lincoln cents until 1998.

Pick-up point: AMERICA.

The 1998-S Proof Lincoln cent can be found both ways—with either widely or closely spaced letters. Finding both is not easy. Only a few hundred Proof 1998-S, Close AM, Lincoln cents are known from the 2,086,507 total coins produced. The vast majority of that total is of the Wide AM variety. Some research suggests that as few as 15,000 Close AM coins, less than one percent of the total mintage, were struck in 1998.

No one knows for sure why the variety exists. One popular theory is that a hub used for creating dies for circulation coins was used; the die then received special preparation for coining Proof coins. This variety is thus sometimes referred to as having the "circulation-style reverse." The quality and appearance of the coin's finish are no different from a regular Proof, but the arrangement of the reverse letters is the same as that seen on circulating coins.

Without explanation, the variety was created again in 1999, and a 1999-S, Close AM, Proof Lincoln cent also exists. It's about four to five times more common than the 1998 version, though. Additionally, a typo in a widely used variety reference suggested that a 2000-S, Close AM, cent also exists. None have yet been reported, and the variety guide has since been corrected, but this original mis-listing is occasionally replicated and quoted.

Mintage: fraction of 2,086,507

	PF-60RD	PF-63RD	PF-65RD	PF-66RD	PF-67RD	PF-68RD	PF-69RD	PF-70RD
Normal	$38	$47	$68	$88	$110	$130	$175	—
Cameo	—	—	—	110	135	155	210	—
Deep Cameo	—	—	94	130	175	195	260	$3,440

52 2019-W AND 2020-W QUARTERS

Designed by John Flanagan (obverse) and various artists (reverses). The obverse portrait of President George Washington, previously a more detailed version in use on the 50 State Quarters, reverted to something closer to Flanagan's original, but the inscriptions remained in place. The reverse design of each represents the designated park or site, enclosed within a wide border bearing the name of site, the state, the national motto, and the year.

Weight: 5.67 grams. *Composition:* Outer layers of .750 copper and .250 nickel over a core of pure copper. *Diameter:* 24.3 mm. *Edge:* Reeded. *GSID:* Lowell, 81700; American Memorial, 81701; San Antonio Missions, 81703; War in the Pacific, 81702; Frank Church–River, 81704; American Samoa, 82010; Weir Farm, 82017; Salt River Bay, 85050; Marsh-Billings-Rockefeller, 85051; Tallgrass Prairie, 85049.

A great lament among long-time coin collectors is that there are few coins of value to be found among coins in circulation. There are exceptions, but these are often subtle die varieties known only to real enthusiasts. Credit is owed to the U.S. Mint for introducing a program in 2019 aimed at encouraging people to look at their pocket change for interesting coins.

Starting in April 2019, the West Point Mint began striking quarters with the W mintmark. These were the first coins with the W mintmark to be struck for circulation. The framework of the program was simple enough: Two million examples of each of the year's five America the Beautiful quarter designs would be produced and mixed into bulk bags of quarters struck at Philadelphia and Denver. These coins would be distributed to banks and financial institutions and then released into circulation with regular coinage. The goal was to introduce scarce coins randomly into pocket change. All five 2019 quarter issues were distributed in this way: Lowell National Historical Park, American Memorial Park, War in the Pacific National Historical Park, San Antonio Missions National Historical Park, and Frank Church River of No Return Wilderness.

The first release was timed with the American Numismatic Association's National Coin Week, and the U.S. Mint promoted the hashtag #WQuarter on social media to generate interest among younger audiences. The promotion was referred to as the Great American Coin Hunt, and the numismatic press reported stories of coin finds, including honoring the first reported finds and recognizing coins found in the first week of release. As most of these quarter

issues have combined Philadelphia-Denver mintages in the 300-plus million range, there was a less than a one–in–one hundred chance of finding one. Spying a coin was indeed worthy of celebration, as many quarters readily traded for as much as $50, with high-grade examples (MS-67 and higher) bringing truly premium prices.

In 2020, the Mint continued the West Point quarter program with an added twist: they included the V75 privy mark to commemorate the 75th anniversary of the end of World War II. This would make the W-mintmark issue even easier to spot. Again, two million coins were struck at West Point with W mintmarks and privy marks for all five 2020 quarter issues: National Park of American Samoa, Weir Farm National Historic Site, Salt River Bay National Historical Park and Ecological Preserve, Marsh-Billings-Rockefeller National Historical Park, and Tallgrass Prairie National Preserve.

The results were similar to the previous year's, although perhaps some enthusiasm had waned. The program ended in 2020. Given their residual value and the comparatively high likelihood of finding one, these 10 W-mintmark quarters remain among the most obvious collectibles to look for in circulating coinage and will be for years to come.

Mintage: 2,000,000 of each design

	AU-50	AU-58	MS-60	MS-63	MS-64	MS-65	MS-66	MS-67	MS-68
Lowell	$16.00	$27.00	$34.00	$47.00	$68.00	$110.00	$155	$405	$6,250
American Memorial	16.00	27.00	34.00	47.00	68.00	110.00	155	405	1,250
San Antonio Missions	16.00	27.00	34.00	47.00	68.00	110.00	155	405	1,250
War in the Pacific	16.00	27.00	34.00	47.00	68.00	110.00	155	405	1,250
Frank Church–River	16.00	27.00	34.00	47.00	68.00	110.00	155	405	1,250
American Samoa	—	—	8.00	11.00	12.00	13.50	32	195	—
Weir Farm	—	—	8.00	11.00	12.00	13.50	47	210	—
Salt River Bay	—	—	8.00	11.00	12.00	20.00	54	390	8,100
Marsh-Billings-Rockefeller	—	—	11.00	27.00	40.00	54.00	130	550	—
Tallgrass Prairie	—	—	8.00	11.00	13.50	21.50	155	405	—

53 1970-D KENNEDY HALF DOLLAR

Designed by Gilroy Roberts (obverse) and Frank Gasparro (reverse). On the obverse, the head of John F. Kennedy faces left. LIBERTY arcs across the top of the obverse; the date arcs along the bottom and IN GOD WE TRUST runs in a straight line beneath Kennedy's head. The reverse features a heraldic eagle, similar to that seen on the 1801 through 1807 and 1892 through 1915 half dollars, within a circle of 50 stars. UNITED STATES arcs around the top and HALF DOLLAR arcs along the bottom of the reverse.

Weight: 11.50 grams. *Composition:* Outer layers of .800 silver and .200 copper over a core of .209 silver and .791 copper. *Diameter:* 30.6 mm. *Edge:* Reeded. *GSID:* 6926.

Nearly every year since 1947, the U.S. Mint has sold Mint sets—annual coin sets that include all the coins struck for circulation in a given year. From 1951 to 1981, they sold sets of some sort each year without interruption, and this became the easiest way for collectors to acquire an Uncirculated example of each coin from each Mint. During these years, these annual coin sets boomed in popularity, growing from 8,654 sets sold in 1951 to two million by the late 1960s.

In 1970, for the first time, these sets contained something of a curiosity. They included the 1970-D Kennedy half dollar—a coin that was never struck for general circulation and can only be found in the 1970 Mint set. Its mintage was only the 2.15 million pieces required for the net sales of 1970 Mint sets. To find an earlier half dollar with a similarly low mintage, one must go all the way back to the 1938-D Liberty Walking half dollar, a classic rarity.

In 1964, the first Kennedy half dollar was introduced with a composition of 90 percent silver. An incredible 273 million examples were struck in Philadelphia, while the Denver Mint struck another 156 million. The Coinage Act of 1965, which suspended the striking of silver coins for circulation, included a special provision for the half dollar, then the largest circulating coin. The act stipulated that the half dollar was to be struck in a silver-clad composition that included 40 percent silver through 1970, and then silver was to be phased out entirely. To meet demand from those who desired silver, half dollars were made in considerable numbers, reaching a peak of 295 million in 1967. The Mint made another 247 million half dollars in 1968, and struck nearly 130 million half dollars for

circulation in 1969. But the very next year, in 1970, not a single half dollar was struck for circulation.

This puts the rarity of the 1970-D half dollar into context. Such a low mintage (only two million struck) would not be seen again until 2006, long after half dollars ceased to have wide use in circulation. By 1970, the production boom had created enough coins to meet demand, and more Kennedy half dollars were not needed for circulation. This is a situation that is being repeated today. Now, Kennedy half dollars are struck almost exclusively for collectors. Sales of Mint sets, rolls, and bags from the Mint directly to collectors account for the entire current production of half dollars. It's thought that present demand for coins in circulation can still be met using a stockpile of coins struck before 2001, as their current use is mostly confined to casino payouts.

Because of its low mintage, the 1970-D is the most valuable Kennedy half dollar in average Uncirculated grades and the key date in the series. Many Kennedys of this era are challenging coins to find in the very highest grades because their production quality was rather low, but examples from all levels are known from Mint sets and from the large quantity of coins struck for circulation. Because of its low original mintage, the 1970-D variety's place among the most important business-strike Kennedy half dollars is unlikely to be challenged.

Mintage: 2,150,000

AU-50	AU-58	MS-60	MS-63	MS-64	MS-65	MS-66	MS-67
$6.30	$7.10	$8.30	$18	$27	$47	$260	$4,250

54 2001-W $50 AMERICAN GOLD EAGLE, PROOF

Designed by Augustus Saint-Gaudens (obverse) and Miley Busiek (reverse). The obverse features a modified rendition of the Augustus Saint-Gaudens design used on U.S. $20 gold pieces from 1907 until 1933. The reverse displays a "family of eagles" motif.

Weight: 33.931 grams. *Composition:* .917 gold,
.030 silver, .053 copper (net weight 1 ounce pure gold).
Diameter: 32.7 mm. *Edge:* Reeded. *GSID:* 10830.

Collector demand for Proof American Gold Eagles always contracts when gold prices decline. Unlike investors, who see dips in prices as buying opportunities, collectors become fickle when prices fall. While this may seem counterintuitive, collectors are slow to return for more when they buy coins from the Mint only to see them trading for discounts in the aftermarket. Collectors of Proof American Gold Eagles experienced this frustration as the price of gold steadily declined from the mid-1990s through 2001.

In 1998, the Mint announced that it would lower the issue price of the one-ounce American Gold Eagle $50 Proof coin from $589 to $570, a rollback that brought its price to the same level it had been at in 1990. "We looked at the substantial fall in gold prices in recent months and concluded that we needed to share these lower costs with our customers," Mint Director Philip N. Diehl said in a U.S. Mint press release announcing the decrease.

In order to further spur sales, the maximum mintage was also lowered from 45,000 to 35,000 examples, a measure that typically appeals to collectors. Buyers responded modestly to lower prices and mintage limits, buoying sales. One major factor is worth noting: in 1990, gold teetered around $400 per ounce, while in 1998, it had slid to the $300-per-ounce mark. Had the Proof American Gold Eagle's prices been adjusted accordingly, much more aggressive sales increases certainly would have been seen.

In the following years—1999, 2000, and 2001—prices remained unchanged and mintage maximums were only slightly increased, up to 40,000 in 1999 and 41,000 in 2000 and 2001. With European central banks selling off gold, however, the metal's value declined further still, bouncing around the $260-per-ounce mark. The Mint did not respond to these new levels, and kept its prices steady.

During this same time, wholesale trading of the one-ounce Proof American Gold Eagles continued at levels of roughly $150 to $200 above the per-ounce

price of gold, but this was still $100 to $150 lower than the U.S. Mint issue price. Fed-up collectors backed away, and only 24,555 of the 2001-W American Gold Eagle $50 Proof were sold, the lowest in the coin's history. As the value of gold increased in 2002 and in each subsequent year, so did the total number of units sold, leaving the 2001 issue as the lowest-mintage one-ounce American Gold Eagle $50 Proof in the series. Since collectors of one-ounce Proof American Gold Eagles commonly seek to build the whole series by date, the 2001-W is emerging as a key date. To avoid years of stagnant prices leading to a decline in sales, the U.S. Mint ultimately revised its pricing policy; starting in 2009, the Mint began re-pricing coins weekly to accord with price movements in precious metals.

Mintage: 24,555

PF-68DC	PF-69DC	PF-70DC	OGP
$2,630	$2,750	$3,380	$3,380

55 1994-P JEFFERSON NICKEL, MATTE "SPECIAL UNCIRCULATED"

Designed by Felix Schlag. The obverse features a bust of Thomas Jefferson facing left. IN GOD WE TRUST appears inside the left edge, and LIBERTY and the date appear inside the right edge. On the reverse, Jefferson's home, Monticello, appears as the central device; E PLURIBUS UNUM arcs above it. The word MONTICELLO captions the building, and the words FIVE CENTS and the legend UNITED STATES OF AMERICA appear below.

Weight: 5.00 grams. *Composition:* .750 copper, .250 nickel.
Diameter: 21.2 mm. *Edge:* Plain. *GSID:* 3602.

In 1993, Thomas Jefferson was honored with a commemorative silver dollar for the 250th anniversary of his birth. As the third president of the United States and the principal author of the Declaration of Independence, Jefferson is an important figure in U.S. history and hence has been honored extensively in numismatic designs. His portrait is featured on the front of the $2 bill, brought back in 1976 for the Bicentennial celebration, and, more famously, his likeness also appears on the five-cent nickel, which replaced the Buffalo nickel in 1938.

Like other modern commemorative coins, the Jefferson 250th-Anniversary silver dollar was available in both Proof and Uncirculated formats. But it was also sold in the Thomas Jefferson Coinage and Currency Set; included in this set were an Uncirculated 1993-P Jefferson 250th-Anniversary silver dollar, an Uncirculated 1994-P Jefferson nickel, and a Series 1976 $2 Federal Reserve Note. In other words, all the current-issue coins and currency featuring Thomas Jefferson were included in the set. Although the commemorative coin bears the date 1993, as a result of a late approval date the authorizing legislation for this coin actually passed in 1994.

The commemorative dollar and the Jefferson nickel are thematically identical, showing a portrait on the obverse and Monticello on the reverse, and are presented side by side in the coin and currency holder. Although the presentation is quite pleasant, that is not what makes this set so special. Rather than selecting regular 1994 nickels for this set, the U.S. Mint struck a special presentation coin for inclusion in this set, a nickel with a special matte finish.

The matte finish had never before been used on a Jefferson nickel and had not been used on any nickel since 1916. In fact, it had not been used on any U.S. coin since 1922! Matte-finish coins are entirely non-reflective and have a dull

textured surface. This effect is created by acid-treating or sandblasting the dies that strike coins to give them a fine-grained, rough surface. Matte coins are made for presentation purposes, and often these coins will receive multiple blows from coinage dies so as to show their detail more crisply. The even surface texture allows the coin's design to be showcased in a special way.

Because of the inclusion of the matte-finish Jefferson nickel, the Coinage and Currency Set was a great seller. In total, 167,703 were sold, accounting for more than half the sales of the Uncirculated Jefferson Anniversary dollar. Single-coin sales of the dollar (not in the sets) were just under 100,000, and more than 330,000 Proof versions were sold. All told, sales of the sets brought the total for the commemorative dollar up to 600,000, the maximum allowed by Congress. Very likely, more sets would have been sold had the limit not been reached—but not because collectors wanted the dollar: they wanted the matte-finish nickel!

The Coinage and Currency Set was the only way to get the matte-finish, special-strike 1994-P Jefferson nickel, and its mintage of 167,703 is the second-lowest mintage for any Jefferson nickel. Its soft, gray-textured finish and crisp, prooflike detail make it a visually exciting specimen, while its low mintage makes it a very scarce and desirable modern issue.

Mintage: 167,703

MS-60	MS-63	MS-64	MS-65	MS-66	MS-67	MS-68	MS-69	MS-70
$9.50	$11.00	$13.50	$15.00	$19.00	$24.50	$35	$54	$325

56 1966 KENNEDY HALF DOLLAR, SMS, NO "FG"

Designed by Gilroy Roberts (obverse) and Frank Gasparro (reverse). On the obverse, the head of John F. Kennedy faces left. LIBERTY arcs across the top of the obverse; the date arcs along the bottom of the obverse and IN GOD WE TRUST runs in a straight line beneath Kennedy's head. The reverse features a heraldic eagle, similar to that seen on the 1801 through 1807 and 1892 through 1915 half dollars, within a circle of 50 stars. UNITED STATES arcs around the top and HALF DOLLAR arcs along the bottom of the reverse.

Weight: 11.50 grams. *Composition:* Outer layers of .800 silver and .200 copper over a core of .209 silver, .791 copper. *Diameter:* 30.6 mm. *Edge:* Reeded. *GSID:* 352004.

The name of this variety tells its story very straightforwardly. The first part of its name is SMS, indicating that it was issued in Special Mint Sets, the coinage sets that replaced Proof sets from 1965 to 1967 so that the U.S. Mint could focus its efforts on the transition from silver to copper-nickel-clad coinage. The "No FG" is an indication that the designer's initials, FG, do not appear on the reverse of the coin as they ought.

On all Kennedy half dollars struck from 1964 to date, the designer's initials are shown on the reverse of the coin. Those examples bearing the standard heraldic eagle design (all but the Bicentennial issue) have an FG placed between the eagle's left leg and tail. The initials stand for Frank Gasparro, the U.S. Mint chief engraver from 1965 to 1981. Gasparro designed the Eisenhower dollar, the Susan B. Anthony dollar, the Memorial cent reverse, and, of course, the reverse of the Kennedy half dollar. He is among the most influential coin designers of the latter half of the 20th century.

Some half dollars found in 1966 Special Mint Sets (SMS) do not show Gasparro's initials, or even any trace of them. Although there is no formal explanation for this omission, it is thought that the initials were simply polished off

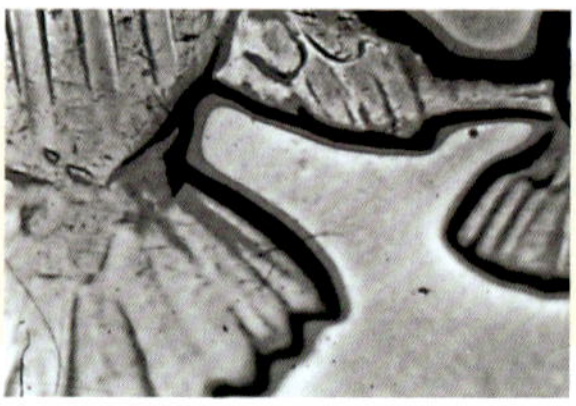

Pick-up point: Area between eagle's tail and leg on reverse.

the dies during their preparation for the production process. The coins in the Special Mint Sets did not receive the care and attention given to Proof coins, though they were struck from highly polished dies that give the coins a mirror-like surface.

There is some history of coins missing initials. It happened previously and with a similar explanation on the Proof 1941 Liberty Walking half dollar, which can be found without its designer's initials. This exact variety of the Kennedy half dollar, without the designer's initials, was created twice more at the Denver Mint in both 1972 and 1982, but those times the mistake was on circulation-strike coins. This 1966 variety is the only time that the omission has occurred on a presentation version of the Kennedy half dollar.

The absent letters make this self-explanatory variety very easy to attribute. Even so, only a few hundred are known, and they can often be lower grade than the typical SMS Kennedy half dollar. Although the most-coveted SMS coins display cameo contrast between the mirrored fields and frosted design elements, this variety is not found with cameo contrast, and not a single cameo coin has been graded by a major service. Because the coins are highly sought after, finding a high-grade example, or an example displaying cameo contrast, would yield the discoverer a nice return.

It is likely that many tens of thousands of 1966 SMS half dollars without designer initials were struck and can still be found in original sets. The 1966 Kennedy half dollar is an exciting issue for collectors because a doubled-die obverse also exists for this year, showing a doubled profile of Kennedy. Cherrypickers can examine the reverse of their coins to determine if it's missing the initials—the most desirable variety of the year—and if that disappoints, they can flip the coin over to examine whether it's a doubled die.

Mintage: fraction of 2,261,583

MS-63	MS-64	MS-65	MS-66	MS-67
$100	$130	$195	$410	$1,500

57 1970, NO S, ROOSEVELT DIME, PROOF

Designed by John R. Sinnock. On the obverse, the head of Franklin Roosevelt faces left. LIBERTY appears in large letters along the left rim; IN GOD WE TRUST appears in small letters at the lower left, and the date appears at the bottom right. The reverse features a lit torch flanked by sprigs of olive and oak. UNITED STATES OF AMERICA arcs above, ONE DIME arcs below, and the motto E PLURIBUS UNUM runs in a straight line through the bottoms of the sprigs and torch.

Weight: 2.27 grams. *Composition:* Outer layers of .750 copper and .250 nickel over a core of pure copper. *Diameter:* 17.9 mm. *Edge:* Reeded. *GSID:* 71685; Cameo, 4975; Deep Cameo, 4976.

The Proof 1970, No S, dime is said to be the most common of all the No S Proof coins, although this by no means makes it common: far fewer than 500 examples are known. Since 1968, all Proof versions of circulating coinage have been struck at San Francisco and included an S mintmark. In at least five instances, the S mintmark was mistakenly omitted from the dies, creating these highly desirable varieties.

First discovered in an original Proof set in early 1971, the 1970, No S, Roosevelt dime was officially confirmed by the Mint. They also acknowledged that they had made 2,200 examples, which were then packaged among the more than 3.2 million Proof sets for that year. In one sense, the small likelihood of finding one of these coins makes it surprising that so many have been found. They are easy to identify, though, and their value makes searching them out worthwhile.

These coins are often in very good, attractive condition, and examples will frequently show mild cameo contrast. Professional authentication is recommended to avoid spurious coins made from circulation-strike 1970 dimes that have been altered to look like Proofs. Proof coins are struck twice from specially prepared dies and have crisp detail and sharp, squared rims. Fortunately, if ever in doubt about a coin's authenticity, it's possible to acquire a regular S mintmark Proof example for comparison, as these are readily available.

The first No S dime was made in 1968 (see no. 8), the first year the Proof dimes included the S mintmark. That first coin is incredibly scarce, with just a few dozen known, compared with a few hundred for this coin. But if this is the most common No S dime, there is no debate over which is the rarest. In 1977, two Proof 1975, No S, dimes were confirmed by prominent numismatists.

Since that time, no other discoveries have been made of the 1975 variety. When the second of the original discovery coins crossed the auction block, it sold for $349,600 and became the highest-value U.S. modern coin ever to sell at auction, earning the 1975, No S, dime number-one ranking on the list of 100 Greatest U.S. Modern Coins. Examples of the 1970, No S, dime in comparable condition trade for over $1,000, making it no slouch—except when compared to its much rarer counterpart.

Mintage: fraction of 2,632,810

	PF-63	PF-64	PF-65	PF-66	PF-67	PF-68	PF-69
Normal	$455	$490	$535	$585	$680	$750	$1,090
Cameo	—	520	570	620	750	845	3,000
Deep Cameo	—	—	845	910	1,090	1,310	3,750

58 2007-P JOHN ADAMS DOLLAR, DOUBLED EDGE LETTERING

Designed by Joel Iskowitz (obverse) and Don Everhart (reverse). The obverse features a portrait of John Adams with the inscriptions JOHN ADAMS, 2nd PRESIDENT, and the dates 1797–1801. The reverse features a rendition of the Statue of Liberty with the inscriptions UNITED STATES OF AMERICA and $1. The date, mintmark, and mottos IN GOD WE TRUST and E PLURIBUS UNUM are incused on the edge.

Weight: 8.1 grams. *Composition:* Outer layers of .770 copper, .120 zinc, .070 manganese, and .040 nickel over a core of pure copper. *Diameter:* 26.5 mm. *Edge:* Lettered. *GSID:* 68748.

During striking of the second coin in the Presidential dollar coin series, the John Adams dollar, the Philadelphia Mint showed that it was determined not to make the same mistake twice. While producing the first coin of the series, the Mint had inadvertently released hundreds of thousands of George Washington dollars before they had passed through the edge-lettering machine (see no. 59). On the edge of the Presidential dollars were supposed to be the date, the mintmark, and required coinage inscriptions IN GOD WE TRUST and E PLURIBUS UNUM.

No one really seemed to care, quite frankly, that the date and mintmark were missing from the coin. It did, however, strike a chord with many that the motto IN GOD WE TRUST had been left off. These George Washington dollars missing edge-lettering quickly earned the moniker "Godless dollars." The U.S. Mint must have been overwhelmed with media requests, as well as letters from the public, because they immediately issued a statement written in response to the public outcry. It read, in part, "The United States Mint understands the importance of the inscriptions. . . . We take this matter seriously." They further stated, "As we adjust this new process, we intend to eliminate any such defects."

The challenge was that the lettering was applied by an edge-lettering machine in a secondary process after the coins were initially struck, so the Philadelphia Mint instituted a new control process to assure that the edge-lettering step would not be missed. They were successful, and the John Adams, Missing Edge Lettering, dollar is, by any comparative measure, a scarce error coin. Subsequent issues of the Presidential dollar coins without edge lettering are scarcer still. But the new control methods were soon found to be overzealous, as a new type of error coin would indicate.

A significant number of 2007-P John Adams dollars show doubled edge lettering! This means that they were passed through the edge-lettering machine twice, which then reapplied the full edge inscription. Indeed, the controls were tight enough that coins were far more likely to pass through the machine twice than to miss the process entirely. According to some estimates, more than 50,000 Doubled Edge Lettering John Adams dollars were made in Philadelphia, while only 10,000 Missing Edge Lettering coins were made. Examples of the John Adams dollar from the Denver Mint are very scarce and only a few hundred are thought to exist.

Because the orientation of the edge-lettering is random, the second inscription can either be in the same direction as or opposite to the first. When the inscriptions both travel in the same direction, they are said to be *Overlapped.* When they are opposite, that is, when one is upside down when compared to the other, they are said to be *Inverted.* Both exist in equal proportion, as would be expected; however, the most readable inscriptions are those that show a close overlapping of the two legends, which then read IINN GGOODD WWEE TTRRUUSSTT.

Mintage: fraction of 112,420,000

MS-63	MS-64	MS-65	MS-66	MS-67	MS-68	OGP
$16	$21.50	$30	$260	—	—	$27

59 (2007) GEORGE WASHINGTON DOLLAR, MISSING EDGE LETTERING

Designed by Joseph Menna (obverse) and Don Everhart (reverse). The obverse features a portrait of George Washington with the inscriptions GEORGE WASHINGTON, 1st PRESIDENT, and the years of his administration, 1789-1797. The reverse features a rendition of the Statue of Liberty with the inscriptions UNITED STATES OF AMERICA and $1. The date, mintmark, and mottos IN GOD WE TRUST and E PLURIBUS UNUM are normally incused on the edge.

Weight: 8.1 grams. *Composition:* Outer layers of .770 copper, .120 zinc, .070 manganese, and .040 nickel over a core of pure copper. *Diameter:* 26.5 mm. *Edge:* Lettered. *GSID:* 68643.

Each modern coin now includes the motto IN GOD WE TRUST, the word LIBERTY, the phrase E PLURIBUS UNUM, the date, and the mintmark in its design. For the new series of Presidential dollar coins, the name of the president, the number denoting the order in which each served, and the years in office were also to appear on the coin. This was so much text that, quite naturally, there was concern about how to still render an attractive design.

In order to leave as much room as possible for a large portrait while nevertheless featuring a great design, a solution was proposed in the Presidential $1 Coin Act of 2005: "In order to revitalize the design of United States coinage and return circulating coinage to its position as not only a necessary means of exchange in commerce, but also as an object of aesthetic beauty in its own right, it is appropriate to move many of the mottos and emblems, the inscription of the year, and the so-called 'mint marks' that currently appear on the 2 faces of each circulating coin to the edge of the coin, which would allow larger and more dramatic artwork on the coins."

Standard edge lettering (left) and blank edges (right).

Opening up the design in this way presented a great opportunity, to be sure, but no circulating coin in the United States had had an edge inscription in more than 170 years! The U.S. Mint simply did not possess the equipment or the experience to repeat this process hundreds of millions of times. They scrambled to find a solution, buying new minting equipment and installing it at the mints in Philadelphia and Denver, where coins for circulation were to be struck. Certainly, the single most compelling characteristic of the newly issued Presidential dollar coins was their edge lettering.

Collectors around the country clamored to get their first look at these coins and their unique incuse, inscribed edge. But only days after the first George Washington dollar coins were released, coins were found with plain edges, having missed the edge-lettering process entirely: the date, mintmark, and other legends were all absent. Names sprung up for these errors, including the Plain Edge or, more colloquially, the Smooth Edge Washington dollar. But because this coin lacked the motto IN GOD WE TRUST, it soon garnered a new nickname—the "Godless dollar." That name, along with the sensation of this new error coin, caught the attention of the national media.

In response, only three weeks after the coin was first released, the U.S. Mint issued a statement indicating that they had struck more than 300 million Washington dollar coins and, due to the implementation of this new complex, high-volume system, the edge-lettering had been missed on an unspecified number of coins. They stated that this error occurred at the Philadelphia Mint.

Today, experts suggest that more than 200,000 George Washington dollar coins were struck without edge lettering. Their high mintage makes them easily obtainable, and many collectors include an example as part of their regular collection. Altered Washington dollars sanded down to simulate the missing inscription are abundant, so third-party authentication is recommended.

Mintage: fraction of 176,680,000

MS-63	MS-64	MS-65	MS-66	MS-67	MS-68	OGP
$27	$30	$32	$57	$310	$715	$34

60 1995, DOUBLED DIE OBVERSE, LINCOLN CENT

Designed by Victor David Brenner (obverse) and Frank Gasparro (reverse). The obverse continues the design of 1909. The reverse shows a frontal view of the Lincoln Memorial with UNITED STATES OF AMERICA and E PLURIBUS UNUM appearing above and ONE CENT below.

Weight: 3.11 grams. *Composition:* .950 copper, .050 tin and zinc. *Diameter:* 19 mm. *Edge:* Plain. *GSID:* Brown, 2303; Red-Brown, 2304; Red, 2305.

In late February 1995, Felix Dausilio of Bridgeport, Connecticut, a 47-year-old school custodian who had been collecting coins for only three years, made a very important discovery. Examining coins from just two rolls of Lincoln cents, he spotted an example with doubled lettering. Although he had not been collecting for very long, he knew exactly what he had found: the first 1995, Doubled Die Obverse, Lincoln cent.

The first weekend in March 1995, the coin was displayed at a major coin convention in Atlanta, Georgia, and word spread throughout the numismatic press. Because the coin's discovery came 40 years after the most visually dramatic Lincoln cent doubled die, the 1955 variety, numerous comparisons were made, further helping to cement the status of the coin among collectors. And then, the national media caught wind of the story, and a number of articles appeared throughout local and national newspapers, including, famously, a front-page mention in *USA Today*. The Associated Press ran a wire story and Dausilio appeared on a Hartford, Connecticut, television station. The nation was captivated by a Lincoln cent that could be found in pocket change and carried a collector value of more than a hundred dollars.

Pick-up point: LIBERTY.

The coin was created, like all doubled dies, when the hub used to create its die rotated between impressions. All examples struck from this obverse die show identical doubling on the design elements. The 1995, Doubled Die Obverse, Lincoln cent shows a clearly doubled and nicely separated impression of the word LIBERTY and slightly less prominent doubling on the motto, IN GOD WE TRUST. From all accounts, it seems likely that a full production run of cents was struck from this die, with typical die life exceeding 600,000 coins. In 1995, the media attention created a frenzy, and collectors began furiously searching for 1995, Doubled Die Obverse, Lincoln cent coins. Surprisingly, they were found in significant numbers. Dealers and collectors probably rounded up more than 50,000 of them from original rolls.

In a sense, it is fortunate that so many examples of these cents have been preserved, making it a popular and findable collectible. Sometimes, exciting discoveries prove too elusive to become collectible. In this instance, high-grade pieces, even MS-68 Red examples, can readily be found, allowing this major variety to become a requirement for a complete set. Virtually all serious collectors of Lincoln Memorial cents will include a 1995, Doubled Die Obverse, in their collection, assuring its long-term desirability.

This coin also continues to garner publicity as one of the most interesting coins that can be found in circulating coinage, although with one billion cents produced each year, the statistical likelihood of finding one in your pocket change is still remote. Having interesting varieties in circulation is one of the essential recruitment tools of numismatics, and this coin helps to meet that need. While there are certainly more valuable error coins in circulation, this coin garnered large amounts of publicity and remains well regarded.

Mintage: fraction of 6,411,440,000

	AU-58	MS-60	MS-63	MS-64	MS-65	MS-66	MS-67	MS-68	MS-69
Brown	$16	$20	$30	$34	$40	$54	$68	$100	—
Red-Brown	—	23	34	47	54	68	81	155	—
Red	—	30	47	54	68	78	100	180	$2,190

61 1982-D GEORGE WASHINGTON HALF DOLLAR COMMEMORATIVE

Designed by Elizabeth Jones. The obverse features George Washington astride a horse. The reverse depicts the eastern façade of Washington's home, Mount Vernon, with a heraldic eagle beneath.

Standards: Weight: 12.5 grams. *Composition:* .900 silver, .100 copper.
Diameter: 30.6 mm. *Edge:* Reeded. *GSID:* 10409.

Many were surprised in 1981 when the George Washington 250th-anniversary half dollar was announced. It had been 27 years since the last commemorative coin was struck, and collectors had all but lost hope that there would be new commemorative-coinage issues. Three factors formed the basis of inspiration for this coin, and together they overcame the long time blockage of new commemorative programs.

First was the occasion. The year 1982 marked the 250th anniversary of George Washington's birth. While commemorative medals were being issued to recognize presidents in recent years, the milestone anniversary of the first president's birth had greater heft and was deemed more deserving of a coin. Secondly, the success of the Bicentennial coinage sold in 1975 and 1976 proved that commemorative-coinage programs could be profitably and successfully managed. Unlike later commemorative issues, proceeds for this coin would not go to a special interest or limited-purpose vehicle; rather, they would be used to pay down the national debt, a use of such general benefit that few could argue against this feature of the coin. And third, there was strong support for this coin from individuals who sought to pass a subsequent bill to make commemorative coins for the 1984 Los Angeles Olympics, which would be a greater challenge if the commemorative program had not already been restored.

The coin itself was to be struck in 90 percent silver, making it the first U.S. coin of this composition since 1964. It was also a half dollar, the denomination that accounted for all but two of the original silver commemorative coins issued between 1892 and 1954. In these ways, this coin was more similar to the early commemorative coins than the subsequent commemoratives. Other features of the program, however, suggested that this was a modern coin and a departure from the earlier issues. First, the coin was to be struck in both Proof and Uncirculated versions; this had contributed significantly to the collector sales of the Bicentennial coinage. Second, a total of 10 million coins were authorized to be struck between the two formats. This figure dwarfed any of the original

commemorative-coin mintages from the earlier period, indicating that this was indeed a coin of the modern era.

The designs, created by U.S. Mint Chief Engraver Elizabeth Jones, show Washington on horseback on the obverse and Mount Vernon, his home, on the reverse. The sales cycle of the coin was not limited in duration and continued into 1985 with a modest price increase in later years. The Proofs were struck at the San Francisco Mint and Uncirculated coins at Denver, with total sales of 4,894,044 and 2,210,458, respectively. The coin and its design were so successful that it was given three awards in the inaugural Coin of the Year competition in 1984 for Most Historically Significant Coin, Most Popular Coin, and Coin of the Year.

Although they were sold individually in cellophane packs inside boxes, the Uncirculated versions did not receive special handling during production (other than multiple strikes to fully render the design). Coins were ejected from dies and allowed to tumble into bins, and thus were marred with contact marks. Later issues would be spared this rough treatment, and thus the Uncirculated 1982 George Washington half dollar is the scarcest modern commemorative at the highest grade levels.

Distribution: 2,210,458

MS-68	MS-69	OGP
$15	$16	$16

62 2014 BASEBALL HALL OF FAME COMMEMORATIVES

Clad half dollar, silver dollar, $5 gold coin. Designed by Cassie McFarland (obverse), and Don Everhart (reverse). The obverse, which is concave, depicts a baseball glove, with LIBERTY, IN GOD WE TRUST, and the date on the palm. The reverse, which is convex, depicts a baseball, with UNITED STATES OF AMERICA and E PLURIBUS UNUM appearing between the top and bottom seams, and the denomination below the lower seam.

Weights: 11.34 grams; 26.73 grams; 8.359 grams. *Compositions:* .917 copper, .083 nickel; .900 silver, .100 copper; .900 gold, .100 copper. *Diameters:* 30.61 mm; 38.1 mm; 21.6 mm. *Edges:* Reeded. *GSID:* Uncirculated—half dollar, 71631; silver dollar, 71624; gold $5, 71623. Proof—half dollar, 73513; silver dollar, 71626; gold $5, 71625.

Founded in 1939, the Baseball Hall of Fame preserves the history of the United States national pastime. In advance of its 75th anniversary, Congress sought to pass legislation to issue commemorative coinage in its honor and for its benefit. Like many other coinage programs before it, this offering would be a three-coin program consisting of a clad half-dollar, a silver dollar, and a $5 gold coin.

There was a great and novel twist in this legislation. Congress requested that the reverse design of all three coins be a baseball. Additionally, they requested that the coin be produced, "in a fashion similar to the 2009 International Year of Astronomy coins issued by Monnaie de Paris, the French Mint, so that the reverse of the coin is convex to more closely resemble a baseball." In other words, they wanted the coin to look like a ball and replicate its curved geometry.

The nature of the request reflects an interesting sentiment. During the last few years, commemorative coinage issues hadn't sold particularly well. Perhaps the United States Mint's offerings needed to be more innovative and keep pace with international coinage issues. The referenced French International Year of Astronomy coin showed the cosmos on its concave side, brightly colored in blue and gold enamel; a footprint on the surface of the moon was on its convex side. The United States had never issued a coin like that!

An open design competition was held to find the obverse design. The winning selection by graphic artist Cassie McFarland was a wonderful and fitting composition: an open glove. The concave shape of the coin would thereby mimic the shape of an actual glove. The purity of concept of the design and the simple

nostalgic appeals of a ball and a glove were very well received and served to quell objection from traditionalists about the dish-shaped coin.

High mintage limits appear in all commemorative coinage legislation, and this program was no exception: 50,000 of the gold $5 coin, 400,000 of the silver dollar, and 750,000 of the clad half dollar in Proof and Uncirculated formats combined. Seldom are the limits reached, but when these coins went on sale on Thursday, March 27, 2014, at noon eastern time, orders poured in. By late afternoon, the gold $5 coin was sold out! On April 9 the silver dollar had also sold out. In the end, over 433,000 half dollars were sold, well short of the mintage limit, but still the best-selling half dollar in 20 years. Surcharges collected during the successful program netted nearly $8 million for the Baseball Hall of Fame.

Coin certification services offered interesting pairings with these coins—including labels signed by Hall of Famers, or authorized facsimiles of baseball greats like Babe Ruth and Ty Cobb—which gave the coins a sustained life in the marketplace. The success of the issue suggests that other commemorative programs proposed by Congress will continue to push boundaries and include requests for more innovation.

Mintage: Unc. Half Dollar, 142,405; Proof Half Dollar, 249,049; Unc. Dollar, 131,910; Proof Dollar, 267,847; Unc. $5 Gold Coin, 17,674; Proof $5 Gold Coin, 32,428

	MS-68	MS-69	MS-70	OGP
Half dollar	$26	$27	$43	$27
Silver dollar	51	54	74	54
Gold $5	—	745	780	750

	PF-68DC	PF-69DC	PF-70DC	OGP
Half dollar	$21.50	$24.50	$62.00	$24.50
Silver dollar	49.00	51.00	120.00	51.00
Gold $5	—	780.00	810.00	780.00

63 2008-W $50 AMERICAN GOLD BUFFALO, PROOF

Designed by James Earle Fraser. The obverse and reverse designs are based on the original 1913 Buffalo nickel, with modified inscriptions on the reverse. The obverse features a portrait of a Native American facing right with the inscription LIBERTY and the date 2008. The reverse features the figure of a bison standing and facing left. The inscription reads UNITED STATES OF AMERICA, E PLURIBUS UNUM, IN GOD WE TRUST, $50, and 1 OZ. .9999 FINE GOLD.

Weight: 31.1035 grams. *Composition:* .9999 gold (one ounce pure gold). *Diameter:* 32.7 mm. *Edge:* Reeded. *GSID:* 68998.

In 2006, the U.S. Mint released the American Buffalo gold coins—the first 24-karat, or .9999 fine, U.S. gold bullion coin. This coin was greatly anticipated after the less-fine American Gold Eagle was first released in 1986. Several other countries had since entered the gold bullion marketplace; most notably, the Royal Canadian Mint began its gold Maple Leaf program in 1988 and the Austrian Mint released its Philharmonic gold bullion coin in 1989. Both of these issues were .9999 fine, while the American Gold Eagle was only .9167 fine, or 22-karat.

Investors throughout the world preferred purer bullion products, which put the original American Gold Eagle at a disadvantage as an investment product. This was partially offset by the desirability of a U.S.-guaranteed coin and U.S. Mint product. In 1990, 1992, 1995, and 1996, the Austrian one-ounce gold coin outsold the American Gold Eagle. In response to the success of purer gold coins in other countries, the first American effort to introduce a pure gold coin was made in 1996, when a bill to authorize this coin passed in the House of Representatives but was not made into law. This was rectified by the Presidential Coin Act of 2005, which included authorization for a coin of 99.99 percent pure gold. The designs were to be those created by James Earle Fraser for the 1913 Type 1 Buffalo nickel. This original design shows a bison on a hill on the reverse and an Indian chief on the obverse.

The coin was issued in one-ounce format as a $50 denomination and was an instant success. The 2006 Buffalo issue outsold the one-ounce 2006 American Gold Eagle by more than 100,000 units. Legislation also allowed for Proof versions to be struck for collectors; the mintage limit was to be prescribed by the secretary of the Treasury in the amount deemed necessary. An astonishing 246,267 were sold, compared with only 37,096 one-ounce American Gold

Eagles. In fact, the only Proof American Gold Eagle with a higher mintage was the first year of issue, the 1986 version, when it was the only Proof gold coin sold by the Mint (along with a single gold commemorative issued that year). Sales for the Proof American Buffalo were strong in 2007, with about 60,000 units sold, but dropped off to only 18,863 units in 2008.

This mintage was surprisingly small and was, by far, the lowest for any Proof one-ounce U.S. gold bullion coin. Since then, its low mintage has been surpassed by only the 2013 American Buffalo. Among Proof bullion coins, the 2008 American Buffalo's low mintage makes this coin an obvious standout.

The low mintage figure is related to U.S. Mint supply channels for the raw materials. With world financial markets experiencing unprecedented volatility, demand for gold spiked in 2008. The Mint had difficulty securing sufficient pure-gold blanks to strike the coins, and had less time to produce them. Consider that in 2007, the Mint produced 140,016 one-ounce American Gold Eagles. In 2008, they would sell 710,000, a five-fold increase. With so few planchets available and little time to produce the coins, the Mint waited until late in the year and released far fewer pieces than normal before declaring a sellout.

Mintage: 18,863

PF-68DC	PF-69DC	PF-70DC	OGP
$3,120	$3,340	$4,120	$3,380

64 1994-P $1 AMERICAN SILVER EAGLE, PROOF

Designed by Adolph A. Weinman (obverse) and John Mercanti (reverse). The obverse features Weinman's Liberty Walking design used on half dollars from 1916 through 1947. Weinman's initials are on the hem of the gown. The reverse design is a rendition of a heraldic eagle.

Weight: 31.101 grams. *Composition:* .999 silver (net weight 1 ounce pure silver). *Diameter:* 40.6 mm. *Edge:* Reeded. *GSID:* 10682.

Along with the introduction of bullion coinage in the United States in 1986, Proof versions sold directly by the Mint to collectors were also introduced. The designs of the American Silver Eagle and American Gold Eagle Proof coins were the same as for the bullion versions intended for investors, although they did include the mintmark, which was omitted from the bullion issues. Proofs were also specially manufactured: they were struck twice on polished blanks from dies that were prepared to impart a mirrored field as well as the frosted devices that lend the American Silver Eagle Proof a rich, cameo-like appearance.

It's clear that collectors were hungry for a one-ounce U.S. silver coin. Before the American Silver Eagle, collectors of modern issues had to buy foreign coins if they wanted silver. This gap in U.S. minted coinage was a contributing factor to the issuance of the American Silver Eagle. The design of the American Silver Eagle was also a strong draw to collectors, as it reused the Liberty Walking design created by A.A. Weinman for the half dollar that was minted from 1916 to 1947. The Liberty Walking half dollar has often been called the most beautiful U.S. silver coin ever produced. For all these reasons, in addition to the fact that this was the first silver dollar to be produced in nearly a decade, sales of the 1994-P Proof American Silver Eagle were strong right out of the gate.

In 1986, an as-yet-unsurpassed 1.4 million Proof American Silver Eagles were sold. In 1987, another 900,000 were sold. Thereafter, sales began to cool. After peaking at more than $10 an ounce in 1987, silver prices declined. Silver traded between $6 and $7 an ounce throughout much of the late 1980s, but would fall below $4 an ounce in the early 1990s, souring collectors on buying coins from the Mint that were trading in the secondary market for less than the $23 issue price.

Sales of the Proof American Silver Eagle hit a new low in 1994, reaching only 372,168 coins—the lowest figure in the series up to that point. In response to

stunted sales, the Mint made several changes in 1995. First, they lengthened the sales period for the Proof American Silver Eagle from just two months to extend throughout much of the year. Second, they issued a special 10th-anniversary coin, the Proof 1995-W American Silver Eagle (no. 5 on the list of 100 Greatest U.S. Modern Coins!). Increased marketing efforts boosted American Silver Eagle sales 10 to 20 percent in subsequent years.

Silver prices flat-lined until the early 2000s, when they began a steadily aggressive upward move. Sales of the Proof American Silver Eagle began to increase, and by 2001 it was doubling its 1994 low each year. The series became increasingly popular with collectors, who seek to assemble complete sets by date. The result is that the 1994 issue has emerged as a key date, often more difficult to locate than the 2006-W Reverse Proof issue, and therefore it can also be more expensive.

Mintage: 372,168

PF-68DC	PF-69DC	PF-70DC	OGP
$110	$150	$780	$130

65 1977-D EISENHOWER DOLLAR, STRUCK IN SILVER-CLAD COMPOSITION

Designed by Frank Gasparro. The head of Dwight Eisenhower faces left on the obverse. LIBERTY arcs around the top of the obverse, and the date appears below the head. IN GOD WE TRUST appears at the lower left. On the reverse, an eagle with an olive branch in its talons alights upon the surface of the moon. A tiny earth can be seen in the background, and 13 small stars surround the eagle. UNITED STATES OF AMERICA and E PLURIBUS UNUM appear above the eagle; ONE DOLLAR appears below.

Weight: 24.59 grams. *Composition:* Outer layers of .800 silver and .200 copper over a core of .209 silver, .791 copper. *Diameter:* 38.1 mm. *Edge:* Reeded. *GSID:* 375898.

On the roster of the 100 Greatest U.S. Modern Coins are a number of die varieties and a couple of errors. It's important to know the difference between these two types of coins. A *die variety* is created when something unusual or distinctive happens to a die that is used to strike coins. The coins it makes can be differentiated from other coins by this distinctive feature they all share, and they are thus collectible. For example, if the die contained two misaligned impressions of the coin's image, all the coins that it struck would be a doubled-die variety.

An *error coin*, by contrast, is produced when something unusual occurs during the process of striking an individual coin, whether mechanical or otherwise. If a coin is struck twice by a die, it is a double-struck error, and only that single coin is affected. It is a coin that was somehow produced improperly, the result of a mistake in its manufacture. This type of error—affecting individual coins rather than an entire group produced from the same die—is what happened to this coin, the 1977-D Eisenhower dollar struck in silver-clad composition. In this case, the wrong type of planchet (or coin blank) was fed into a coin press, and thus a silver coin was produced when the Mint intended to make coins of copper-nickel.

The bill that authorized the Eisenhower dollar specified that for circulation purposes the dollar was to be struck in copper-nickel-clad, the same composition as the circulating dime, quarter, and half dollar. It also allowed for silver-clad versions (40 percent silver in composition) to be produced for sale to collectors. Uncirculated versions of the silver coin were struck at San Francisco and sold for $3 each.

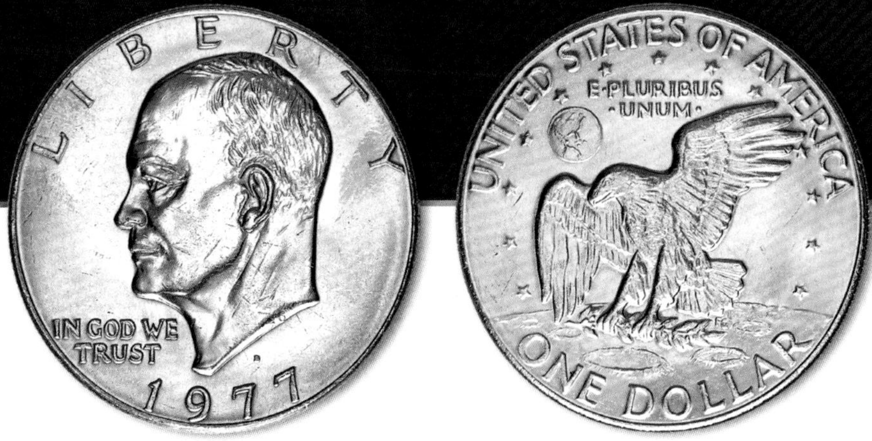

The Denver Mint was given the dual responsibilities of preparing planchets for San Francisco's production of silver coins as well as making copper-nickel-clad planchets for its own coins. Although Denver itself was meant to strike only the copper-nickel coins, silver blanks became inadvertently mixed with the copper-nickel blanks and were accidentally used to strike coins in Denver. Silver Denver Mint Eisenhower dollars are coins that were never meant to be.

Interestingly, this error has occurred on a number of occasions. Silver Denver Mint Eisenhower dollars are known for the 1974-D, 1976-D, and 1977-D issues, with the 1977-D being the rarest of these error coins: only an estimated few dozen are known. The reason for its scarcity is obvious. Production of silver Eisenhower dollars began in 1971 and ceased in 1976 with the Bicentennial issue. No silver dollars were intended to be produced in 1977 at all (and certainly not in Denver). These coin blanks must have been left over from the previous year's production, and only a handful remained to find their way to the coinage press.

Mintage: unknown

Value cannot be speculated, due to the extreme rarity of this variety.

66

1990-S, DOUBLED DIE OBVERSE, WASHINGTON QUARTER, PROOF

Designed by John Flanagan. The obverse features the head of George Washington facing left, the word LIBERTY above his head and the date below. The motto IN GOD WE TRUST appears in small letters in the left field. On the reverse, an eagle with wings outspread perches on a tight bundle of arrows. Two olive sprigs are joined beneath the eagle. The outer legends include UNITED STATES OF AMERICA above and QUARTER DOLLAR below. The motto E PLURIBUS UNUM appears in smaller letters above the eagle's head.

Weight: 5.67 grams. *Composition:* Outer layers of .750 copper and .250 nickel over a core of pure copper. *Diameter:* 24.3 mm. *Edge:* Reeded. *GSID:* 375896.

This coin is almost too rare to be included among the 100 Greatest U.S. Modern Coins. Because fewer than 20 examples have been identified since it was first discovered nearly two decades ago, this coin has failed to create the publicity that has been generated by a number of its counterparts on this list. It is unquestionably one of the best doubled dies in the Washington quarter series.

One thing that makes this coin so interesting for specialists is its attribution diagnostics. *Diagnostics* are the specific details of a coin that distinguish it. Doubled dies are created when a working die receives two impressions of the coin's design as the die is created. Usually, this occurs when the hub or die has rotated. Close to the pivot point of the rotation, doubling will be minor. It will widen farther away from the pivot. The exact features of the doubling will be identical on all the coins struck by the doubled die.

The doubling is most visible in two areas of this particular coin. First, it can be seen on the date, where a second impression sits northeast of the first date. Second, doubling can be seen most prominently on the mintmark, which shows two S's, one slightly above and to the right of the other one that sits underneath it. It is just the lucky way in which this doubled die was created that imparted this trait, the diagnostic feature that makes this coin so exciting.

Doubling on the mintmark wasn't seen on a doubled-die before this coin. Until 1985, mintmarks were added to Proof dies after they were hubbed in a separate process. Starting in 1968, a small mintmark punch would add the S mintmark for San Francisco, where all Proof versions of circulating coinage were made. If the mintmark was doubled, that doubling was confined to the

mintmark—a variety called a *repunched mintmark*. By 1990, however, since the mintmark was now imparted in the same process as the rest of the coin's design, a doubled mintmark meant something else—a true doubled die. Not only is the diagnostic exciting, but the amount of separation is significant. The doubling is readily visible with the naked eye, but, like with most die varieties, the coin is best observed under magnification to really appreciate its drama.

The other shocking aspect of the coin is that so few have been found. It was first discovered by New Hampshire coin dealer Jim Carr not long after the Proof set's release. The 1990 Proof set and 1990 Prestige Proof set are home to three great varieties, including the 1990, No S, Lincoln cent (no. 10 on this list), this doubled-die, and a doubled-die Jefferson nickel (see no. 71). Because of all the wonderful coins that can be found in this set, 1990 Proof sets are probably examined more closely than any other date of modern Proof set. It's estimated that there are 2,000 to 2,500 of these coins spread among the 3.2 million Proof and Prestige Proof sets issued in 1990. Even though these quarters are widely distributed, it's still hard to explain why so few have been found. Some have begun to speculate that the mistake was discovered at the Mint prior to release and many of the coins were destroyed. If this is true, the estimated mintage number will need to be revised downward.

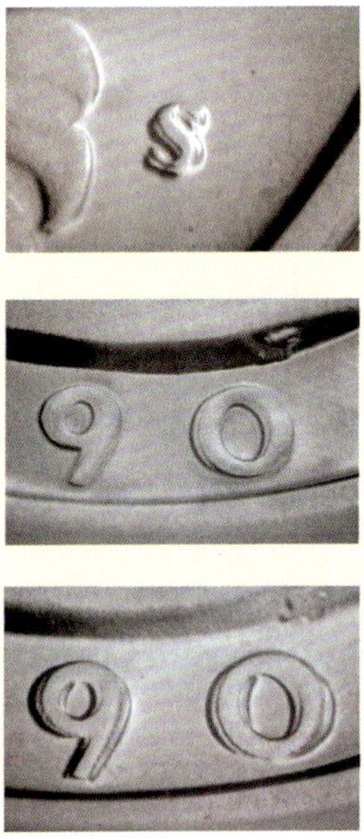

Pick-up points: Date, mintmark.

Mintage: fraction of 3,299,559

PF-68DC	PF-69DC	PF-70DC
$310	$570	$4,380

67 1984, DOUBLED DIE OBVERSE, LINCOLN CENT

Designed by Victor David Brenner (obverse) and Frank Gasparro (reverse). The obverse continues the design of 1909. The reverse shows a frontal view of the Lincoln Memorial with UNITED STATES OF AMERICA and E PLURIBUS UNUM appearing above and ONE CENT below.

Weight: 2.5 grams. *Composition:* Outer layers of pure copper over a core of .992 zinc, .008 copper. *Diameter:* 19 mm. *Edge:* Plain. *GSID:* Brown, 2272; Red-Brown, 2273; Red, 2274.

The 1984, Doubled Die Obverse, Lincoln cent has a nickname that is also the key to its attribution—sometimes it's called the "Doubled Ear Lincoln cent." Rather unusually, the doubling of this coin appears almost exclusively on the bust of Lincoln, instead of on the lettering that surrounds him. It is so dramatic that the doubling creates a fully duplicated and well-spaced earlobe beneath Lincoln's full ear. Doubling can also be seen on Lincoln's beard, giving him a full double chin and a rather portly appearance. Variety expert Ken Potter notes that the widest doubling is seen on Lincoln's bowtie, although this feature usually gets less mention.

The discovery of this coin mirrored that of the 1983, Doubled Die Reverse, cent (see no. 35), with both being found in large caches. Because these two coins appeared in consecutive years, it seems natural to compare them. Since the variety's discovery in 1984, experts have speculated that the 1984, Doubled Die Obverse, is more common than the previous year's Doubled Die Reverse. A large find by a single coin dealer, believed to number 2,000 pieces, contributed to this thinking. Over time, certification reports have yielded additional insights, and it now appears that the two coins are of comparable rarity, with about 4,000 examples of each known to collectors.

Compared to its 1983 counterpart, the 1984, Doubled Die Obverse, does not exhibit severe planchet flaws nearly as frequently. Many of the problems

Pick-up point: Ear.

that the Mint experienced beginning in 1982 in creating Lincoln cents from a copper-layered zinc-core planchet were resolved by 1984, and therefore spotting and corrosion are less severe on this issue. As a result, higher-condition examples are much more plentiful, and the average grade of this cent is a full grade point higher than for the 1983 variety. Hence, at any given grade level, the 1984 issue trades for much less than the 1983, although overall interest level and availability are again similar. Both coins are considered requirements of a complete set of Lincoln Memorial cents.

It is also very important to note that there are other collectible doubled-die obverses for this date, although the doubled-ear variety described here is by far the most valuable of them. One of the major pitfalls of variety collecting is that less-frequently collected varieties have significantly lower values, and, at one point or another, most variety collectors mistakenly purchase a coin that he or she believes is more desirable (and therefore more valuable) than it actually is. When purchasing this coin, especially when the example has not been attributed by a major grading service, make sure that the coin is indeed the doubled-ear example described here.

Mintage: fraction of 8,151,079,000

	MS-60	MS-63	MS-64	MS-65	MS-66	MS-67	MS-68
Brown	$130	$145	$155	$170	$180	$260	—
Red-Brown	155	190	195	210	235	310	—
Red	155	200	215	230	290	490	$1,750

68 2006-W $1 AMERICAN SILVER EAGLE

Designed by Adolph A. Weinman (obverse) and John Mercanti (reverse). The obverse features Weinman's Liberty Walking design used on half dollars from 1916 through 1947. Weinman's initials are on the hem of the gown. The reverse design is a rendition of a heraldic eagle.

Weight: 31.101 grams. *Composition:* .999 silver (net weight 1 ounce pure silver). *Diameter:* 40.6 mm. *Edge:* Reeded. *GSID:* 70901.

Since the start of the American Eagle Bullion program, coins were issued in two formats: for the most part, they were sold by the Mint to officially authorized distributors as bullion coins and priced at only a small premium to their intrinsic metal value. Also, American Eagle Bullion coins were available as Proof coins, sold by the Mint directly to collectors. The Proof versions, with special finish and packaging, sold at a premium to their metal value. In 2006, the U.S. Mint took the unprecedented step of additionally producing Uncirculated American Eagle Bullion coins, a new version of the coins for sale directly to collectors and priced in between the bullion and the Proof coins.

Although the finish of the Uncirculated coin is essentially indistinguishable from the bullion issue's, there are two notable differences. First, and most importantly, the Uncirculated coins featured a W mintmark, indicating their origin at the West Point Mint. The second difference was identified in a curious statement from the U.S. Mint: the coins were said to be struck on specially burnished blanks. With little additional information, collectors speculated wildly about what this could mean, and the 2006-W Uncirculated American Eagle Bullion coins became popularly known as "burnished coins."

All coin blanks are burnished prior to striking. The process of burnishing blanks normally involves tumbling or spinning a number of blanks with stainless steel balls or other media. It's a rough treatment that brightens the coin blanks while removing scaling and other surface irregularities. Chemicals, lubricants, and anti-tarnishing agents are often added during this step. The exact process for burnishing coin blanks has not been revealed by the Mint, so it is unknown what exactly makes the burnishing process for the 2006-W Uncirculated American Eagle Bullion coins special. The planchets (or coin blanks) for the bullion-issue American Silver Eagles are thought to be purchased fully ready for coining, and thus no burnishing is performed at the West Point Mint prior to striking these coins.

When the Uncirculated American Eagle Bullion coins came out in 2006, there was a plethora of new American Eagle products in celebration of the 20th anniversary of the American Silver Eagle. Accordingly, the 2006-W Uncirculated American Silver Eagle was available for purchase from the Mint in one of three different ways. It was included in the Three-Piece American Silver Eagle 20th-Anniversary Set and the Two-Piece American Gold Eagle and American Silver Eagle 20th-Anniversary Set. These two product options went on sale on August 30, 2006. Later in the year, on September 28, the coin was sold by itself for $19.95, priced in between the Proof and bullion coins.

The coin market was hungry for the new Uncirculated American Silver Eagle with the W mintmark, and it felt like there were never enough. Individual pieces traded for more than $50 even as they were still being sold by the Mint for $20. Order fulfillment on these coins became so backed up that they continued to ship into 2007. The prices kept on increasing after all of the coins were shipped, and the coins have since sustained their value.

Although this coin is sought after as the first mintmarked Uncirculated-finish American Silver Eagle, part of the justification for the price premium comes from the variety's low mintage: a total of only 466,573. Only 198,553 were sold as single coins and the balance were sold as part of the anniversary sets. Assuming that a great number of these sets remain intact, it is suspected that few individual coins are still available.

Mintage: 468,020

MS-68	MS-69	MS-70	OGP
$48	$68	$130	$62

69 2007-W, 2008-W, AND 2010-W $10 FIRST SPOUSE GOLD, "LIBERTY" DESIGNS

Jefferson: **The obverse features a reproduction of Liberty as originally used on the Draped Bust cent minted from 1796 to 1807, originally designed by Robert Scot.** ***Jackson:*** **The obverse features a reproduction of Liberty as used on the Capped Bust, Lettered Edge half dollar minted from 1807 to 1836, designed by John Reich.** ***Van Buren:*** **The obverse features a reproduction of Liberty as originally used on the Liberty Seated dime minted from 1837 to 1891, designed by Christian Gobrecht.** ***Buchanan:*** **The obverse features a reproduction of Liberty as originally used on the Liberty Head quarter eagle ($2.50) minted from 1840 to 1907, designed by Christian Gobrecht.**

Weight: 15.55 grams. *Composition:* .9999 gold (net weight 1/2 ounce pure gold). *Diameter:* 26.49 mm. *Edge:* Reeded. *GSID:* Uncirculated—Jefferson's Liberty, 68816; Jackson's Liberty, 70429; Van Buren's Liberty, 70430; Buchanan's Liberty, 71031. Proof—Jefferson's Liberty, 68815; Jackson's Liberty, 70890; Van Buren's Liberty, 70894; Buchanan's Liberty, 71039.

It is fitting that when honoring the presidents, the first spouses should be similarly honored. The Presidential $1 Coin Act of 2005 also brought into being the First Spouse Gold Coin Program. Concurrent with the issuance of each Presidential dollar, a $10 coin made of one half-ounce of .9999 fine gold was to be sold by the Mint honoring each president's respective spouse.

Many questioned the need for this program. It had its advantages, however; Congress was actively seeking to introduce .9999 fine gold (or 24 karat) bullion, as American Eagles are only .9167 fine, and most nations were already producing bullion gold coins of much higher fineness.

Of course, not all presidents were married while in office. For program continuity, the authorizing legislation stipulated that a design emblematic of Liberty be shown on the obverse of the coin in the first four instances when there was no first spouse. Depictions of Liberty were taken from coinage that circulated during their time in office. For Thomas Jefferson, whose wife died before he became president, the Draped Bust Liberty design chosen was that used on the cent coins that circulated from 1800 to 1808. Jefferson's Liberty proved to be the most popular coin in the series at its time of issue, selling out in Proof and Uncirculated formats, with a net mintage of 19,815 and 19,823, respectively.

The popularity of the First Spouse program rapidly waned after this issue. The seventh coin in the series was Andrew Jackson's Liberty. (Jackson's wife died a few months before he was inaugurated as president.) The obverse of the

coin shows Liberty as borrowed from the Capped Bust half dollar that circulated from 1808 to 1836. Only 4,754 Uncirculated examples were sold and 7,806 Proofs.

The next Liberty coin in the series was Martin Van Buren's Liberty. Van Buren had been a widow for 18 years when he became president in 1837, and his coin features Christian Gobrecht's Seated Liberty design, as used on the dime from 1837 to 1891. The coin was a dud at time of sale: just 3,826 Uncirculated and 6,807 Proof coins sold.

The last Liberty coin in the series is James Buchanan's Liberty, issued in 2010. For the "Bachelor President," another Gobrecht design was chosen—this one the Liberty head from the quarter eagle. By this time, collectors were already pursuing the "Liberty Gold" independently from the main set. To make them yet more attractive to collectors, in 2010, mintage limits were cut from 40,000 to 15,000 coins. Sales rose slightly for this coin: 5,162 Uncirculated coins and 7,110 Proofs were sold.

It may seem a bit sexist that the most coveted coins in the First Spouse series don't honor first spouses at all. But really, collectors like them because of the way they honor numismatic history, recasting old designs in a new way. Mintage levels for First Spouse coins continued to dwindle as the series came to a close, with the notable exception of the Jacqueline Kennedy coin, which sold more Uncirculated and more Proof examples than any other First Spouse coin issued after the first year of the program. The final coin in the series, picturing Nancy Reagan, showed a slight, though significantly smaller, bump in sales as well. Nonetheless, for most collectors and dealers, the Liberty coins are truly the greatest First Spouse gold coins.

Mintage: Jefferson Uncirculated, 19,823; Proof, 19,815. Jackson Uncirculated, 4,281; Proof, 7,454. Van Buren Uncirculated, 3,443; Proof, 6,187. Buchanan Uncirculated, 5,162; Proof, 7,110.

	MS-69	MS-70	OGP
2007-W, Jefferson's Liberty	$1,530	$1,550	$1,530
2008-W, Jackson's Liberty	1,530	1,610	1,530
2008-W, Van Buren's Liberty	1,530	1,550	1,530
2010-W, Buchanan's Liberty	1,530	1,550	1,530

	PF-69DC	PF-70DC	OGP
2007-W, Jefferson's Liberty	$1,530	$1,610	$1,530
2008-W, Jackson's Liberty	1,530	1,610	1,530
2008-W, Van Buren's Liberty	1,530	1,610	1,530
2010-W, Buchanan's Liberty	1,530	1,610	1,530

70 2000-P SACAGAWEA DOLLAR, "GOODACRE PRESENTATION" VARIETY

Designed by Glenna Goodacre (obverse) and Thomas D. Rogers (reverse). The front of the coin features the Indian guide Sacagawea and her infant son. LIBERTY appears above her head; IN GOD WE TRUST appears on the left, and the date appears on the right side. The reverse features an eagle in flight surrounded by 17 stars. UNITED STATES OF AMERICA arcs around the upper reverse, while ONE DOLLAR arcs around the bottom. E PLURIBUS UNUM appears in small letters in the left field.

Weight: 8.1 grams. *Composition:* Outer layers of .770 copper, .120 zinc, .070 manganese, and .040 nickel over a core of pure copper. *Diameter:* 26.5 mm. *Edge:* Plain. *GSID:* 7991.

Artist Glenna Goodacre designed the obverse of the Sacagawea dollar. She accepted her $5,000 commission for her work for the Mint in the form of "sacks of golden dollars," according to a press release for the April 5, 2000, event held at her New Mexico studio. Rather than giving her standard circulation-issue coins, however, she was given specially prepared presentation coins.

Not long after the presentation, Goodacre submitted a large group of her coins to a certification service for grading and encapsulation. At that time, the full details of the coin's special attributes were revealed to the numismatic community. First, these coins had been burnished by the Mint after they were struck, evident from their high-gloss sheen, and they were treated with an anti-tarnishing agent. The coins were largely high grade and had few contact marks, suggesting that they had received extra-attentive handling after striking. The Goodacre Presentation coins were well-struck, which led to some speculation that higher striking pressure was used. Of the 5,000 coins, slightly more than a hundred appeared to have not been burnished. Examination of these unburnished coins revealed that the Goodacre Presentation coins had been struck on polished or Proof blanks from specially finished dies, information that could not have been readily discerned from the burnished coins themselves.

Of the 5,000 coins that she was presented, Goodacre retained 2,000. The other 3,000 she sold for $200 each. In the secondary market since then, their value has continued to grow. These coins are visually distinctive. Unlike so many other modern rarities, their full story and origin is also very well known. The direct association with the coin's designer also contributes to collector demand.

Goodacre's design shows Sacagawea, the Shoshone woman who served as guide and interpreter on the Lewis and Clark Expedition, carrying her baby, Jean Baptiste, who was born during the journey. Since no contemporary image of Sacagawea exists, the portrait is really the likeness of a Shoshone woman named Randy'L He-dow Teton, who sat for Goodacre. The coin is distinctly American, and the design was well received.

Goodacre was also fortunate to receive payment in coin form the way that she did. With less forethought, a designer might have simply requested payment by check! The designer of the reverse, Thomas Rogers, was not eligible to receive a similar commission because he was a U.S. Mint employee. The total value of the $5,000 in coins paid to Goodacre in 2000 exceeds $2 million in today's market, a handsome commission by any measure.

It is best to buy examples that have been certified. Since all of the Goodacre Presentation dollars were originally sold in third-party certification holders, it's logical to question the provenance of any example that was removed from its holder. Also, deceptively altered coins can appear to be burnished in a similar way, and thus it's important to have a properly authenticated coin.

Mintage: 5,000

MS-65	MS-66	MS-67	MS-68	MS-69
$340	$415	$585	$715	$4,380

71 1990-S, DOUBLED DIE OBVERSE, JEFFERSON NICKEL, PROOF

Designed by Felix Schlag. The obverse features a bust of Thomas Jefferson facing left. IN GOD WE TRUST appears inside the left edge, and LIBERTY and the date appear inside the right edge. On the reverse, Jefferson's home, Monticello, appears as the central device, while E PLURIBUS UNUM arcs above. The word MONTICELLO captions the building, and the words FIVE CENTS and the legend UNITED STATES OF AMERICA appear below.

Weight: 5.00 grams. *Composition:* .750 copper, .250 nickel.
Diameter: 21.2 mm. *Edge:* Plain. *GSID:* 375895.

If ever there were a Proof set that has been a boon to collectors of modern U.S. coins, it is the 1990 Proof set. Three very significant varieties can be found in it, including the 1990, No S, Lincoln cent (see no. 10), the 1990-S, Doubled Die Obverse, quarter (see no. 66), and this coin.

Like other doubled-die coins, its genesis can be traced to a blunder that occurred when the die was made. It received a duplicate, and misplaced, impression from the hub that imparted the design. All the coins struck from this doubled die show doubling in the same exact way, and these distinct diagnostic features are used to identify the variety. This example exhibits moderate doubling on the motto, IN GOD WE TRUST. Stronger doubling is evident on the designer's initials, showing nearly complete separation between the two sets. Light doubling is also visible on the profile of Jefferson, most readily of his top eyelid. Examination with a loupe is recommended to see these pick-up points properly so as to confirm attribution.

Of course, Proof coins are made with great care and attention and receive a number of inspections at the Mint. As a result, moderate doubled dies of this type are uncommon, and this is unquestionably the best Proof doubled-die Jefferson nickel of the modern coinage time period, if not the entire series. Each obverse die is used to strike only 2,500 nickels, and sometimes far fewer than that to keep the quality high. That figure is the maximum estimated mintage of this coin, but fewer than 50 are known in total. Considering that 1990 Proof sets are carefully examined for varieties by specialists, it's very surprising that so few are known.

This coin was reported to the numismatic community in 1999, a late date for such a grand discovery. It was first identified in 1997 by collector Charles Clark III. He shared the discovery with just a small network of friends in hopes that

more coins could be found to confirm and validate the discovery. It's not unusual for new varieties to be initially kept quiet by their discoverer in the hope that more examples will be found that can be sold in the wake of the first reporting. After two years of searching for, but failing to find, a second example, Clark had the coin authenticated at a Texas Numismatic Association convention in 1999. He then reported the confirmed discovery to CONECA, an organization that records varieties and promotes them within the hobby.

Even after more than a decade since first being reported, 1990-S, Doubled Die Obverse, Jefferson nickels are very scarce. When they are found, as with virtually all 1990 Proof coinage, they exhibit very strong cameo contrast and are in the highest states of preservation. Certainly, more examples are out there to be found in Proof sets and Prestige sets. The hunt for this variety remains well underway.

Mintage: fraction of 3,299,559

PF-68DC	PF-69DC	PF-70DC
$245	$365	—

72 2014 KENNEDY HALF DOLLAR, 50TH ANNIVERSARY ISSUES

GSID: 2014-P—Clad, 82061; 2014-D—Clad, 82062, Silver, 198230; 2014-S, Silver, Enhanced Uncirculated—84799, Prooflike, 84800, Deep Mirror Prooflike, 84801.

To celebrate the 50th anniversary of the Kennedy half dollar, the Mint pulled out all the stops. For the 50th anniversary of the Roosevelt dime they produced a single coin, the 1996-W Roosevelt dime that was included in Mint Sets of that year. By contrast, for the Kennedy's anniversary, the Mint issued seven different coins in three different sets. They were struck at all four Mints. Never had the Mint celebrated a coin with so much fanfare.

The first anniversary set to be released was the called the 50th Anniversary Kennedy Half-Dollar Uncirculated Coin Set. It featured two clad half dollars in standard copper-nickel clad composition, one struck in Philadelphia and the other in Denver. The design was modified from standard issue 2014 Kennedy half dollars by recreating the original relief and detail of Gilroy Roberts's 1964 design for the coin. The production limit for this offering was capped at 200,000 sets.

Being the golden anniversary, a gold coin was also offered. It is seen by many as the centerpiece of the anniversary offerings. It was struck at West Point in proof finish. A dual date, 1964–2014, was used, and an inscription describing the coin's composition was added to the reverse, "3/4 OZ. .9999 FINE GOLD." Sold singly, no mintage limit was revealed at time of its initial release; it was ultimately capped at 75,000 pieces.

On its first day of issue, in addition to being sold online, the gold coin was available for sale at the American Numismatic Association's World's Fair of Money, held in Chicago that year. It was also sold onsite at the Philadelphia and Denver Mints and at the Mint's executive office in Washington, D.C. It was also pre-announced that coins purchased at the locales would be designated as "First Day of Issue" by the coin grading services.

Since these physical location purchases were limited to one-per-customer, some enterprising coin dealers thought to hire people to wait in line and purchase coins using pre-paid debit cards. One clever dealer even contracted with a casting company in Denver to find actors to purchase coins while also acting "excited" about the product release. From a marketing standpoint, it worked. The resulting frenzy surrounding the purchase and release of these coins made

national news headlines. Ultimately, however, safety concerns related to the crowds forced the Mint to suspend physical location sales.

Later in the year, following the clad and gold coins, the Mint released a silver set. The 50th Anniversary Kennedy Half Dollar Silver Coin Collection included 90 percent silver coins in four different finishes struck at four different Mints: a Reverse Proof struck at West Point, a Proof coin struck at Philadelphia, an Enhanced Uncirculated coin struck at San Francisco, and an Uncirculated coin struck at Denver. This design was also rendered with close adherence to Gilroy Roberts's original design. Production limit for the offering was 300,000 sets.

Although for many, many years the half dollar has not been widely used in commerce, it had a massive anniversary celebration. In retrospect, these offerings are less about the Kennedy half dollar and more a demonstration of the Mint's capabilities to coordinate multi-Mint product offerings and its proficiency with a variety of metals and coin finishes. These are vitally important considerations.

Mintage: 2014-P Clad Unc., 197,608; 2014-P Silver Proof, 221,134; 2014-D Clad Unc., 197,608; 2014-D Silver Unc., 221,134; 2014-S Silver Enhanced Unc., 221,134; 2014-W Silver Reverse Proof, 221,134; 2014-W Gold Proof, 73,772

	MS-65	MS-66	MS-67	MS-68	MS-69	MS-70	OGP
2014-P, Clad	$24.50	$30.00	$34.00	$54.00	$210.00	—	$32.00
2014-D, Clad	11.00	12.00	21.50	61.00	110.00	—	$10.50
2014-D, Silver	19.00	19.00	19.50	20.50	21.50	$30	—
2014-S, Silver, Enhanced Unc.	—	19.00	19.50	20.50	21.50	51	—
2014S, Silver, Enhanced Unc., Prooflike	—	22.00	23.00	24.50	34.00	100	—
2014-S, Silver, Enhanced Unc., Deep Mirror Prooflike	—	24.50	30.00	46.00	100.00	520	—

73 1971-S, DOUBLED DIE OBVERSE, LINCOLN CENT

Designed by Victor David Brenner (obverse) and Frank Gasparro (reverse). The obverse continues the design of 1909, featuring a bust of Lincoln facing right, the word LIBERTY to his left, and the date in the field in front of his coat. The legend IN GOD WE TRUST appears above his head. The reverse shows a frontal view of the Lincoln Memorial with UNITED STATES OF AMERICA and E PLURIBUS UNUM appearing above and ONE CENT below.

Standards: Weight: 2.5 grams. *Composition:* Outer layers of pure copper over a core of .992 zinc, .008 copper. *Diameter:* 19 mm. *Edge:* Plain. *GSID:* Brown, 2227; Red-Brown, 2228; Red, 2229.

Rare and interesting coins that form a short, compact grouping are sometimes able to take on special significance. For instance, collectors of classic coinage refer to the four issues of Carson City Liberty Seated dollars minted from 1870 through 1873 with great affection. Similarly, during the four-year span from 1969 through 1972, collectors were gifted with the production of four exciting doubled-die Lincoln cents.

This four-coin run began with the 1969-S, Doubled Die Obverse, the "King of the Lincoln Cent Doubled Dies" and by far the most valuable (and no. 2 on this list). Next is the 1970-S, Large Date, Doubled Die Obverse, another dramatic coin that ranks no. 47 on this list. Next is the best doubled-die Proof in the series, the 1971-S, Doubled Die Obverse (more on this coin, the focus of this entry, to follow). Finally, capping off this unbeatable sequence is the 1972, Doubled Die Obverse, the most visually splendid doubled die of the entire Memorial cent series and no. 12 on this list.

Proof-coin doubled dies are made in the same way as circulation issues. The working die that is used to strike coins receives unintentional, misaligned blows from the working hub that imparts the coin's design. Because Proof dies receive so much special attention, as do the coins that they strike, dramatic varieties are relatively rare. There is, of course, a grand exception. In 1971, the San Francisco Mint released *three* different doubled-die obverse cents.

The first was discovered by Philadelphia coin dealer Harry Forman in 1975, and variety expert John Wexler discovered a second, but even more dramatic, variety in 1982. Both of these coins show strong doubling on the word LIBERTY. The first variety shows a small amount of doubling on the date, while the second shows no doubling on the date but good doubling on the motto,

IN GOD WE TRUST. A third, minor doubled die was later discovered and is worth much less than the two major varieties described.

As with all Proof-coin varieties, these coins are found only in Proof sets. Approximately 2,300 coins were struck from each Proof Lincoln cent obverse die at this time, making that the presumed mintage of each of these coins. The second variety has proven more elusive than the first and carries a greater value today. While most references try to list varieties from most important to least important, this progression can be violated to follow discovery order. It's vital to consult references to make sure varieties are properly attributed and that their value and rarity are being related accurately.

Mintage: fraction of 2,632,810

Pick-up point: LIBERTY.

	MS-60	MS-61	MS-62	MS-63	MS-64	MS-65	MS-66
Brown	$130	$150	$170	$195	$235	$390	$1,250
Red-Brown	145	160	180	210	275	585	1,750
Red	160	175	195	230	325	845	2,250

74 2013-W $50 AMERICAN GOLD BUFFALO, REVERSE PROOF

Designed by James Earle Fraser. The obverse and reverse designs are based on the original 1913 Buffalo nickel, with modified inscriptions on the reverse. The obverse features a portrait of a Native American facing right with the inscription LIBERTY and the date 2013. The reverse features the figure of a bison standing and facing left. The inscription reads UNITED STATES OF AMERICA, E PLURIBUS UNUM, IN GOD WE TRUST, $50, and 1 OZ. .9999 FINE GOLD.

Weight: 31.1035 grams. *Composition:* .9999 gold (one ounce pure gold). *Diameter:* 32.7 mm. *Edge:* Reeded. *GSID:* 71495.

There was never a time that collectors weren't asking for a Reverse Proof American Buffalo gold coin. The coin debuted in 2006, the same year as the 20th-anniversary Reverse Proof American Gold Eagles and American Silver Eagles. As new Reverse Proof American Silver Eagles came out in 2011 and 2012, collectors were asking, "Where is the Reverse Proof Buffalo?!"

Fortunately, the year 2013 provided the occasion. It marked the centennial anniversary of James Earle Fraser's Type 1 Buffalo nickel design. The Buffalo nickel circulated for 25 years, from 1913 to 1938, although the Type 1 design was used only in 1913.

The Type 1 design shows the buffalo standing on a raised mound. The words FIVE CENTS and the mintmark appear in relief on the mound. It was quickly realized that these inscriptions would be the first area to wear off the coin during circulation. The nickel design was accordingly modified to place the buffalo on flat ground with the denomination and mintmark within a recessed exergue.

The American Buffalo gold coin is modeled after this original design. The most significant modification is the addition of the motto, IN GOD WE TRUST, which did not appear on the original coin. The design of the Reverse Proof is the same as that of other Proof American Buffalo gold coins; only its surface finish is different. The fields are matte-like, while the design elements have a mirror-like reflectivity.

The coin was produced to meet demand. It was sold for $1,740 during an ordering period from August 8 to September 5, 2013, with the U.S. Mint posting sales figures each day. Opening day sales were 21,000 units, more than the entire total of Proof Gold Buffaloes sold in 2012! Sales remained steady at an average of nearly 1,000 coins a day for the entire order period, closing at 47,836

coins. That figure amounts to more than $83 million in total sales, nearly $3 million in Reverse Proof American Buffalo gold coins sold each day!

Things were different with the Reverse Proof American Buffalo gold coin. First, the Mint elected to sell coins at the American Numismatic Association's (ANA) World's Fair of Money held in Chicago from August 13 to 17, 2013. This gave the public their first glimpse of the coins in person and created a sensation at the show. When submitted for certification, grading services accommodated collectors' requests to have these coins labeled as "Chicago ANA Releases."

Also, in the past, the Mint didn't begin shipping until after an ordering period had closed. However, the Mint began shipping Reverse Proof American Buffalo gold coins purchased online on August 22, while the ordering period was open. The early availability of the coin at the ANA convention and in the marketplace cut down on the activity of speculators. The coin didn't experience an aggressive price spike or decline. Rather, it routinely trades at a modest increase to its original issue price, although examples labeled "Chicago ANA Releases," especially those graded PF-70, command hefty premiums.

The pent-up demand meant that sales were strong enough to satisfy near-term demand. As the only Reverse Proof in the series and without another on the horizon, the long-term outlook for this issue to remain one of the 100 Greatest U.S. Modern Coins is very good.

Mintage: 47,836

PF-68	PF-69	PF-70	OGP
$3,210	$3,310	$3,410	$3,320

75 2021-W $100 AMERICAN LIBERTY HIGH RELIEF GOLD

Designed by Beth Zaiken (obverse) and Richard Masters (reverse). The obverse features Liberty as a wild American Mustang horse, bucking off a western-style saddle. The reverse depicts a close-up view of an eagle with an open beak.

Standards: Weight: 31.108 grams. *Composition:* .9999 gold (one ounce pure gold). *Diameter:* 30.61 mm. *Edge:* Reeded. *GSID:* 193333.

Desiring to repeat or even build on the success of the 2009 Ultra High Relief gold coin, in 2015 the U.S. Mint introduced the American Liberty series of $100 coins struck in pure gold and high relief. (The lone exception has been the 2018 issue, which was a $10 tenth-ounce coin.) Each coin would feature a modern, allegorical depiction of Liberty on the obverse. Although novel designs were selected, the first four coins in the series, issued in 2015, 2017, 2018 and 2019, featured a depiction of the female goddess Liberty. In other words, the coins were thematically like most non-commemorative U.S. coins issued in the past.

The numismatic community was therefore aflutter when the designs for the fifth installment in the series were presented for review by the Citizens Coinage Advisory Committee in October 2019. They showed a wild departure from the previous issues, and they included designs of coins with butterflies, torch flames, and even a "shining city on a hill." Most exciting were a pair of designs that featured a horse, captioned with the design description, "A wild American Mustang horse, bucking off a western-style saddle, evoking the throwing off of the yoke of British rule during the American Revolution. The Mustang horse is presented both as native to this land, yet simultaneously an immigrant to the nation as we know it today. The ancestor to all true horses alive today evolved here in North America. Those horses inexplicably disappeared at the end of the last Ice Age, only to be accidentally re-introduced in their domesticated form by the Spanish in the 1500s."

The coin was given the moniker "Bucking Bronco" by eager collectors before it went on sale at noon on August 19, 2021. There was a mintage limit of 12,500 and an order limit of one per household. By late afternoon, they were unavailable. First-day sales totaled 11,992. After order review and reconciliation was completed, a second sales window opened briefly, closing when sales reached the mintage limit. The final net mintage figure for this coin is 12,471.

Although it sold quickly, it wasn't quite gone in a flash as were other hotly anticipated U.S. Mint issues. That's due in part to its high issue price of $2,715. On the same day, the spot price of gold was only $1,788, and some prospective buyers were skittish about the high price premium given the modest aftermarket performance of the previous American Liberty gold issues. Enthusiastic buyers were rewarded, however, because the price of the coin has never fallen below its issue price. Instead, today the coin routinely trades for more than three times its initial cost!

The success of this coin marked a sea change for the U.S. Mint and the Citizens Coinage Advisory Committee, emboldening them to step away from convention and tradition when a truly exciting design alternative is presented. The Mint's forward thinking was further validated in 2023, when the coin received Krause Publication's Coin of the Year Award for Best Gold Coin, and now it has also earned a coveted spot among Whitman's 100 Greatest U.S. Modern Coins.

Mintage: 12,471

PF-68DC	PF-69DC	PF-70DC	OGP
$5,800	$6,250	$8,750	$6,250

76 2021-W NATIONAL LAW ENFORCEMENT MEMORIAL $5 COMMEMORATIVE, UNC

Designed by Frank Morris (obverse) and Ronald D. Sanders (reverse). The obverse depicts male and female officers in profile saluting. The reverse depicts a folded flag with three roses beneath symbolizing remembrance.

Standards: Weight: 8.359 grams. *Composition:* .900 gold, .060 silver, .040 copper. *Diameter:* 21.6 mm. *Edge:* Reeded. *GSID:* 85122.

The framework of the 2021 National Law Enforcement commemorative coin program was identical to those of so many in the past. Three coins would be issued: a copper-nickel-clad half dollar, a silver dollar, and a gold $5 coin, each in both uncirculated and Proof formats, with maximum mintage limits of 750,000, 400,000 and 50,000 respectively. Broadly speaking, the 2021 commemoratives would have a law-enforcement theme. At the time of authorization, the United States had nearly 800,000 sworn law-enforcement officers supported by nearly half a million more civilian personnel. This program should have had broad appeal and the coins should have sold well.

Despite the potential for thematic resonance, the coinage program had a few flaws, and one was that it was not designed to support local law enforcement. Most law-enforcement officers in the United States are employed by municipalities, not federal agencies. This commemorative coinage program provided funding for exhibits and operations of the National Law Enforcement Museum in Washington, D.C., which had just opened in 2018. The likely target audience for this coin was police officers, but during the COVID-19 pandemic they were unmotivated to support a coin that did not offer local law-enforcement programs any direct benefit. Making matters worse, sales of the coin began on January 28, 2021. The museum had been closed because of COVID-19 since March 15, 2020, and would not reopen until August 27, 2021. No promotional events or direct sales efforts could be made. The coin couldn't even be sold at the museum gift shop.

Against the backdrop of the pandemic, the designs of the $5 gold coin further lessened its appeal. It was clearly a memorial coin. It showed a funerial scene: the heads of two police officers saluting on the obverse and, on the reverse, a flag folded into a triangle alongside roses. By contrast, the dollar and half dollar coins reflected the core motto of U.S. law enforcement, Serve and Protect, with the half dollar having playful designs of a police badge emblem on the obverse paired with a fingerprint and magnifying-glass detective theme on the reverse.

And last, this commemorative coinage program was overshadowed by incredibly popular programs running concurrently. The $1 American Silver Eagle was redesigned, doubling the number of bullion and collectibles versions for collectors to buy. The release of the popular 2021 Morgan and Peace silver dollar coins (nos. 28 and 29, respectively) also overshadowed this coin.

For all of these reasons, the gold coin failed to attract interest. Sales were so poor that when they closed on December 31, 2021, a mere 1,754 coins had been sold—the lowest of any modern commemorative coin. The mintage figure is only a few coins away from one of the rarest and most significant U.S. coins ever produced, the 1794 dollar, with 1,758 minted. Many numismatists have joked that they wished four more had sold. It is already evident that the small mintage will make this issue a key coin for collectors of modern commemoratives.

Mintage: 1,754

MS-69	MS-70	OGP
$780	$845	$780

77 2022-W NEGRO LEAGUES BASEBALL SILVER $1 COMMEMORATIVE

Designed by Matt Swaim (obverse) and Don Everhart (reverse). The obverse design depicts a pitcher in mid-throw with the baseball in the foreground, enclosed in a border of baseball stitching. The reverse design depicts a pitcher's-eye view of the ball being delivered to the catcher at the plate.

Standards: Weight: 26.718 grams. *Composition:* .999 silver.
Diameter: 38.1 mm. *Edge:* Reeded. *GSID:* 188855.

It's no secret that many commemorative coinage programs have underperformed in recent years, selling only a fraction of their authorized mintages. The prices of these coins include surcharges to be paid to designated beneficiaries, and many programs result in only modest payments.

To its credit, the marketing department of the Mint has innovated by offering new product formats to generate additional interest. In some cases the result has been to transfer net sales from one coin to another, creating a low-mintage anomaly. That's what occurred for the 2022 Negro Leagues Baseball silver dollar in uncirculated format, the lowest-mintage commemorative silver dollar issued to date.

The Negro Leagues Baseball silver dollar was issued as part of the Negro Leagues Baseball Commemorative Coin Program. It celebrated the centennial of the formation of the Negro National League, the first successful, organized professional African-American baseball league in the United States. It was formed in 1920 in Kansas City, Missouri, in response to African-American baseball players' being banned from the major leagues, and it lasted until integration in the early 1950s.

As with other commemorative programs, a clad half dollar, silver dollar, and $5 gold coin were issued. The silver dollar had an authorized mintage of 400,000 pieces across product types, including both uncirculated and Proof versions. For the Negro Leagues Baseball silver dollar, however, the Mint increased the product options in a couple of novel ways.

First, the Proof dollar could be bought singly for $79 ($74 introductory price), and a total of 22,695 were sold in this format. Second, the Proof dollar could be bought as part of the three-coin Proof set with the other denominations. The price for the set, based largely on the gold metal price, closed at $787.25, and a modest 3,823 sets were sold. Last, the Proof coin could be bought with a dollar-sized silver version of the 2003 Jackie Robinson medal, and 10,668

of these sets were sold, bringing the total number of Proof silver dollars sold to 37,186.

The Mint wasn't finished. Additionally, they offered the Proof dollar in a privy-marked version, which included a small "100" emblem within a baseball diamond added to the obverse. Privy marks have appeared on other U.S. coins recently, but they have a notable history among early U.S. commemorative issues. In fact, one of the keys to the early commemorative issues is a privy-marked coin that was struck exactly 100 years before the Negro Leagues commemorative. The 1922 Grant Memorial half dollar exists with a star privy mark, and its low mintage of 4,256 coins makes it one of the most coveted issues of the series. The privy-marked Negro Leagues coin was a strong success, selling out its full 20,000-coin issue at a premium price of $85, adding an additional net mintage of 19,687 to the silver dollar sales.

The uncirculated silver dollar was a different story. Offered singly at $74 ($69 introductory price), the low-priced product option failed to gain traction. While over 56,000 Proof dollars had sold in various product offerings, just 8,445 uncirculated dollars were purchased, leading to the lowest mintage figure of any U.S. commemorative silver dollar. Although comparatively less desirable at the time of issue, compared to the other coins in this series the uncirculated silver dollar commands the most meaningful premium today.

Mintage: 8,445

MS-69	MS-70	OGP
$95	$95	$115

78 1996-W SMITHSONIAN $5 COMMEMORATIVE

Designed by Alfred Maletsky (obverse) and James T. Ferrell (reverse). The obverse features a bust of James Smithson. The inscriptions include FOR THE INCREASE AND DIFFUSION OF KNOWLEDGE, IN GOD WE TRUST, the dual date 1846–1996, JAMES SMITHSON, and LIBERTY. The reverse features the Smithsonian sunburst logo with SMITHSONIAN beneath. The inscriptions include UNITED STATES OF AMERICA, E PLURIBUS UNUM, and the denomination FIVE DOLLARS.

Weight: 8.359 grams. *Composition:* .900 gold, .100 copper (net weight .2418 ounces pure gold). *Diameter:* 21.6 mm. *Edge:* Reeded. *GSID:* 10583.

In 1995 and 1996, the number of commemorative-coinage issues swelled to reach unprecedented numbers. Counting Mint State and Proof issues, a combined total of 46 different coins were issued in those two years. The 1996 Atlanta Olympics commemorative-coinage program, consisting of 32 coins, overshadowed the other, concurrent issues. There were so many coins to buy in the mid-1990s that collectors were overwhelmed, and the last several coins didn't sell particularly well. The 1996 Smithsonian $5 gold coin, released in August 1996, was among the biggest duds of all. It is precisely because this coin didn't sell well at the time that it's so desirable today.

Although a combined 100,000 coins could be struck under Congressional authorization in Proof and Mint State formats, fewer than 30,000 sold in total. The Uncirculated-finish coin, issued at a slightly higher price, sold a mere 9,068 pieces, making it the single worst-selling commemorative at that time, and the tenth-rarest modern commemorative issue including all issues that have followed it.

The Smithsonian $5 coin has a relatively straightforward design, jointly credited to U.S. Mint sculptor-engravers Alfred Maletsky (who designed the obverse) and T. James Ferrell (who designed the reverse). The obverse shows a bust of James Smithson with the inscription FOR THE INCREASE AND DIFFUSION OF KNOWLEDGE. Hardly a household name in the United States, Smithson was an Englishman who bequeathed his large fortune to the United States in 1829 in order to form a museum institution in his name. The fascinating mystery is that no one knows why he did so. Smithson never traveled to the United States, nor is there evidence that he corresponded with anyone in the country. His considerable generosity, albeit mysterious, is unquestionably

worthy of his portrayal on a commemorative coin. However, as a little-known figure and a foreigner, a coin featuring his likeness was not destined to be a best seller.

In the commemorative tradition of celebrating sesquicentennials, the 1996 issue of this coin marked the 150th anniversary of the Smithsonian Institution, as 1846 was the year President James K. Polk finally signed the long-debated act of Congress establishing the Smithsonian. Today, the Smithsonian is the world's largest museum complex and the national museum of the United States. Its National Numismatic Collection is worthy of being the country's coin collection, as it is among the most important and most valuable coin collections housed in private hands. Included among the museum's countless rarities are all three classes of the 1804 dollar, two 1933 $20 gold pieces, a 1913 Liberty Head nickel, and the unique 1849 $20 coin, considered the most valuable coin in existence.

The Smithsonian $5 gold commemorative coin, always a worthy issue, is only now starting to garner more respect. It is among the more sought-after issues in the series but still doesn't trade at price levels in line with its overall scarcity. Many who avidly follow this series describe it as a "sleeper" issue. Whenever it finally wakes up, it will become a hard coin to find.

Distribution: 9,068

MS-69	MS-70	OGP
$745	$810	$750

79 1996-S CENTENNIAL OLYMPICS (SWIMMING) HALF DOLLAR COMMEMORATIVE

Designed by William Krawczewicz (obverse) and Malcolm Farley (reverse). The obverse design features a male swimmer with the inscriptions LIBERTY and IN GOD WE TRUST, along with the date 1996. The reverse features symbols of the Olympic Games, including a torch, rings, a Greek column, and the number 100, representing the 100th anniversary of the modern Olympic Games. The inscriptions around the edge read UNITED STATES OF AMERICA, E PLURIBUS UNUM, and ATLANTA 1996.

Weight: 11.34 grams. *Composition:* Outer layers of .750 copper and .250 nickel over a core of pure copper. *Diameter:* 30.6 mm. *Edge:* Reeded. *GSID:* 10435.

A number of modern commemoratives appear on this list of the 100 Greatest U.S. Modern Coins, and for the most part they fall into two categories: First are coins that are thematically relevant, so that there is always a strong base of demand. Second are coins that proved unpopular at the time of issue and, as a result, few examples were coined. Their low mintage makes them desirable to collectors—those coins that originally proved unpopular become the most coveted. The Uncirculated 1996-S Olympic Swimming half dollar is among the most significant of the coins that fall into the latter category, because it heralded wide-sweeping changes in the commemorative-coinage program.

As the Olympic Games were being held in Atlanta, there was reason to think that the commemoratives would be popular. For the 1996 Olympics commemorative half dollars, a maximum mintage of three million coins was authorized by Congress for the Proof and Uncirculated versions combined. Being one of the most popular sports at the Games and having the most events, swimming was a logical sport to choose for a commemorative. The United States is also dominant in Olympic swimming, having won a total of 607 medals in competition over the years, followed by Australia in second place with 230. The coin design itself was also pleasing and modern.

The slow sales of the Swimming half dollar were recognized immediately. The coin design and theme were not to blame. The cause was the sheer number of commemorative coins that were issued in the mid-1990s. The 1995 and 1996 Atlanta Olympic Games commemorative-coinage program consisted of 16 different coins (or 32 if both Proof and Uncirculated versions are counted). Furthermore, during those same two years, there was a three-coin Civil War

Battlefields commemorative program, a Special Olympics dollar, a National Community Service dollar, and the two-coin Smithsonian commemorative program. Counting Proof and Uncirculated versions, this is 46 total commemorative coins in just two years. Adding to the list, the Olympics had already been the theme for commemorative coins in 1983, 1984, 1988, and 1992, accounting for 23 additional Olympic coins over the span of 10 years.

On August 1, 1997, sales were progressing so slowly that the U.S. Mint issued a press release. Of the three million coins authorized, it said, only 49,571 Swimming half dollars had sold. "The consequences of the low demand. . . is that collectors still have the opportunity to purchase coins that will have among the lowest mintages of all the modern commemoratives," said Mint Director Philip N. Diehl. "Some mintages are remarkably low, especially among the uncirculated coins, and many of these were sold overseas in 32-coin sets that are unlikely to be broken up. We want our collectors to be aware of this unique opportunity while the Olympic coins are still available from the Mint."

This was a unique opportunity for collectors, but poor sales meant that the U.S. Mint was losing money. The Mint reported a $3.2 million loss for the Olympics program as of March 31, 1996, according to a U.S. Government Accountability Office report titled "Commemorative Coins Could Be More Profitable," published in 1996. The report also outlined a series of recommendations that included limiting the number of commemorative programs and limiting their mintages. For the most part, the recommendations were instituted and have contributed to the resurgence in popularity of modern commemoratives over the past decade. The low mintage of the Swimming half dollar makes it by far the most valuable of all the commemorative half dollars, and, as an agent of change in the U.S. Mint commemorative program, it has an important place in the annals of numismatics.

Distribution: 49,533

MS-68	MS-69	MS-70	OGP
$46	$47	$54	$47

80 2014-D NATIVE AMERICAN / PRESIDENTIAL DOLLAR MULE

Designed by Glenna Goodacre (obverse) and Don Everhart (reverse). The obverse features the Shoshone guide Sacagawea and her infant son. The reverse shows the Statue of Liberty, viewed from ground level.

Weight: 8.1 grams. *Composition:* Outer layers of .770 copper, .120 zinc, .070 manganese, and .040 nickel over a core of pure copper. *Diameter:* 26.5 mm. *Edge:* Plain. *GSID:* 375897.

A mule occurs when two things are combined that don't naturally belong together. That's precisely the case with the 2014-D Native American / Presidential dollar mule. The obverse was struck using a Native American dollar die, showing designer Glenna Goodacre's lauded design of the young Shoshone woman with her child. The reverse, however, was not struck from the die for the Native American dollar as intended. Instead, it was paired with the Presidential dollar reverse showing the Statue of Liberty. The date and mintmark appear on the edge of the coin.

This was a highly unusual and unexpected discovery. By 2014, dollar coins were not being struck for circulation. Large production figures in earlier years had grown the Treasury's stockpile of dollar coins enough that new coins were no longer needed to meet demand for circulation. Beginning in 2012, both the Native American and Presidential dollar coins were produced as noncirculating legal tender for inclusion in Mint Sets and Proof Sets. They were also sold to collectors in bags and rolls, but were never released into circulation by the U.S. Mint.

The owner of this coin reported that it was discovered in a mixed bag of dollars obtained from a bank in 2019. The discovery came to light only when the coin was submitted to NGC before being offered for sale by Heritage Auctions. It shows light evidence of handling and was graded AU-58.

If the collecting public didn't expect this discovery, the Mint did. U.S. Mint spokesman Michael White told *Coin World* in a 2021 statement, "We are aware of this error coin from the past. Since 2014 we have implemented multiple controls and mistake-proofing measures both within the Coining Die Vault and Numismatics operations which will prevent a similar error from occurring again."

Of course, this was not the first time something like this had occurred. In 2000, the newly issued Sacagawea dollar reverse was paired with a Washington

quarter dollar obverse (see no. 4), creating one of most celebrated mint errors among modern coins in U.S. history, commanding six-figure prices and legendary status.

When the 2014 Native American / Presidential dollar mule was offered for sale on April 24, 2021, the auction listing was viewed over 10,000 times and the coin received over 45 bids, realizing a healthy and hefty $84,000. Today it remains unique—the discovery coin is the only known example. David Camire, NGC finalizer and noted mint-error authority, made the most prescient comment of all when the coin was first announced: "Now, the hunt is on to see whether additional specimens can be found. Happy hunting!"

Mintage: unique

AU-58
$96,000

81 1982 LINCOLN CENT, SMALL DATE, COPPER-PLATED ZINC

Designed by Victor David Brenner (obverse) and Frank Gasparro (reverse). The obverse continues the design of 1909. The reverse shows a frontal view of the Lincoln Memorial with UNITED STATES OF AMERICA and E PLURIBUS UNUM appearing above and ONE CENT below.

Weight: 2.5 grams. *Composition:* Outer layers of pure copper over a core of .992 zinc, .008 copper. *Diameter:* 19 mm. *Edge:* Plain. *GSID:* Brown, 312897; Red-Brown, 312898; Red, 71111.

The considerable expense of producing a mostly copper cent was recognized in the early 1970s, yet the composition of 95 percent copper and 5 percent zinc persisted until 1982. That fateful year marked the transition from a mostly copper cent to the copper-plated zinc coin that we have today (97.6 percent zinc and 2.4 percent copper). Also in 1982, a hub variation was introduced with slightly lower relief and sharper detail that made the coin easier to strike. Since the newly modified design had a smaller date, collectors named it the Small Date and the old style was called the Large Date.

All told, the change in composition and the new hub design created seven major varieties of circulating cents in 1982:

1. Bronze 1982, Large Date
2. Bronze 1982, Small Date
3. Bronze 1982-D (all are Large Date)
4. Copper-Plated Zinc 1982, Large Date
5. Copper-Plated Zinc 1982, Small Date
6. Copper-Plated Zinc 1982-D, Large Date
7. Copper-Plated Zinc 1982-D, Small Date

Although the original alloy for the bronze 1982 cents no longer contained tin, and was therefore technically brass, collectors still commonly referred to its composition as bronze, the original composition of the Lincoln cent. The first Lincoln cent was released in 1909, and never before had such a variety of cent coins been released in a single year. Because no Mint sets were issued in 1982, many marketers issued seven-coin sets of their own. This remains one of the easiest and most economical ways to purchase all seven varieties.

Telling the seven coins apart isn't challenging. First, there are the different date styles: the Small Date is much smaller and further from the rim. Its 9 is

pointed at its lower terminus and the top loop of the 8 is round rather than oval. To distinguish the metal types, it is easiest to weigh the coins. Bronze cents weigh 3.1 grams, while zinc cents weigh 2.5 grams. Some may even be able to spot bubbles underneath the surface of the copper-plating, which is another sure way to identify zinc cents.

In fact, the Mint faced a serious challenge in creating these cents with the new, zinc-heavy alloy. Air pockets underneath the plating create the appearance of a rough, blemished surface. Black spots of corrosion can also be seen on many 1982 cents. Quality control appears to have been slightly better at Denver, and the toughest coin to acquire in gem Uncirculated condition is the Philadelphia Mint copper-plated zinc 1982, Small Date, variety. Although not an expensive coin per se, it carries the biggest premium of the seven different cent varieties that were minted in 1982.

In the very highest grade levels, all seven coins will pose a challenge. Through 1983, the Mint struggled with the copper-plating, and both 1982 and 1983 zinc cents suffer from production issues. The 1982, Small Date, copper-plated zinc cent was the first cent produced of this composition, the first of this new hub style, and the scarcest cent of that year, all of which combine to earn it a place on the list of 100 Greatest U.S. Modern Coins.

Mintage: fraction of 10,712,525,000

	MS-64	MS-65	MS-66	MS-67	MS-68	MS-69
Brown	$0.85	$2.60	$4.70	—	—	—
Red-Brown	1.10	3.40	5.40	—	—	—
Red	1.50	4.10	9.50	$68	$455	$15,000

82 2003-W FIRST FLIGHT CENTENNIAL $10 COMMEMORATIVE

Designed by Donna Weaver (obverse) and Norman E. Nemeth (reverse). The obverse features portraits of Orville and Wilbur Wright. The surrounding inscriptions read LIBERTY, IN GOD WE TRUST, the centennial dates 1903–2003, ORVILLE & WILBER WRIGHT, and FIRST FLIGHT CENTENNIAL. The reverse features the Wright 1903 Flyer in flight with an eagle overhead. Inscriptions include UNITED STATES OF AMERICA, E PLURIBUS UNUM, and TEN DOLLARS.

Weight: 16.718 grams. *Composition:* .900 gold, .100 copper (net weight .48375 ounces pure gold). *Diameter:* 27 mm. *Edge:* Reeded. *GSID:* 10604.

The historic legislation that created the 50 State Quarters® Program and the Sacagawea dollar also created a three-coin commemorative program to honor the 100th anniversary of the first flight, the Wright brothers' successful airplane flight at Kitty Hawk, North Carolina, on December 17, 1903. The authorization was approved in December 1997, six years before the coins were to be issued. The lead time was far longer than many coins enjoyed, and suggested the austerity and importance of the occasion.

Uncharacteristically, the program consisted of a clad half dollar, a silver dollar, and a $10 gold coin, the first time commemoratives had been issued together in this arrangement. Normally, $5 gold commemorative coins are issued; this coin was only the second $10 gold commemorative since the resumption of the commemorative-coinage program in 1982 (or the third if the bimetallic Library of Congress issue is counted). But that wasn't the only peculiarity of the legislation. Another requirement stipulated that the First Flight Foundation would receive proceeds from the surcharges collected upon the sale of the coins only if they had received a similar amount of donations from private sources. This condition was a first among coinage legislation.

In the wake of the terrorist attacks of September 11, 2001, and a modified, less-ambitious plan for the visitors' center at the site of the first flight, the foundation had trouble raising anything close to the predicted $9 million in surcharge receipts that the coin's sales would generate. Concerned that the foundation would receive nothing, North Carolina senator John Edwards introduced a legislative fix just three months before the coin went on sale to make sure that at least $2.5 million of the funds raised from the coins' surcharges would go to

the foundation. Ultimately, the foundation would receive more than $3.5 million in proceeds from the sale of the coins.

But sales were soft, especially for the $10 gold piece. Most previous issues of commemorative gold coins were of a $5 denomination and contained 7.5 grams of pure gold. These coins contained double the amount of gold of a $5 coin and therefore were nearly twice as expensive. The 2002-W Salt Lake City Olympics $5 Uncirculated coins sold for $180, and the Proofs sold for $195. By contrast, the U.S. Mint priced the First Flight $10 coin at $340 for the Uncirculated and $350 for the Proof, and sold 10,009 and 21,676 examples, respectively. The mintage of 10,009 pieces makes the 2003-W First Flight $10 Uncirculated coin one of the most elusive in the series and also one of the most valuable today.

On the obverse, the coin shows side-by-side facing busts of Orville and Wilbur Wright wearing high-collared early-20th-century–style suits. The arrangement of two superimposed, three-quarters busts, created by U.S. Mint sculptor-engraver Donna Weaver, is somewhat atypical, giving the impression that the two men are standing very close to one another. The reverse shows their plane, the Wright Flyer, and an eagle soaring above it. Collectors will note that the soaring eagle resembles the bird that appears on the reverse of the American Platinum Eagle bullion coin. References and recast imagery occur numerous times in the annals of U.S. coinage design, especially when a commemorative can borrow a design element that has been implemented successfully elsewhere.

Distribution: 10,009

MS-68	MS-69	MS-70	OGP
$1,430	$1,500	$1,530	$1,500

83 1976 WASHINGTON QUARTER

Designed by John Flanagan (obverse) and Jack L. Ahr (reverse). The obverse features the normal design for the Washington quarter, except that the date now reads 1776–1976. On the reverse, a colonial drummer faces left. A torch of freedom, surrounded by 13 stars, appears in the field before the drummer. The outer legends include UNITED STATES OF AMERICA above and QUARTER DOLLAR below. The motto E PLURIBUS UNUM appears in small letters below the torch.

Weight: 5.67 grams. *Composition:* Outer layers of .750 copper and .250 nickel over a core of pure copper. *Diameter:* 24.3 mm. *Edge:* Reeded. *GSID:* 5714.

While not a rare coin in any of its forms, the Bicentennial quarter is squarely among the most important of all modern U.S. coinage issues. As a coin, it established the framework for future commemorative-coinage issues, and, as the first thematic circulating coin of its type, it also paved the way for the statehood quarters and America the Beautiful™ quarters.

Near the end of 1973, an open contest was announced to select designs for the Bicentennial coinage to be issued in celebration of the 200th anniversary of U.S. independence. This announcement came after a long year of debate. Everyone, it seemed, was in agreement that the event was worthy of recognition, but many thought that a commemorative coin went against the primary purpose of the country's coinage program: to produce coins that would be used readily in commerce. Based on that goal, no U.S. commemorative coin had been issued since 1954, and in recent years, from 1965 to 1967, coins had not had mintmarks so as to discourage hoarding. Now, it was proposed that coins would have a special design, making them sure candidates for hoarding.

Initially, proponents of Bicentennial coinage sought to have all coins from the cent to the dollar redesigned. This proposal met strong resistance, and focus shifted to a redesign of only the half dollar and the dollar. Since these two denominations were less-used in commerce, plans proceeded with little resistance. As debate came into full swing, U.S. Mint director Mary Brooks and John Jay Pittman, director of the American Numismatic Association, pressed to have the quarter included in the redesign as well. With the numismatic press supporting them, they argued that Americans should have a coin in their pocket that represented the ideals of the country and told its story. Some, too, must have

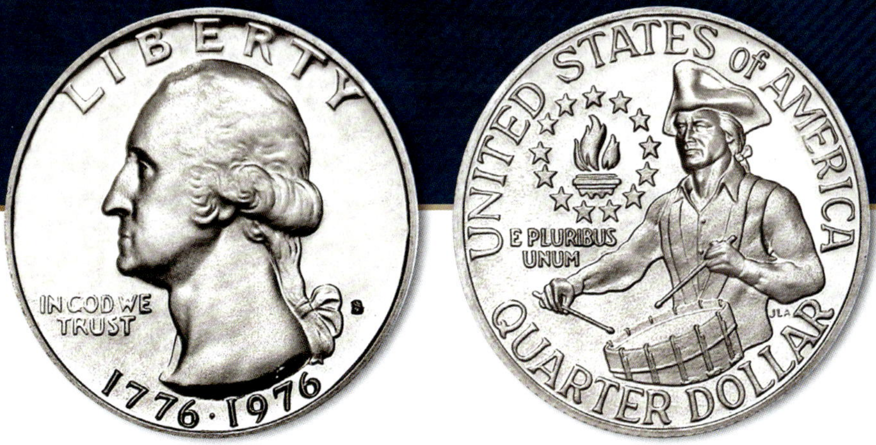

sensed the obvious omission if the quarter were not included—Washington, after all, was a great Revolutionary War general, but the Bicentennial coins being redesigned, the Kennedy half dollar and Eisenhower dollar, both featured 20th-century figures.

When the design was announced, a plan was laid out that would be replicated by many future programs. Competitions are now regularly held to find and select new designs. The winner for the Bicentennial design was Jack L. Ahr's reverse design of a colonial drummer and a torch surrounded by 13 stars. The obverse of the coins bore the dual date 1776–1976. To prevent hoarding and any potential interruption in commerce, a large number of coins were struck in advance of their 1975 release. Coins were released in both 1975 and 1976, with a special legislative allowance granted so that post-dated coins could circulate.

There are, in fact, five different Bicentennial quarters. More than 800 million pieces were struck at both the Philadelphia and Denver Mints for circulation in the standard copper-nickel-clad composition, while regular copper-nickel Proof coins struck at San Francisco were included in the 1975 and 1976 Proof sets. Silver-clad examples were also struck at San Francisco in both Proof and Uncirculated formats that were each sold to collectors in three-coin sets alongside silver examples of the Bicentennial half dollar and dollar.

All five different quarters are widely available today, with the Proof silver-clad version being the most valuable. Very high-grade examples of the circulating coins can also be surprisingly elusive.

Mintage: 1976 Uncirculated, 809,784,016; 1976-D Uncirculated, 860,118,839; 1976-S Proof, 7,059,099; 1976-S Silver Uncirculated, 11,000,000; 1976-S Silver Proof, 4,000,000

MS-60	MS-63	MS-64	MS-65	MS-66	MS-67
$0.55	$0.75	$1.10	$4.10	$20.00	$68

84 1986 $1 AMERICAN SILVER EAGLE

Designed by Adolph A. Weinman (obverse) and John Mercanti (reverse). The obverse features Weinman's Liberty Walking design used on half dollars from 1916 through 1947. Weinman's initials are on the hem of the gown. The reverse design is a rendition of a heraldic eagle.

Weight: 31.101 grams. *Composition:* .999 silver (net weight 1 ounce pure silver). *Diameter:* 40.6 mm. *Edge:* Reeded. *GSID:* 10644.

The American Silver Eagle was an instant success and has become the most popular silver bullion coin in history. The first release of this coin came on November 24, 1986, when each of the 28 authorized distributors bought their full allocation of 50,000 examples, adding up to a maximum sellout of 1.4 million coins. To meet demand, the Mint announced it would produce five million coins by the end of 1986. In addition to striking coins at West Point, new production lines were added at the Denver and San Francisco mints. The total mintage of the 1986 American Silver Eagle exceeded 5.39 million coins. Since the coin is struck without mintmark, it is not possible to distinguish coins from different mints.

The coin was introduced as a silver investment vehicle and sold at a small premium to its precious-metal content, one ounce of pure silver. It reuses the obverse design crafted by A.A. Weinman for the Liberty Walking half dollar (struck from 1916 to 1947), often called the most beautiful U.S. silver coin. The reverse shows a modern re-imagining of the heraldic eagle designed by U.S. Mint engraver John Mercanti. It also has a symbolic one-dollar face value, even though it trades based on the value of its silver metal content.

Sales of the coin continued unabated into 1987, reaching more than 11 million coins—a record that would not be surpassed until 2008. In 1988, however, when sales declined by more than half of the previous year's totals, blame was placed on the small distribution network, and legislators advocated an open-sales system. Distributors countered that the novelty of the coin had worn off, and that current levels reflected investor interest—a claim that seems justified because sales of the coin had been steady since the first 1986 issue. No change to the distributor network was ever instituted, although the Mint does now sell Uncirculated versions of bullion coins directly to collectors.

More than 340 million American Silver Eagles have been sold to date, including a record 40 million in 2011 prompted by silver's surge in value. The price

of silver nearly tripled from 2007 to 2011 and increased in value fivefold from decade lows. While this reflects investor interest, the American Silver Eagle is also among the most widely collected modern coins, and Proof coins and other special issues are avidly collected alongside the bullion issue.

The silver used to make the original American Silver Eagles was taken from the national defense silver stockpile managed by the Defense Logistics Agency, and sales of the coin have generated hundreds of millions of dollars for the agency. Because of the enduring popularity of the American Silver Eagle, the silver stockpile was depleted in 2002. This prompted legislation that allows the Mint to purchase silver from domestic sources so as to continue production without interruption, ensuring that American Silver Eagles will be produced well into the future. This 1986 bullion issue that makes the list of the 100 Greatest U.S. Modern Coins is the coin that started it all.

Mintage: 5,393,005

MS-68	MS-69	MS-70	OGP
$81	$100	$960	$100

85 1984-W LOS ANGELES OLYMPIAD $10 COMMEMORATIVE

Designed by John Mercanti and James Peed (obverse) and John Mercanti (reverse). The obverse depicts two runners holding aloft the Olympic torch. Inscriptions include LIBERTY, IN GOD WE TRUST, LOS ANGELES, the date 1984, and OLYMPIAD XXIII at the base of the coin. The reverse features an adaptation of the Great Seal of the United States. Inscriptions include UNITED STATES OF AMERICA, TEN DOLLARS, and E PLURIBUS UNUM on two banners above the eagle.

Weight: 16.718 grams. *Composition:* .900 gold, .100 copper (net weight .48375 ounces pure gold). *Diameter:* 27 mm. *Edge:* Reeded. *GSID:* 10600.

The $10 gold coins struck to commemorate the 1984 Olympic Games were a collection of firsts. They were the first U.S. gold coins struck since 1933, and, to conform to this earlier coinage, they were identical in composition to the circulating $10 gold coins made more than 50 years earlier. Further, this coin was the first, and still remains the only, commemorative issue in U.S. history to be struck at four different mints. Of significant note to collectors, the West Point issue was also the first U.S. coin to ever bear the W mintmark.

The obverse, designed by U.S. Mint artist James Peed and executed by engraver John Mercanti, shows a male and a female athlete gripping a torch that they run to the Games. Mercanti also designed the Great Seal adaptation for the reverse. Originally, the $10 gold coin was struck only at the West Point Mint and offered in Proof and Uncirculated versions. Demand was robust through the entire sales period, and when sales were closed at the end of 1984, a total of 381,085 of the Proof and 75,886 of the Uncirculated versions had been purchased.

Released mid-way through the coinage program, additional Proof versions of the $10 coin were also struck at Philadelphia, Denver, and San Francisco. As had been true during the classic commemorative programs of the past, these mintmark variants were offered to prompt additional sales specifically to collectors, and they foreshadow the abuses of the Olympic commemorative coinage that would come for the 1996 Atlanta Games. These additional gold coins were greeted much less enthusiastically, and only 30,000 to 50,000 of each were sold, with the highest sales belonging to the San Francisco issue—no doubt buoyed by California residents enthusiastic about the locally held Games. A unique

feature of the sales effort for these coins was that banks and S&L's participated, receiving coins on consignment from the Mint to then sell to their customers. While institutions across the country participated, California led the sales effort.

Total surcharges received from the sale of the Olympic gold coin were $28,668,200. This places it third on the list of most successful single commemorative issues in terms of surcharges raised; only the Statue of Liberty dollar and the Constitution Bicentennial $5 gold coin eclipse it. Counting the silver coins as well, the 1984 Olympic commemorative-coinage program raised more than $73 million to fund athlete training and offset costs of the Games, and it was deemed a major factor in closing the Games on budget.

Although some of the other mints' Proof coins are lower mintage and can carry a higher price premium, the Uncirculated West Point issue is the only coin of this format released. Of note to advanced collectors, this coin is found with two subtly different surface finishes: a heavy matte surface and a satin, semi-prooflike sheen. While researchers at coin grading service NGC were investigating these different surface characteristics in 2006, they identified a doubled-die obverse variety that can be found on the satin surface type. A surprise to many collectors, the doubled die took more than 20 years to be discovered.

Distribution: 75,886

MS-69	MS-70	OGP
$1,500	$1,530	$1,500

86 2015-P TRUMAN AND EISENHOWER PRESIDENTIAL DOLLARS, REVERSE PROOF

Weight: 8.1 grams. *Composition:* Outer layers of .770 copper, .120 zinc, .070 manganese, and .040 nickel over a core of pure copper. *Diameter:* 26.5 mm. *Edge:* Lettered. *GSID:* Truman, 76508; Eisenhower, 76506.

The Mint is always walking a delicate balance. They want to ensure that coins are available to everyone who wishes to purchase them. At the same time, collectors naturally desire items that are limited. For collectors, the lower the mintage the better. The Mint, therefore, doesn't want mintage limits to be any larger than they need to be. When they misgauge collector interest, they can create a messy situation. In 2015, they made a big blunder and created two rarities in the Presidential $1 coin series.

For each Presidential $1 coin, a Coin & Chronicles Set has been issued. These sets consist of a dollar coin in a handsome folio and other collectibles of numismatic relevance, along with a booklet describing the President's life and time in office. Throughout the series they met with modest demand. For example, the last set of 2014, the Franklin Delano Roosevelt Coin & Chronicles set, sold just a little over 13,000 of its product limit of 20,000 pieces.

To entice collectors, the Mint decided that the 2015 Coin & Chronicles Sets would include Reverse Proof versions of the Presidential $1 coins. They would be available exclusively in these sets and were to be the first Reverse Proof coins in the series.

The first such set of 2015 was the Harry S. Truman Coin & Chronicles Set. Along with the Reverse Proof Truman $1 coin were a silver inaugural medal and a Truman 8¢ postage stamp from 1973. The Mint set the product limit at 17,000, above the sales levels of the previous sets. The set was priced at $57.95. With a limit of five sets per household, it went on sale on June 30, 2015, at noon. At 12:15 p.m., it was sold out!

What happened? Quite simply, the Reverse Proof happened. Collectors were excited about the very first Reverse Proof $1 coin in the series and, more specifically, its astonishingly low mintage of just 17,000 coins. For comparison, 4.9 million Truman $1 coins were struck for circulation in Philadelphia, and 3.5 million were struck in Denver. Over 1.1 million standard Proof coins were struck. Yet just 17,000 Reverse Proof examples were made.

Sets quickly resold in the secondary market for three to four times the issue price.

Not wanting to repeat the blunder, for their next offering, the Dwight Eisenhower Coin & Chronicles Set, the Mint dropped the household order limit to two sets. Otherwise, the set was similar. It included a postage stamp, a silver medal, and the exclusive Reverse Proof dollar. It also was capped at 17,000 sets and priced at $57.95.

If there was a difference this time, it was that many more people had been alerted to buy this coin because of the surge in demand (and market value) of the previous issue. The set went on sale at noon on August 11. Fifteen minutes later, there were no more to be had.

Despite frustration about the low production limits and a flawed ordering system, collectors didn't take their frustration out on the coins. Subsequent issues had higher mintages, and these two coins, now standalone keys, have held their value.

Mintage: Truman, 16,812; Eisenhower, 16,744

	PF-65	PF-67	PF-68	PF-69	PF-70	OGP
Truman	$34	$43	$46	$51	$780	$94
Eisenhower	34	43	46	51	2,000	68

87 2012-S $1 AMERICAN SILVER EAGLE, REVERSE PROOF

Designed by Adolph A. Weinman (obverse) and John Mercanti (reverse). The obverse features Weinman's Liberty Walking design used on half dollars from 1916 through 1947. Weinman's initials are on the hem of the gown. The reverse design is a rendition of a heraldic eagle by John Mercanti.

Weight: 31.101 grams. *Composition:* .999 silver (net weight 1 ounce pure silver). *Diameter:* 40.6 mm. *Edge:* Reeded. *GSID:* 71592.

If the Mint has learned anything in recent years, it's that collectors love Reverse Proof American Silver Eagles. The first of these coins was issued in 2006 as part of a three-coin American Silver Eagle set struck in celebration of the American Silver Eagle's 20th anniversary. The second formed part of the five-coin American Silver Eagle set offered in 2011 to celebrate the American Silver Eagle's 25th anniversary. Both sets were rapid sellouts. The 100,000 sets offered to collectors in 2011 were entirely accounted for just five hours after going on sale. Despite the success of their sales effort, however, the Mint received considerable criticism for mismanaging the ordering process. Once again, too many collectors couldn't get through to place their orders online or by phone until it was too late.

In 2012, the Mint needed to do something different to make their coveted products more widely available. They announced both a novel coinage set and a novel ordering process.

First, the coins. The Mint announced the 2012 American Eagle San Francisco Two-Coin Silver Proof Set. Included were two American Silver Eagles: a 2012-S Proof, the first Proof American Silver Eagles minted at San Francisco since 1992, and a 2012-S Reverse Proof, the third Reverse Proof in the series and the first to be struck at San Francisco. These coins definitely excited collectors, even if it wasn't entirely clear why a special San Francisco set was being offered. The third and current Mint building at San Francisco opened in 1937, so 2012 marked the 75th of production at this facility. But the 75th anniversary of the third San Francisco Mint building is hardly an auspicious occasion. It seems more likely that San Francisco had more capacity to handle the minting of these coins, since the new ordering system required an open-ended mintage.

Following several recent sellouts, the Mint needed to make a change. They unveiled a new ordering process that would ensure that everyone who wanted a set could get one. The set would go on sale at noon on June 7, 2012, and remain on sale for a month, until 5:00 p.m. on July 5, 2012. There was no household

order limit. Sales figures would be posted on the Mint's web site and be updated daily. That way, collectors could gauge how low the mintage would be if this was a factor in deciding to purchase sets.

It worked like a charm. Several web sites tracked daily sales, and numerous posts on coin discussion boards tried to guess what the final figure would be. First-day sales were impressive. It was announced on June 8 that more than 85,000 sets had been sold the first day. Sales then dropped to a trickle until spiking toward the end of the ordering process. The final number: 251,302 sets. While higher than the mintage of other Reverse Proofs, this figure stood as the fourth-lowest mintage of any Proof American Silver Eagle and one of only three Reverse Proof American Silver Eagles ever issued—making the Reverse Proof 2012-S $1 American Silver Eagle one of the greatest U.S. coins of recent vintage.

The Mint, too, had managed to right previous wrongs with a new ordering system and open-ended mintage—until they blundered again. Collectors had been led to believe that both 2012-S coins would be available only in this two-coin set. But on July 31, after sales had closed, the Mint announced that they would offer a coin and currency set that included a Proof 2012-S American Silver Eagle and a Series 2009 $5 note. While the Reverse Proof was unique to the two-coin set, the regular Proof was not, and up to 100,000 more could be issued. The Mint released a statement that said, in part: "In retrospect, it may have been appropriate to announce our intentions to produce the coin and currency set earlier in the year or perhaps simultaneously with the two-coin set." While the Mint created great products, they hadn't quite gotten the formula down for creating happy customers.

A final and unexpected announcement came on December 6, 2012, that buoyed the spirits of those who had purchased the two-coin Proof set. After the processing of returns and order cancellations, net orders slid back to 224,998, pushing the rarity of this coin ahead of the 2006-P Reverse Proof.

Mintage: 224,981

PF-68	PF-69	PF-70	OGP
$82	$94	$180	$94

88 1996 $1 AMERICAN SILVER EAGLE

Designed by Adolph A. Weinman (obverse) and John Mercanti (reverse). The obverse features Weinman's Liberty Walking design used on half dollars from 1916 through 1947. Weinman's initials are on the hem of the gown. The reverse design is a rendition of a heraldic eagle.

Weight: 31.101 grams. *Composition:* .999 silver (net weight 1 ounce pure silver). *Diameter:* 40.6 mm. *Edge:* Reeded. *GSID:* 10676.

Without question, the most common way to collect any given type of modern coin is to complete the series. That means buying every different issue of the coin that is available. When collecting by series, the date of the lowest mintage normally emerges as the *key date*—the toughest example to acquire and also the most expensive. For the first 20 years of the American Silver Eagle, the 1996 issue was the key. Although its status has since been eclipsed by coins issued in 2006 and after, it still remains among the most desirable issues even today.

As we see repeatedly in this book, during the mid to late 1990s, demand dwindled for a number of U.S. Mint products. That is certainly true of the American Silver Eagle, which had depressed mintage figures from 1994 to 1998. These coins are struck to order, and in 1996, only 3,603,386 were made to satisfy the diminished demand. This figure is about 600,000 fewer coins than were struck for any other date, and well less than half of the number that would be struck for most bullion issues in the period from 1999 to the present, when mintage figures have approached or surpassed 10 million coins every year.

While the fluctuation might not seem extreme, it was noticeable, and the relative scarcity of 1996 issues was recognized almost immediately. One prominent trader of the period recalled a conversation in which he stated, "We just knew they were going to be worth a premium. You just never saw them." He was aware that some dealers had personally stashed a few monster boxes of 1996 American Silver Eagles, knowing that they would be worth a premium one day. By the late 1990s, dealers were paying a few extra dollars per coin for 1996 American Silver Eagles irrespective of grade. Today, it is not unusual for dealers to pay two to four times the prevailing rate for American Silver Eagles for coins dated 1996!

Buying 1996 American Silver Eagles does come with some hazards. Like other issues from the mid to late 1990s, they are prone to spotting, and even coins in unopened boxes can develop a speckled, milky-white haze, frequently

called "milk spotting." The spotting is irreversible and will usually prevent a coin from grading any higher than MS-68 at the major certification services. Concern regarding spotting dissuades dealers from bidding too aggressively on these issues and keeps their price in check, despite their scarcity. This creates an opportunity for collectors who can take the extra time to search out a pristine example.

Mintage: 3,603,386

MS-68	MS-69	MS-70	OGP
$44	$80	$2,500	$80

89 1981-S SUSAN B. ANTHONY DOLLAR, CLEAR S (TYPE 2), PROOF

Designed by Frank Gasparro. A bust of Susan B. Anthony faces right within an angular border. LIBERTY appears above her head and the date is below, while 13 stars are arranged on the left and right sides. IN GOD WE TRUST appears in small letters at the lower right. The reverse is a miniature version of the design on the regular Eisenhower dollar, also within an angular border.

Weight: 8.1 grams. *Composition:* Outer layers of .750 copper and .250 nickel over a core of pure copper. *Diameter:* 26.5 mm. *Edge:* Reeded. *GSID:* 7985.

Until 1999, there were only three years of Proof issues of the Susan B. Anthony dollar: 1979, 1980, and 1981. With such a scant number of issues, it is easy to see why collectors sought out varieties to collect, expanding opportunities and interest in the series.

Fortunately, great mintmark varieties do exist! When first issued, the 1979-S Proof Susan B. Anthony contained an S mintmark that was little more than a blob, with the upper and lower portions mashed into a thick, ill-defined base. This coin is numismatically named Type 1 since it was the first version issued, and it also bears the more descriptive name Filled S. Later that year, a better-defined mintmark punch was used instead, the Type 2 or Clear S variety. Its use persisted through all of 1980 and into 1981.

In 1981, a further refinement of the mintmark was attempted and an even clearer version was created. Since this happened well into the year, the original is called the Type 1 or, popularly, the Filled S version—even though it had the exact opposite name in 1979! The new version, showing wider loops and bulbous terminations at both ends of the S, is called the Type 2 or Clear S variety. One should note that the major certification services use the Type 1 and Type 2 naming schema, while most published resources refer to Filled S and Clear S.

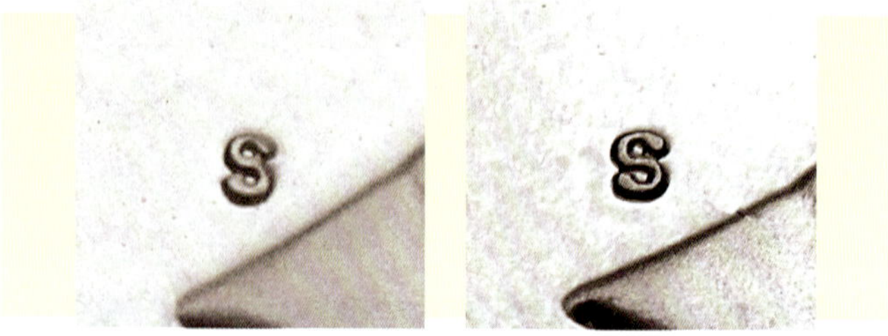

Filled S (Type 1) mintmark (left) and Clear S (Type 2) mintmark (right).

Although clarity is a relative measure, there are ways to tell the two mintmarks apart without the other type present for comparison. One conclusive way to tell the marks apart is that the high points of the Type 1 S are rounded like an arch when viewed in cross-section, while the top of the Type 2 S is flattened, and thus its cross-section will resemble a mesa or step. Also, if you see thickened bulbs at the ends of the S and a circular shape to the top loop, you have a Type 2 coin. The Type 1 mintmark has smaller, rounded serifs, and the loop at the top of the S pinches together, making it appear elliptical in shape. On the Type 1 variety, the ends of the S will often, but not always, touch the center portion of the S, while the ends of the S on a Type 2 are most often, but not always, detached. One should use a magnifier to examine these fine details.

Although more than four million Proof Susan B. Anthony dollars were produced in 1981, less than 10 percent are the Clear S or Type 2, making the estimated mintage approximately 350,000. This is a low mintage for any widely collected variety, and means that Type 2 examples trade for five times (or more) the value of a Type 1. An exciting aspect of these coins is that they can be found in 1981 Proof sets, so it's possible to be rewarded with a valuable find just by looking through these sets.

Also of note, when production of the coin resumed in 1999, it seems there was no need to revisit the mintmark issues of the past. The coin was struck in Philadelphia and bears the P mintmark.

Mintage: fraction of 4,063,083

PF-67DC	PF-68DC	PF-69DC	PF-70DC	OGP
$74	$88	$110	$325	$88

90 2007-W $25 AMERICAN GOLD EAGLE

Designed by Augustus Saint-Gaudens (obverse) and Miley Busiek (reverse). The obverse features a modified rendition of the Augustus Saint-Gaudens design used on U.S. $20 gold pieces from 1907 until 1933. The reverse displays a "family of eagles" motif.

Weight: 16.966 grams. *Composition:* .917 gold, .030 silver, .053 copper (net weight 0.500 ounces pure gold). *Diameter:* 27 mm. *Edge:* Reeded. *GSID:* 68650.

Almost every year that American Gold Eagles are on sale, the half-ounce or $25 American Gold Eagles are the worst sellers. Over the 31-year history of the American Gold Eagle, mintage figures are available for 65 different half-ounce American Gold Eagles, including coins issued in all three different formats (Proof, Uncirculated, and bullion). In all but 12 instances, the half-ounce $25 denomination was the lowest-mintage denomination of its respective year and type.

So, in other words, the half-ounce is the dud American Gold Eagle. But this is also where one of the greatest modern coins of recent vintage can be found: the Uncirculated 2007-W $25 American Gold Eagle. It has, by a good margin, the lowest mintage of any half-ounce American Gold Eagle at just 11,455 pieces.

Wherever there are low mintages, there are usually collectors. Collectors are attracted to lower mintage figures for two reasons. First, they mean a scarcity, a challenge, a harder coin to come by. Second, many collectors of American Gold Eagles like these coins as a way to own gold. In this respect, they are investors as well as collectors. Collectors use their numismatic knowledge to identify coins they feel have a superior opportunity for price appreciation. Topping this list are low-mintage issues—or half-ounce American Gold Eagles. King among them is the 2007-W.

Why the 2007-W $25 American Gold Eagle sold poorly isn't too hard to ascertain. Starting in 2006, the Mint offered Uncirculated American Gold Eagles directly for sale to collectors. These coins look similar to the bullion versions but include a W mintmark for West Point, where they are produced. For devoted collectors of half-ounce American Gold Eagles, instead of just needing to buy the Proof and the bullion versions, there was now a third coin to buy. Sales of the 2006-W coins weren't great, and they fell even more in 2007.

The 2007 mintage figures for the four Uncirculated American Gold Eagles are as follows: $50, 18,608 coins; $25, 11,455 coins; $10, 12,766 coins; $5, 22,501 coins. The Mint, maybe in part as a response to poor sales of the half-ounce coin, engineered a new sales initiative. In 2008, it offered something called the 8-8-08 Double Prosperity Set. The set included a half-ounce Uncirculated American Gold Eagle along with a half-ounce Uncirculated American Buffalo gold coin and was aimed at Asian buyers who associate the number 8 with wealth and prosperity. Certainly, it ranks among the more unusual packaging options offered by the Mint.

Sales of the Prosperity set weren't great, at 7,622 units. But as a result of the set, something uncharacteristic happened. Mintage figures for 2008-W Uncirculated American Gold Eagles set are as follows: $50, 11,908 coins; $25, 15,683 coins; $10, 8,883 coins; $5, 12,657 coins. For the first time ever, the half-ounce American Gold Eagle had the highest mintage figure of any denomination American Gold Eagle for its date and type. But the special sales push wasn't enough to satisfy the Mint. Because of low demand, they cancelled the program entirely for 2009 and 2010.

Because the half-ounce $25 denomination is popular with collectors, the low-mintage key 2007-W easily merits its spot among the 100 Greatest U.S. Modern Coins.

Mintage: 11,455

PF-68DC	PF-69DC	PF-70DC	OGP
$825	$895	$960	$895

91 2013-W $1 AMERICAN SILVER EAGLE, ENHANCED UNCIRCULATED

Designed by Adolph A. Weinman (obverse) and John Mercanti (reverse). The obverse features Weinman's Liberty Walking design used on half dollars from 1916 through 1947. Weinman's initials are on the hem of the gown. The reverse design is a rendition of a heraldic eagle by John Mercanti.

Weight: 31.101 grams. *Composition:* .999 silver (net weight 1 ounce pure silver). *Diameter:* 40.6 mm. *Edge:* Reeded. *GSID:* 71533.

Mints around the world today are presenting collectors with a rich variety of never-before-seen offerings: colorful coins painted with enamel, coins embedded with semiprecious stones, and even coins struck in unusual shapes and sizes. Their goal is to win over collectors and to demonstrate their own capabilities. Although it sells more coins than any other mint, the U.S. Mint also faces pressure to push the envelope.

Since the Mint has considerable control over which American Eagle coins are issued to collectors, they decided to issue a new-format American Silver Eagle, in part, to showcase their mastery of modern coin minting. The 75th anniversary of the West Point Mint's construction served as the occasion to issue a two-coin American Silver Eagle set including a Reverse Proof and the first-ever Uncirculated coin with an Enhanced finish.

Right away, this coin became known as the "Enhanced Uncirculated" American Silver Eagle, and collectors immediately began to speculate on what this term might mean. It was an entirely novel term for the Mint, and "Enhanced" appears in quotation marks in their own January 2013 announcement.

In March, online coin columnist James Bucki was able to see examples of the coin being struck during a visit to the West Point Mint. He was allowed to release photos, giving the public their first glimpse.

The coin mixes three finishes selectively applied to various portions of the design to accentuate its details. For example, on the obverse, the blue portion of the flag is rendered in a shallow mirrored finish while the stars within it are heavily frosted. The entire design and legends are similarly rendered in reflective areas that contrast with the heavy white frost. The fields are rendered in a lightly frosted finish, a treatment new to this coin.

The 2013 American Eagle West Point Two-Coin Silver Set went on sale from May 9 to June 6, 2013. The coins would be produced based on demand and customers could order as many sets as they wanted. The price was fixed at $139.95

and the set was scheduled to ship in mid-June after the order period closed. Each day, the total units sold was reported on the catalog order page.

The Mint designed this ordering process to prevent customers from being shut out of low-mintage issues. Opening week sales were 180,000 units. When the ordering period closed, 281,310 sets had sold, making the Enhanced Uncirculated American Silver Eagle, along with 2013-W Reverse Proof, the best sellers of the Mint's special finish (Reverse Proof and Enhanced) American Eagle coins. The Mint succeeded in ensuring that everyone was able to buy the coins that they wanted from the Mint; however, an unintended consequence emerged.

In October 2013, the Mint released revised figures of sets sold: 235,689 units, an enormous downward revision. Some of the reduction is due to cancellations by the Mint. For example, an order is canceled when the Mint cannot process a credit card. However, the vast majority were cancellations by speculators who'd purchased coins during the order period. They waited to see what the coins sold for once they were no longer available from the Mint. If the coins were trading for a premium, they would have completed their orders. Since they were not, they canceled them.

Unfortunately, the new ordering system created to ensure wide availability of the coins instead created a glut in the marketplace, causing the coins to lose value immediately after they were released. However, owing to their uniqueness, these coins have rebounded above their issue price. They are almost always sold with their Reverse Proof counterpart.

Mintage: 235,689

MS-68	MS-69	MS-70	OGP
$88	$110	$130	$110

92 2010-P GRAND CANYON 5 OZ. SILVER QUARTER, LIGHT FINISH

Designed by John Flanagan (obverse) and Phebe Hemphill (reverse). The obverse features Flanagan's Washington quarter design used beginning in 1932. The reverse design features a view of the granaries above the Nankoweap Delta in Marble Canyon near the Colorado River.

Weight: 155.5 grams. *Composition:* .999 silver (net weight 5 ounces pure silver). *Diameter:* 76.2 mm. *Edge:* Lettered. *GSID:* 76807.

The legislation that authorized the recent quarter dollars series, the America's Beautiful National Parks Quarter Dollar Coin Act of 2008, contains the strangest provision of any coinage legislation in the history of the United States. The law dictates that circulating quarters will be issued with designs that celebrate America's national parks, one from each state, in order of the selected parks' establishment. Normal enough. But "Section 201. Silver Bullion Coin" is where it gets weird. It reads in part:

> (1) IN GENERAL. —The Secretary shall strike and make available for sale such number of bullion coins as the Secretary determines to be appropriate that are exact duplicates of the quarter dollars issued under subsection (t), each of which shall—
> (A) have a diameter of 3.0 inches and weigh 5.0 ounces;
> (B) contain .999 fine silver.

That's right. Lawmakers demanded that quarters three inches in diameter and weighing five ounces of pure silver must be produced as well. Beyond the sheer oddity of creating huge legal-tender silver quarters, seemingly little consideration was given to how these coins would be produced and distributed. Those two considerations created mountains of frustration at the Mint, as well as for dealers and collectors.

Putting that aside, collectors looked forward to something truly new and different from the U.S. Mint. Oversized, multi-ounce precious-metal coinage had been released from mints around the world for a number of years. And now it was the U.S. Mint's time to get into the action.

A Light Finish quarter (left) shown next to an example of the standard matte bullion finish (right).

In addition to the bullion five-ounce quarters, which were sold through the American

Eagle Bullion distributor network, the Mint eventually offered examples for sale directly to collectors. Unlike the bullion examples, these collector coins had a P mintmark for Philadelphia, where they were produced. Further, these coins had a special flat, matte finish, created by a process called vapor blasting. After the coins were struck, they were hand treated with equipment that imparted this special surface. Because of this special handling and matte finish, these coins are referred to as Specimens to distinguish them from the satin-finish Uncirculated bullion coins.

Due to production difficulties, it wasn't until July 2011 that the Specimen 2010-P Grand Canyon five-ounce silver quarters were released. This was the fourth issue in the series, preceded by Hot Springs, Yellowstone, and Yosemite. Unlike the previously released coins, the Grand Canyon coins exhibited unusual variations in the texture of their finish. Most had the typical coarse, matte finish, but a small number, estimated at 15%, had a finer, slightly reflective finish, called Light Finish. It was easy to distinguish between both types, especially when viewed side by side. Because of the light finish, handling marks show more readily on these coins, impairing their condition and causing them to grade much lower than their heavy-finish counterparts.

The cause of the variation, the Mint claimed, was wear to equipment that had been retrofitted to apply the granular finish to the Grand Canyon bullion coins. The Mint ordered new equipment that would better handle the demand and allow them to better integrate vapor blasting into coin production, eliminating the manual process. The change of equipment proved effective, because this surface variation cannot be seen on coins issued after the Grand Canyon. A maximum mintage of 27,000 Grand Canyon five-ounce silver Specimen quarters was sold, and approximately 4,000 are of the Light Finish variety.

Mintage: fraction of 27,000

MS-68	MS-69	MS-70	OGP
$255	$260	$295	$230

93 2008-W $10 AMERICAN BUFFALO GOLD

Designed by James Earle Fraser. The obverse and reverse designs are based on the original 1913 Buffalo nickel, with modified inscriptions on the reverse. The obverse features a portrait of a Native American facing right with the inscription LIBERTY and the date 2008. The reverse features a figure of a bison standing, facing left. The inscription reads UNITED STATES OF AMERICA, E PLURIBUS UNUM, IN GOD WE TRUST, $10, and 1/4 OZ .9999 FINE GOLD.

Weight: 7.776 grams. *Composition:* .9999 gold (0.250 ounces pure gold). *Diameter:* 21.5 mm. *Edge:* Reeded. *GSID:* 70888.

When the Liberty Head nickel design was first released in 1883, a large V, signifying the Roman numeral for 5, was the only indication of its value. The word "cents" did not appear on the coin. There are stories that some miscreants plated the new nickels with gold, hoping to pass them off as $5 gold pieces. These gold-plated nickels are still sold as novelties today and are called "racketeer nickels." The dimensions of the nickel and the $5 gold piece, each a little more than 21 mm in diameter at the time, were similar enough to enable this illusion to pass.

Size is one of the features that make the 2008-W American Buffalo $10 gold coin so special. It is 22 mm and struck in a quarter ounce of pure, .9999 fine gold. Its design faithfully replicates the design of the 1913 Buffalo nickel, making it a true representative of the original—a sort of racketeer nickel in reverse.

The gold Buffalo coins were first authorized in 2005, and they were the first U.S. pure gold bullion coins. The design is nearly identical to James Earle Fraser's original composition for the Buffalo nickel that was made from 1913 to 1938. The obverse shows a Native American chief in profile, said to be a composite of three models who sat for Fraser: Chief Iron Tail of the Oglala Lakota, Chief Two Moons of the Cheyenne, and a third whose identity Fraser could not recall (who may have been Chief "Big Tree" Adoette of the Kiowa). The American bison on the reverse is said to be modeled after Black Diamond, an animal kept at New York's Central Park Zoo, although there are other potential models.

Two years after the introduction of the one-ounce gold American Buffalo gold coin, fractional denominations were introduced. They were offered in the same weights and denominations as the coins in the American Gold Eagle series, only with the higher metal fineness of the Buffalo. The coins were sold as bullion, in

Proof versions, and also in Uncirculated versions. The Uncirculated coins had the same finish as their bullion counterparts but also included the W mintmark and were sold directly to the public. They were expensive, as the price of gold was high in 2008 and a surcharge was added. The Uncirculated varieties were also available only in limited quantities. The quarter-ounce coin and the half-ounce coins sold in the least numbers, 9,949 and 9,286, respectively.

To date, the 2008-W is the only quarter-ounce Uncirculated version of the gold Buffalo coin and, with fewer than 10,000 examples, it's an attractive scarcity. Because its size so closely mimics the Buffalo nickel that served as its model, the quarter-ounce coin is in higher demand than the even-lower-mintage half-ounce coin. The fractional gold American Buffaloes were not issued in 2009. Based on the low sales figures in 2008 and the current high demand for bullion coinage, it's uncertain when collector versions of the fractional gold American Buffalo coins will be offered again.

Mintage: 9,949

PF-68DC	PF-69DC	PF-70DC	OGP
$1,120	$1,250	$2,250	$1,250

94 1992-D XXV OLYMPIAD (BASEBALL) DOLLAR COMMEMORATIVE

Designed by John R. Deecken (obverse) and Marcel Jovine (reverse). The obverse features a pitcher about to throw a ball to a batter. Inscriptions read LIBERTY, IN GOD WE TRUST, USA with the Olympic logo, and 1992. The reverse features a shield, intertwined Olympic rings, and olive branches. Inscriptions include UNITED STATES OF AMERICA, E PLURIBUS UNUM on a scroll, ONE DOLLAR, and USA within Olympic rings.

Weight: 26.73 grams. *Composition:* .900 silver, .100 copper (net weight .77344 ounces pure silver). *Diameter:* 38.1 mm. *Edge:* Lettered on a reeded background. *GSID:* 10474.

The 1992 Olympic Commemorative Coin Act sought to raise money to support the training of athletes participating in the 1992 Olympic Games. Three coins were authorized: a copper-nickel-clad half dollar, a silver dollar, and a $5 gold coin. The only stipulation regarding the design of the silver dollar in the legislation was that "the design of the $1 coins shall be emblematic of the participation of American athletes in the 1992 Olympic Games."

Secretary of the Treasury Nick Brady openly solicited designs for the coins and selected the winners after consultation with the United States Olympic Committee and the Commission of Fine Arts. The winning design for the Olympic dollar featured a baseball pitcher firing a ball to home plate. Baseball isn't normally identified as an Olympic sport, and in previous games it had only been included as an exhibition. The 1992 Olympic Games in Barcelona were the first ever to include it as an official sport for which medals would be awarded. In light of this, it seemed fitting that the design selected for the dollar coin should highlight America's national pastime, baseball.

The coin's design was created by artist John R. Deecken, and it shows a right-handed pitcher in the midst of motion. A maximum mintage of four million coins was authorized. Sales totals were 187,552 for the Denver Mint's Uncirculated version and 504,505 for the San Francisco Mint's Proof version. The Denver Mint coin is known for an unusual feature: it bears a lettered edge—the phrase XXV OLYMPIAD was impressed into its edge four times—and was the first edge-lettered coin to be issued in the United States since 1933. It was not this feature, however, that generated excitement among the numismatic press.

After the coin's release, collectors noticed an uncanny resemblance between the pitcher shown on the coin and the image on the Nolan Ryan 1991 Fleer baseball card. Every detail in the photograph of Ryan perfectly matched the pitcher's image on the coin, including the position of Ryan's arms, glove, and stride—even down to the crane of his neck and the wrinkles on his jersey. Ryan's unofficial depiction caused some controversy, and the coin's legality was even called into question. There was never any formal inquiry, however, because Mint officials and Deecken himself fervently denied that the resemblance was intentional.

For some time in the secondary market, the coin took on a nickname: the Nolan Ryan dollar. Since this dollar was produced, baseball has thrice returned as a theme for U.S. commemorative coins. The sport is depicted on the 1995-S Olympic half dollar, struck for the 1996 Olympic Games; on the 1997 Jackie Robinson commemorative dollar and $5 gold coins (see no. 18); and on the commemorative coins (no. 62). Unfortunately, the sport has not fared so well at the Olympics. It was voted out of the Olympics for the 2012 London games, becoming the first sport to be removed from competition since 1936, when polo was eliminated.

Distribution: 187,552

MS-68	MS-69	MS-70	OGP
$36	$39	$135	$39

95 1970-S LINCOLN CENT, SMALL DATE

Designed by Victor David Brenner (obverse) and Frank Gasparro (reverse). The obverse continues the design of 1909. The reverse shows a frontal view of the Lincoln Memorial with UNITED STATES OF AMERICA and E PLURIBUS UNUM appearing above and ONE CENT below.

Weight: 3.11 grams. *Composition:* .950 copper, .050 tin and zinc. *Diameter:* 19 mm. *Edge:* Plain. *GSID:* Brown, 312831; Red-Brown, 312832; Red, 2374.

Throughout the entirety of U.S. coin collecting, there are dozens of coins described as being Small Date or Large Date, a reference to the size of the digits used on the date of the coin. There are two principle reasons why the Mint might change the size of a coin's date. First, as the coin's design varies, there may be aesthetic reasons to modify this particular aspect of the design. More often with modern coins, though, modifying the date is a way to improve die life and production quality. Such was the case in 1960, when the date on the Lincoln cent was enlarged in the middle of the year because the small 0 was determined to cause breaking and wearing of the dies. To balance out a larger 0, the rest of the date was reconfigured in a larger size, creating two very collectible varieties, the 1960, Small Date, and 1960, Large Date, cents, each struck at both mints that produced Lincoln cents that year.

Ten years later, in 1970, coins struck at the San Francisco Mint were produced in two date styles, Small Date and Large Date. There is no record, though, of why or when this change occurred, and many simply believe that two different hubs with minor variations were used by the Mint to create dies from the very beginning of the year. Coins of both the 1970-S Small and Large Date varieties were found early in 1970 and far from California in the Northeast and the South. Numismatic researcher and author David W. Lange suggests that these

Pick-up point: Date (left, normal date; right, small date).

coins were widely distributed throughout the country to combat hoarding by speculators. It became clear right away that the Small Date variety was much scarcer than the Large Date. Since then, the 1970-S, Small Date, Lincoln cent has emerged as one of the key Lincoln cents of the era.

The 1970-S, Small Date, Lincoln cent is rather scarce and valuable but is not as well known as other Lincoln cent varieties, including the 1960 Small Date and Large Date coins. One reason may be that this variety can be difficult to attribute. The size difference between the two date styles isn't significant enough to "eyeball" to determine whether a coin is Large or Small Date. Oftentimes, when a collector encounters either variety, he or she doesn't have an example of the other variety with which to compare it, either. Understanding Small and Large Date varieties is an essential skill for the collector of U.S. coins because variations in date size have occurred dozens of times. Almost always one date size is far more valuable than the other, and knowing how to accurately attribute varieties in isolation is important.

The 1970-S Lincoln cent offers some attribution clues that make it possible to identify the Small and Large Date varieties with 100 percent accuracy. First, the position of the 7 should be examined. On the Small Date cent, the top of the 7 is aligned with the tops of the 9 and 0 that surround it. On the Large Date cent, the top of the 7 is lower than the 9 and 0. For this reason, sometimes these varieties will be referred to as the "High 7" for the Small Date and the "Low 7" for the Large Date. Additionally, on the Small Date variety the word LIBERTY is usually, but not always, indistinct and mushy, while on the Large Date the word LIBERTY will be crisp. Knowing these diagnostics makes easy work of attributing this elusive Lincoln cent.

Mintage: fraction of 690,560,004

	MS-60	MS-63	MS-64	MS-65	MS-66	MS-67
Brown	$13.50	$27	$34	$49	$94	—
Red-Brown	18.50	35	43	68	120	—
Red	30.00	47	61	92	145	$650

96 1997-P LAW ENFORCEMENT OFFICERS MEMORIAL DOLLAR COMMEMORATIVE

Designed by Alfred Maletsky. The obverse depicts two U.S. Park Police officers making a rubbing of a fellow officer's name, based on a photo by Larry Ruggeri. The inscriptions include NATIONAL LAW ENFORCEMENT OFFICERS MEMORIAL, IN GOD WE TRUST, LIBERTY, and the date 1997. The reverse of the coin features a shield with a rose across it, evocative of the sacrifices made by the officers. Inscriptions include UNITED STATES OF AMERICA, TO SERVE AND PROTECT, E PLURIBUS UNUM, and ONE DOLLAR.

Weight: 26.73 grams. *Composition:* .900 silver, .100 copper (net weight .77344 ounces pure silver). *Diameter:* 38.1 mm. *Edge:* Reeded. *GSID:* 10520.

In an unusual stroke, the same legislation that authorized the 1997 National Law Enforcement Officers Memorial coin established the National Law Enforcement Officers Memorial Maintenance Fund. The fund was created to cover the costs of maintaining the memorial in Washington, D.C., and to provide educational scholarships to family members of officers killed in the line of duty. The 500,000 coins, authorized at the same time, were each to be sold with a $10 surcharge, thereby contributing $5 million to the newly established fund. Sadly, these well-laid plans were not realized, as, like all the other commemorative issues of 1997, the coin did not sell well. Only 139,003 were sold, yielding less than $1.4 million for the fund.

Proof examples comprised the majority of the gross sales, and only 28,575 Uncirculated pieces were sold, putting this coin among the lowest-minted commemorative dollars in the series. In combination with the low mintage, its evocative theme makes the 1997-P Law Enforcement Officers Memorial Uncirculated dollar one of the most coveted coins in the series and, therefore, one of the most valuable.

Designed by U.S. Mint sculptor-engraver Alfred Maletsky, the coin's obverse is based on a photograph by Larry Ruggeri showing two police officers making a rubbing of a name off of the National Law Enforcement Memorial wall. The reverse shows the memorial's emblem, a shield and a solitary rose, above the phrase TO SERVE AND PROTECT.

This coin does not commemorate a specific date or event, and it certainly would have performed better had it been issued at a different time. In the late 1990s, collectors were fed up with the glut of commemorative coins, all of which traded for less than their issue price soon after the Mint's sales period ended. As

a result, the coin's sales suffered. The Proof coin was sold paired with an enamel pin and patch in the Insignia Set, and the Mint offered the Uncirculated coin attached by a bezel to a sterling-silver money clip. These programs contributed enough for the U.S. Mint to deem the coin a success. As stated in the 1998 Mint report, "The National Law Enforcement Memorial silver dollar ended with Proof and Uncirculated (gross) sales of $4,898,000, a good showing given recent commemorative coin trends. Strong management closed this program with a profit."

In later years, greater restraint was exercised in approving new commemorative issues for mintage, which increased the success of the U.S. commemorative-coinage program. The Law Enforcement Memorial theme brought new collectors to the hobby and expanded demand—as is often the case on low-mintage commemorative issues. Numismatic author David L. Ganz comments that the Law Enforcement Officers Memorial dollar is evidence that Congress has the ultimate say regarding which coins are made: this coin was the fifth in the modern commemorative program to fund a national memorial. Previous issues included the Vietnam Veterans' Memorial, the Women in the Military Memorial at Arlington National Cemetery, the Battle of Normandy Foundation Memorial Wall in France, and the Korean War Memorial on the National Mall, and more would follow.

Distribution: 28,575

MS-68	MS-69	MS-70	OGP
$37	$40	$110	$40

97 2016-W AMERICAN SILVER EAGLES, LETTERED-EDGE 30TH ANNIVERSARY ISSUES

GSID: 74076.

In recent years, American Silver Eagles minted to celebrate their own anniversary have been among the most important and widely collected of all U.S. modern coinage. The 1995-W American Silver Eagle, struck in recognition of the coin's tenth year of issue, garners a high ranking on the list of 100 Greatest U.S. Modern Coins. The 2006 set issued for the coin's 20th anniversary included the first Reverse Proof. The 25th anniversary set included the first American Silver Eagle struck at San Francisco. They are all wildly popular coins.

For the 30th anniversary, something big was planned. Rather than issue a special set, every single 2016 American Silver Eagle sold directly to the public—both the Proof and Uncirculated (or so-called "Burnished") issues—would be an anniversary coin. The standard reeded edge for the 2016 numismatic issues would be replaced with a lettered edge with the incuse inscription, "30TH ANNIVERSARY." The bullion issue coin was left unchanged. In 2017, the edge would again revert to standard reeding.

Since the reeded edge is part of the legal specifications of the American Silver Eagle, this change required Congressional authorization. In December of 2015, wording to this effect was added to the Fixing America's Surface Transportation (FAST) Act, which in addition to being a $305 billion funding bill for transportation infrastructure projects, included some last-minute housekeeping amendments.

While previous anniversary sets always seemed to involve some form of melee when they went on sale, this coin's release was rather more subdued. From the outset it was known the coins would be struck to meet demand and therefore

Edge lettering.

the final mintage was unlimited. Further, there would not be a household limit restriction. These two features served to quell speculator demand.

These coins were sold by the Mint singly and in combination with several set options throughout the year. Unlike the bullion coin, they are sold directly to the public and bear a mintmark. Both of these coins were struck at West Point and include the "W" mintmark. In the last few years prior to issue, about 900,000 Proof American Silver Eagles and roughly 225,000 Uncirculated American Silver Eagles have sold each year.

Just over 650,000 Proof and 216,000 circulating coins were sold. These figures were certainly lower than many predicted. The biggest single factor in sales for the 30th Anniversary coin was its high issue price. In 2015, Proof and Uncirculated American Silver Eagles were sold by the Mint for $48.95 and $39.95, respectively. The anniversary coins were $53.95 and $44.95. This is a significant premium for an unlimited mintage one-ounce silver coin considering that during 2016 silver traded for an average of $17 per ounce.

Overall sales numbers don't seem to tell the whole story. These are the only lettered-edge American Silver Eagles. A major design change, enacted by Congress, allowed the 30th anniversary to be celebrated in a big way. Maybe best of all, since there were no production limits in place, everyone who really wanted one of these coins was able to acquire one.

Mintage: Uncirculated, 216,501; Proof, 651,453

PF-68DC	PF-69DC	PF-70DC	OGP
$74	$81	$125	$81

98 2023 LINCOLN CENT, "EXTRA V" VARIETY

Designed by Victor David Brenner (obverse) and Joseph Menna (reverse). The obverse continues the original design of 1909. The reverse features a Union shield with 13 vertical stripes and the national motto in a horizontal bar above. ONE CENT appears in a banner draped across the shield.

Weight: 2.5 grams. *Composition:* Outer layers of pure copper over a core of .992 zinc, .008 copper. *Diameter:* 19 mm. *Edge:* Plain. *GSID:* 375894.

From time to time in numismatics, there is a mystery that cannot be solved. This is the case with a discovery by Buffalo, New York–based collector Dave Santiago. While searching rolls of Lincoln cents, he discovered coins with an extra, incused V spaced slightly after the initials V.D.B. on the bust truncation. This variety was initially called "VDBV" before the name "Extra V" became preferred. What caused this anomaly is unknown.

Error coin and variety expert Mike Diamond documented the discovery in a March 2023 *Coin World* column. There he speculated that the additional design element was most likely carved into a hub, perhaps intentionally. The reason he suspected a hub was altered is that the design element is incused, or depressed into the surface. That means the extra V is raised on the coinage die. The scenarios that add extra, raised metal in this shape and position to a coinage die are less likely than the simple cutting of a V-shaped notch into a hub that is then used to make dies.

All Extra V cents also display a small, rectangular, raised die flaw on the leading edge of Lincoln's forehead, a pronounced die feature that makes these coins easier for the roll searcher to spot. This is further evidence that this variety may be die specific (i.e., caused by one die pair) rather than a hub anomaly present on several dies; but in time this question will be resolved. Another possible scenario is that this was caused during the die-making process when foreign material was trapped between the hub and the die.

Collectors immediately got excited about this variety. It's easy to identify, and the seemingly deliberate nature of the anomaly recalls other popular die varieties in the modern series, like the Wisconsin Extra Leaf quarters. Soon, anything related to the VDB became noteworthy. "VDB" are the initials of Victor David Brenner, designer of the bust of Lincoln. In 1909, these initials appeared at the bottom of the reverse of the coin, with periods after each letter. They were too prominent, and outcry caused them to be removed and then

restored more subtly on the base of the bust. The result was that the first issue from San Francisco that includes the initials, the 1909-S V.D.B., is a scarcity in the Lincoln cent series and one of the most highly coveted Lincoln cents. Now, 114 years later, collectors are still getting excited about these initials.

Santiago's initial search yielded 75 coins, and an estimated 3,000 have been found today. When certified at the superb gem MS-67 Red grade level, these coins command thousand-dollar price tags; the more abundant MS-65 Red gems trade for $300. Raw examples can be found for around $100. Collectors should be cautious of misrepresented examples being offered in the $20 to $50 range. While the coins are not difficult to attribute, many examples offered online as the Extra V cent are wrongly described and are not worth any more than their face value.

Mintage: 3,000 (estimated)

MS-63RD	MS-64RD	MS-65RD	MS-66RD	MS-67RD
$68	$100	$160	$195	$415

99 2009-W $100 AMERICAN PLATINUM EAGLE, PROOF

Designed by John Mercanti (obverse) and Susan Gamble (reverse). The obverse features a portrait of Lady Liberty. The reverse design is emblematic of the principle "To Form a More Perfect Union" as written in the Preamble to the Constitution, and features four faces representing the diversity of our nation.

Weight: 1.0005 ounces. *Composition:* .9995 platinum.
Diameter: 32.7 mm. *Edge:* Reeded. *GSID:* 70872.

Ever since the American Platinum Eagle coins were first issued in 1997, they were available in four weights and in both bullion and Proof formats. This remained the case for 12 years without interruption. In 2009, however, the production of platinum coinage was suspended. The extreme volatility in both the metals markets and the broader financial markets caused demand for American Silver Eagles and American Gold Eagles to swell unexpectedly, putting enormous pressure on the Mint to produce those issues. Platinum bullion coinage, a niche product in comparison, was put on hold. Only a single platinum coin was issued in 2009, the one-ounce Proof American Platinum Eagle.

Beyond its being the only platinum coin issued in 2009, the coin was a departure in other ways as well. In that year, a new six-year design program was introduced for the Proof American Platinum Eagle, with each year memorializing one of the six principles found in the preamble to the Constitution, beginning with "To Form a More Perfect Union" in 2009. The design selected for this issue shows four heads in profile—each of a different race—symbolizing the diversity of the United States. They form a circular arrangement, with their hair intertwined to suggest how different people have come together to create the nation. Within the circle is the legend A MORE PERFECT UNION.

Designed by U.S. Mint artist Susan Gamble and sculpted by Phebe Hemphill, this coin lacks something that all other American Platinum Eagle reverse designs have had: an eagle. Although no law requires this coin to include an eagle, other coins are required to have this design element. Additionally, the coin forms part of the American Eagle Bullion program, and thus an eagle motif is appropriate, if not apt. To overcome the omission, the design includes a "privy mark," or small symbol of an eagle's head based on an original coin punch in the archives of the U.S. Mint at Philadelphia. This mark was simply meant to indicate that the coin is indeed an American Eagle Bullion coin.

Since then, Proof American Platinum Eagle issues have included a small eagle mark, giving artists greater space and freedom on the coin. This is the first privy mark to appear on a U.S. bullion coin. The feature is employed routinely by a number of other countries, however, to produce special-purpose limited editions of their bullion coinage without requiring a separate commemorative program or incurring the costs of creating a whole new design. A similar design element appeared on the reverse of the Franklin half dollar beginning in 1948: although the Liberty Bell is the prominent design feature, a small eagle appears beside it, as its inclusion was required by law.

A total of 8,000 examples of the 2009-W $100 American Platinum Eagle were scheduled for sale, and the issue sold out despite the relatively high issue price of $1,792. Although this figure is comparable to earlier issues, the 2009 coin is both the only platinum coin issued for the year and the first coin in a six-part series. The emphasis on artistry and the freedom allowed in the allegorical representations has produced some exciting coins. The price of platinum metal and the quality of the designs will be the key elements in assessing future demand for other subseries.

Mintage: 7,945

PF-68DC	PF-69DC	PF-70DC	OGP
$1,460	$1,590	$1,650	$1,590

100 1996-D CENTENNIAL OLYMPICS (HIGH JUMP) DOLLAR COMMEMORATIVE

Designed by Calvin Massey (obverse) and Thomas D. Rogers (reverse). The obverse features an athlete performing the Fosbury Flop maneuver. The inscriptions include LIBERTY, IN GOD WE TRUST, 1996, and the U.S. Olympic logo. The reverse portrays the Atlanta Committee for the Olympic Games logo with torch and flame. The inscriptions read UNITED STATES OF AMERICA, ONE DOLLAR, E PLURIBUS UNUM, ATLANTA 1996, and CENTENNIAL OLYMPIC GAMES.

Weight: 26.73 grams. *Composition:* .900 silver, .100 copper (net weight .77344 ounces pure silver). *Diameter:* 38.1 mm. *Edge:* Reeded. *GSID:* 10512.

The high jump has been contested at every modern summer Olympic Games. Most of the coins from the 1996 Olympic commemorative series depicted sports, such as swimming or cycling, that covered several disciplines or accounted for a number of contested events. Just 87 medals have been awarded to men and 61 to women for high jump in all modern Olympic Games since the first in 1896. There are other jumping events held at the Games, including the long jump, the triple jump, and the pole vault, all of which have also been contested at every Olympics.

One reason that this sport may have been chosen for a commemorative was the wonderful design created by artist Calvin Massey for the coin. Seventy years old at the time his design was selected, Massey had created hundreds of medallic designs, including some he made while working as a staff member of the Franklin Mint. He was well known for his portrayal of African-American women in bas-relief and painting.

The coin's obverse shows an African-American female athlete in mid-execution of the "Fosbury Flop," a high jumping technique popularized by Dick Fosbury in the 1968 Olympics. The wonderful aspect of the composition is that, while jumping, the athlete arches her back as her legs dangle on the opposite side of the bar, her body forming an arch that matches the roundness of the coin. The word LIBERTY is spelled out above her, matching her shape, while USA and the Olympic rings are below.

The masterful design, alas, could not rescue the coin from suffering the same fate as the other 1996 Olympic commemoratives. Far too many coins were issued, and collector apathy took over. To spur sales, Congress lowered the authorized mintage from 1,000,000 coins to 500,000, but this had little effect.

As with virtually all commemorative issues, the Proof version struck at the San Francisco Mint proved much more popular than the Uncirculated variety. The Proof version totaled 124,502 sales, while the Denver Mint's Uncirculated version only sold 15,697, the second-lowest mintage of any silver commemorative dollar. Today, its low mintage and popular design combine to make the 1996-D Olympic High Jump dollar the most valuable of all the Uncirculated dollars in the series.

Distribution: 15,697

MS-68	MS-69	MS-70	OGP
$140	$145	$310	$145

ABOUT THE AUTHORS

Scott Schechter is the son of a collector and has been involved in numismatics since childhood. In his early teens, he started traveling to numismatic conventions around the country and began collecting U.S. commemorative coins. This area of numismatics remains a core interest. While still in high school, he had his first formal job in numismatics as an intern at the Smithsonian's National Museum of American History, working with the National Numismatic Collection. Throughout college, he cataloged ancient coins at the Semitic Museum. After graduating from Harvard with a degree in history of science in 2000, he joined Pinnacle Rarities and became a dealer in U.S. coins.

In 2005, he began work at Numismatic Guaranty Corporation, and now serves as chief numismatist and grading finalizer. He has worked extensively on the development of the NGC Registry and online collection-management tools. He is particularly proud of his role in the project to upgrade the preservation of the National Numismatic Collection, which involved the creation of a custom conservation-grade holder for the Smithsonian's coins, bringing his professional experience full circle. He has lectured on modern coins for the Professional Numismatists Guild, contributed to *Coin World* and *Coin Dealer Newsletter*, and written extensively for NGC. He has also spoken about coin certification at many conventions in the United States and abroad, including the Beijing International Coin Expo in China and the World Money Fair in Germany.

Scott's wife, Sonia, while not a collector herself, is very supportive of his seemingly endless fascination with numismatics. They live in Sarasota, Florida, with their two children.

Jeff Garrett began his coin collecting in 1969, when a family friend gave him a Lincoln cent board. Since then, coins have been the focus of his life. Growing up in the Tampa Bay area in Clearwater, Florida, Garrett became very active in several local clubs, serving as a junior officer of the Clearwater Coin Club in the 1970s. He was mentored at an early age by many of the area's dealers, among them Ed French and Jeff Means. Garrett attended his first ANA convention in 1974 in Miami with Ed French and has not missed one since. He has been a member of the ANA for more than 25 years and is a past president of the organization, with life membership number 3124.

At the age of 17, Garrett was offered a position with Florida Coin Exchange, one of the dominant firms of the day. Two years later, he became a partner. In 1984, Garrett founded Mid-American Rare Coin Galleries, which continues to operate today. He is also co-owner of the Sarasota Rare Coin Gallery. During the 1980s, he was a partner in Mid-American Rare Coin Auctions, which sold many important collections and earned Catalogue of the Year in 1986 from the Numismatic Literary Guild. Several years later, Garrett organized the Bluegrass Coin Club in Lexington, Kentucky. Because local coin clubs were so important in his early life, Garrett wanted to foster the same atmosphere of enthusiastic collectors that he enjoyed as a youth. Today, the club is very healthy, with more than 30 members in attendance each month.

Garrett describes his expertise as being a "dealer's dealer." With a network of professionals he has established over 25 years, he helps with financing, research, and acquisitions sales. Over the course of his career, Garrett has handled nearly every U.S. rarity. During the ANA Convention in 2003, he was one of the experts called upon to authenticate the long-lost 1913 Liberty Head nickel. Ten years later, Garrett purchased the coin for more than $3 million at public auction. In 2004 he handled one of the greatest gold collections ever assembled, the famed Dukes Creek set of Georgia gold, a collection that sold for nearly $4 million.

Another important aspect of his career is his membership in the Professional Numismatists Guild, to which he has belonged since 1982. Today, Garrett is a former president of the prestigious organization. In 2003, the PNG awarded him the Abe Kosoff Founders Award, that organization's highest honor, for work promoting the hobby and organization. In 2003, the first edition of *100 Greatest United States Coins* was given the Best Book award by both the NLG and the PNG. Although he spends most of his time buying and selling coins, Garrett enjoys research and the study of rare coins. He is coauthor of *The Official Red Book of Auction Records* and of the award-winning *Encyclopedia of United States Gold Coins 1795–1933*, a project done in cooperation with the Smithsonian Institution. Garrett is currently the senior editor for *A Guide Book of United States Coins* (the Red Book), published annually by Whitman.

Living in Lexington, Kentucky, he enjoys golf, travel, and spending time with his family: his wife Mary Lynn, their daughter Morgan, and their son Ben, who runs his own rare-coin business in Sarasota, Florida.

About the Foreword Author

David J. Ryder served as the 34th director of the U.S. Mint from 1992 to 1993 under President George H.W. Bush and President William J. Clinton. He returned to the Mint as its 39th director from 2017 to 2021 under President Donald J. Trump. Ryder is the only two-time director of the Mint in more than a century.

Prior to returning to the Mint, Ryder was the global business-development manager and managing director of currency for Honeywell's Authentication Technologies group. Previously, Ryder served as CEO of Secure Products Corporation, a spin-off from the Sarnoff Corporation, which developed highly advanced anti-counterfeiting technologies for the protection of global currencies and other valued documents. The Honeywell Corporation acquired Secure Products in 2007.

Ryder's prior government positions include Deputy Treasurer of the United States, Deputy Chief of Staff to Vice President Dan Quayle, and special assistant to Vice President George H.W. Bush. Ryder was also the Commissioner General–Director, U.S. Pavilion at the Louisiana World Exposition, United States Department of Commerce.

Ryder was born in Billings, Montana; grew up in Boise, Idaho; and attended Boise State University. Currently the president of the Aureus Group, LLC, a consulting company in Alexandria, Virginia, Ryder is married with two children.

ACKNOWLEDGMENTS

I would like to thank my wife, Sonia, whose love and support truly made this book possible.

—Scott Schechter

I want to thank my wife, Mary Lynn, and my daughter, Morgan, for allowing me to take the time away from my family required to write these books.

—Jeff Garrett

CREDITS

Creative Director, *Matt Jeffirs* • ***Editorial Director,*** *Diana Plattner*
Graphic Designers, *Matt Heller and Thinh Bui*
Pricing Editors, *John Feigenbaum and Patrick Ian Perez*

Assistance with images was provided by Numismatic Guaranty Company photographer Doug Plasencia; Mid-American Numismatic Rarities photographer Tom Mulvaney; photographer Cassidy DuHon; Heritage Auction Galleries; *Coin World* (www.CoinWorld.com); and the Library of Congress. Cover image courtesy of Professional Coin Grading Service (PCGS.com).

The following books in the Whitman library were also valuable resources for images, data, and other information: *A Guide Book of United States Coins; MEGA RED—A Guide Book of United States Coins, Deluxe Edition; Cherrypickers' Guide to Rare Die Varieties of United States Coins; 100 Greatest U.S. Error Coin; A Guide Book of Franklin and Kennedy Half Dollars; A Guide Book of United States Commemorative Coins; A Guide Book of Lincoln Cents;* and *A Guide Book of Modern U.S. Proof Coin Sets.*

Rank Changes from the Fourth Edition

The fifth edition of *100 Greatest U.S. Modern Coins* saw sweeping changes over the prior edition. Fewer than one-fourth of all coins held their rank. Ten items are all-new; nine from the previous list dropped off, and two former entries were merged. Sixty-seven items changed rank, most of them by at least two places; fewer than a third of those that moved did so by only one place. Seven actually moved by 10 or more places. Exciting Mint programs are represented among the new list items, along with fresh error-coin discoveries and two commemoratives that hold low-mintage records.

It is interesting to analyze the full list and look for patterns: new directions on the part of the United States Mint, volatility among commemoratives, and the waxing and waning popularity of various error coins are three questions that come to mind. (The reader may think of many others.) To that end, this appendix now includes all the coins that have made the rankings since the first edition, making it a truly comprehensive record of every coin that has ever been listed among the 100 Greatest U.S. Modern Coins.

Coin	Fifth Edition	Rank Change 4th Ed. to 5th Ed.	Fourth Edition	Third Edition	Second Edition	First Edition
1975, No S, Roosevelt Dime, Proof	1	↔	1	1	1	—
1969-S, Doubled Die Obverse, Lincoln Cent	2	↔	2	2	2	1
1976, No S, Bicentennial Eisenhower Dollar, Proof	3	↔	3	3	3	8
2000 Sacagawea Dollar / Washington Quarter Mule	4	↑1	5	5	4	2
1995-W $1 American Silver Eagle, Proof	5	↓1	4	4	5	4
1964 Special Mint Set	6	↑1	7	8	9	12
2009 (MMIX) Ultra High Relief Double Eagle	7	↑4	11	16	16	16
1968, No S, Roosevelt Dime, Proof	8	↔	8	7	8	3
2007-W American Platinum Eagle, Proof, "Frosted FREEDOM" Variety	9	↑4	13	13	13	—
1990, No S, Lincoln Cent, Proof	10	↓1	9	11	11	13
2006-W $50 American Gold Eagle, Reverse Proof	11	↓5	6	6	6	7

Coin	Fifth Edition	Rank Change 4th Ed. to 5th Ed.	Fourth Edition	Third Edition	Second Edition	First Edition
1972, Doubled Die Obverse, Lincoln Cent	12	↓2	10	10	10	10
2000-P Sacagawea Dollar, "Cheerios" Variety	13	↓1	12	12	12	14
2008-W $1 American Silver Eagle, Reverse of 2007	14	↑3	17	17	17	17
1999-S Silver Delaware Quarter, Proof	15	↔	15	14	14	9
1997-P Jefferson Nickel, Matte "Special Uncirculated"	16	‹ ›	16	15	15	15
2020-W $1 Silver and $50 Gold American Eagles, V75 Privy Mark, Proof	17	New entry	—	—	—	—
1997-W Jackie Robinson $5 Commemorative	18	↓4	14	9	7	5
2004-D, Extra Leaf, Wisconsin Quarters	19	↔	19	19	19	18
2011-P $1 American Silver Eagle, Reverse Proof	20	↓2	18	18	18	—
1999-W $5 and $10 American Gold Eagles, From Unpolished Proof Dies*	21	↓1, ↑8	20, 29	25, 30	25, 31	24, 34
1972 Eisenhower Dollar, Variety 2	22	↓1	21	21	21	20
1998-S Kennedy Half Dollar, Silver, Matte Finish	23	↔	23	23	23	22
2001-P American Buffalo Dollar Commemorative	24	↔	24	28	28	27
2008-W American Gold Eagle Set, Uncirculated	25	↔	25	27	27	—
2000-W Library of Congress $10 Commemorative, Bimetallic	26	↔	26	26	26	25
1965–1967 Special Mint Set Coinage, Ultra Cameo	27	↔	27	33	40	43
2021 Morgan Dollars	28	New entry	—	—	—	—
2021 Peace Dollar	29	New entry	—	—	—	—
1996-W Roosevelt Dime	30	↓8	22	22	22	21
1971, No S, Jefferson Nickel, Proof	31	↓3	28	29	30	30
1982, No Mintmark, Roosevelt Dime	32	↓2	30	24	24	23

Coin	Fifth Edition	Rank Change 4th Ed. to 5th Ed.	Fourth Edition	Third Edition	Second Edition	First Edition
2006-P $1 American Silver Eagle, Reverse Proof	33	↓2	31	31	32	11
2006 $100 American Platinum Eagle	34	↓2	32	32	33	26
1983, Doubled Die Reverse, Lincoln Cent	35	↓2	33	34	34	31
1964 Kennedy Half Dollar, Accented Hair, Proof	36	↓1	35	35	35	33
1964-D Washington Quarter, Reverse of 1965	37	↑2	39	39	41	42
2008-W $50 American Platinum Eagle	38	↔	38	38	36	32
2016-W Centennial Gold Coins	39	↓2	37	—	—	—
2000-D Sacagawea Dollar, "Millennium" Variety	40	↔	40	40	38	37
2021-W $10 American Gold Eagle, From Unpolished Proof Dies	41	New entry	—	—	—	—
1983-P Washington Quarter	42	↓6	36	36	29	29
1983, No S, Roosevelt Dime, Proof	43	↓2	41	41	37	36
1992 and 1992-D Lincoln Cent, Close AM	44	↓10	34	37	39	38
2008 $50 American Platinum Eagle, Proof	45	↓3	42	42	42	35
1999 Lincoln Cent, Wide AM	46	↓3	43	43	44	41
1970-S, Doubled Die Obverse, Lincoln Cent, Large Date	47	↓3	44	44	45	—
2001-W Capitol Visitors Center $5 Commemorative	48	↓3	45	45	43	40
2011-S $1 American Silver Eagle	49	↓2	47	46	46	—
1991 $25 American Gold Eagle	50	↓2	48	48	48	45
1998-S Lincoln Cent, Close AM, Proof	51	↓2	49	49	49	48
2019-W and 2020-W Quarters	52	New entry	—	—	—	—
1970-D Kennedy Half Dollar	53	↓3	50	50	50	49
2001-W $50 American Gold Eagle, Proof	54	↓3	51	51	51	50
1994-P Jefferson Nickel, Matte "Special Uncirculated"	55	↓3	52	47	47	44
1966 Kennedy Half Dollar, SMS, No "FG"	56	↓3	53	67	75	75

Coin	Fifth Edition	Rank Change 4th Ed. to 5th Ed.	Fourth Edition	Third Edition	Second Edition	First Edition
1970, No S, Roosevelt Dime, Proof	57	↓3	54	54	54	54
2007-P John Adams Dollar, Doubled Edge Lettering	58	↓1	57	57	58	57
(2007) George Washington Dollar, Missing Edge Lettering	59	↑1	60	52	52	53
1995, Doubled Die Obverse, Lincoln Cent	60	↓4	56	56	56	55
1982-D George Washington Half Dollar Commemorative	61	↓6	55	55	55	39
2014 Baseball Hall of Fame Commemoratives	62	↓16	46	—	—	—
2008-W $50 American Gold Buffalo, Proof	63	↔	63	63	63	63
1994-P $1 American Silver Eagle, Proof	64	↓5	59	60	60	59
1977-D Eisenhower Dollar, Struck in Silver-Clad Composition	65	↔	65	65	65	71
1990-S, Doubled Die Obverse, Washington Quarter, Proof	66	↓5	61	61	61	51
1984, Doubled Die Obverse, Lincoln Cent	67	↓5	62	62	62	61
2006-W $1 American Silver Eagle	68	↓4	64	64	64	64
2007-W, 2008-W, and 2010-W $10 First Spouse Gold, "Liberty" Designs	69	↓11	58	58	59	84
2000-P Sacagawea Dollar, "Goodacre Presentation" Variety	70	↓4	66	66	66	70
1990-S, Doubled Die Obverse, Jefferson Nickel, Proof	71	↓2	69	69	69	60
2014 Kennedy Half Dollar, 50th Anniversary Issues	72	↓1	71	—	—	—
1971-S, Doubled Die Obverse, Lincoln Cent	73	↔	73	73	74	28
2013-W $50 American Gold Buffalo, Reverse Proof	74	↔	74	74	—	—
2021-W American Liberty High Relief Gold Coin	75	New entry	—	—	—	—
2021-W National Law Enforcement Memorial and Museum $5 Commemorative, Uncirculated	76	New entry	—	—	—	—

Coin	Fifth Edition	Rank Change 4th Ed. to 5th Ed.	Fourth Edition	Third Edition	Second Edition	First Edition
2022-W Negro Leagues Baseball Silver $1 Commemorative, Uncirculated	77	New entry	—	—	—	—
1996-W Smithsonian $5 Commemorative	78	↓11	67	59	57	56
1996-S Centennial Olympics (Swimming) Half Dollar Commemorative	79	↓9	70	53	53	52
2014-D Native American / Presidential Dollar Mule	80	New entry	—	—	—	—
1982 Lincoln Cent, Small Date, Copper-Plated Zinc	81	↓13	68	68	68	47
2003-W First Flight Centennial $10 Commemorative	82	↔	82	82	82	80
1976 Washington Quarter	83	↓5	78	71	72	65
1986 $1 American Silver Eagle	84	↓1	83	83	83	46
1984-W Los Angeles Olympiad $10 Commemorative	85	↓1	84	84	84	81
2015-P Truman and Eisenhower Presidential Dollars, Reverse Proof	86	↓1	85	—	—	—
2012-S $1 American Silver Eagle, Reverse Proof	87	↔	87	87	90	—
1996 $1 American Silver Eagle	88	↓8	80	78	79	67
1981-S Susan B. Anthony Dollar, Clear S (Type 2), Proof	89	↔	89	79	77	58
2007-W $25 American Gold Eagle	90	↔	90	90	92	—
2013-W $1 American Silver Eagle, Enhanced Uncirculated	91	↑1	92	92	—	—
2010-P Grand Canyon 5 oz. Silver Quarter Dollar, Light Finish	92	↑1	93	93	93	—
2008-W $10 American Gold Buffalo	93	↑1	94	94	94	90
1992-D XXV Olympiad (Baseball) Dollar Commemorative	94	↑1	95	95	95	89
1970-S Lincoln Cent, Small Date	95	↑1	96	96	96	97
1997-P Law Enforcement Officers Memorial Dollar Commemorative	96	↓24	72	72	73	69
2016-W Silver Eagles, Lettered Edge 30th Anniversary Issues	97	↔	97	—	—	—

Coin	Fifth Edition	Rank Change 4th Ed. to 5th Ed.	Fourth Edition	Third Edition	Second Edition	First Edition
2023 Lincoln Cent, "Extra V" Variety	98	New entry	—	—	—	—
2009-W $100 American Platinum Eagle, Proof	99	↓1	98	98	98	94
1996-D Centennial Olympics (High Jump) Dollar Commemorative	100	↓25	75	75	70	66
Other Coins from Prior Editions						
1974 Aluminum Lincoln Cent	—	—	—	—	—	6
1971 Eisenhower Dollar	—	—	—	—	67	62
1996-S National Community Service Dollar Commemorative	—	—	79	70	71	68
1981-S Lincoln Cent, Clear S (Type 2), Proof	—	—	—	91	91	72
1979-S Susan B. Anthony Dollar, Clear S (Type 2), Proof	—	—	—	—	—	73
1973-P and D Eisenhower Dollars	—	—	77	77	78	74
2005-D Jefferson Nickel, "Speared Bison" Variety	—	—	—	80	80	76
1996-D Centennial Olympics (Paralympics) Dollar Commemorative	—	—	—	76	76	77
1996-W Centennial Olympics (Flag Bearer) $5 Commemorative	—	—	81	81	81	78
1979-P Susan B. Anthony Dollar, Wide Rim	—	—	86	86	86	79
2004-P Doubled-Die Obverse Peace Medal Nickel	—	—	—	85	85	82
1964-D/D Kennedy Half Dollar	—	—	—	—	87	83
1996-W Centennial Olympics (Cauldron) $5 Commemorative	—	—	—	—	—	85
2005-P Marine Corp 230th Anniversary Dollar Commemorative	—	—	—	—	—	86
1996-D Centennial Olympics (Tennis) Dollar Commemorative	—	—	88	88	88	87
1974-D Doubled-Die Obverse Kennedy Half Dollar	—	—	—	89	89	88

Coin	Fifth Edition	Rank Change 4th Ed. to 5th Ed.	Fourth Edition	Third Edition	Second Edition	First Edition
1976-S Eisenhower Dollar, Variety 1, Clad, Proof	—	—	—	—	—	91
1986-S Statue of Liberty Half Dollar Commemorative	—	—	100	97	97	92
1999-W Washington $5 Commemorative, Proof	—	—	—	99	100	93
1995-S Kennedy Half Dollar, Silver, Proof	—	—	—	—	—	95
1996-D Centennial Olympics (Rowing) Dollar Commemorative	—	—	—	—	—	96
1981-S Susan B. Anthony Dollar	—	—	—	100	99	98
2010-D Zachary Taylor Dollar, Misdated	—	—	—	—	—	99
1987-P and D Kennedy Half Dollars	—	—	—	—	—	100
2016-W National Park Service $5 Commemorative	—	—	76	—	—	—
2014-D Sacagawea Dollar, Enhanced Uncirculated	—	—	91	—	—	—
1982-D Lincoln Cent, Small Date, Bronze Planchet Error Coin	—	—	99	—	—	—

The Future of
Coin collecting
BROUGHT TO YOU BY
TraderBea ONLY ON
whatnot
WWW.TRADERBEA.COM